Camelia

Camelia

SAVE YOURSELF BY TELLING THE TRUTH
—A MEMOIR OF IRAN

Camelia Entekhabifard

Translated from Persian by George Mürer

SEVEN STORIES PRESS

New York | Toronto | London | Melbourne

A Seven Stories Press First Edition

Selections from this book have appeared, in different form, in the following publications: the *Village Voice* ("Unveiled Threats," March 28, 2001), and *Mother Jones* ("Behind the Veil," May/June 2001).

Lines from Ahmad Shamlu's poem *"Paria"* (Fairies) are from his collection *Havaye Taze* (Fresh Air), translation © 2007 by George Mürer. Lines by Hafez are from *The Divan of Hafez*, translation © 2007 by George Mürer. Lines by Sadegh Ahangran are from his song *"Ay Leskar-e Saheb-e Zaman, Amadeh Bash, Amedeh Bash"* (Oh Army of the Master of Time, Get Ready, Get Ready), translation © 2007 by George Mürer. Lines from "Camelia in Chains" by Mandana Sadeqi and excerpts from her unpublished letters are used with permission of the author, translations © 2007 by George Mürer. Lines from Forugh Farrokhzad's poem "Another Birth" are from *Another Birth: Selected Poems of Forugh Farrokhzad*, translation © 1981 by Hasan Javadi and Susan Sallée.

Some names have been changed to protect individual identities.

Seven Stories Press, 140 Watts Street. New York, NY 10013
www.sevenstories.com

In Canada: Publishers Group Canada, 559 College Street, Suite 402, Toronto, ON M6G 1A9

In the UK: Turnaround Publisher Services Ltd., Unit 3, Olympia Trading Estate, Coburg Road, Wood Green, London N22 6TZ

In Australia: Palgrave Macmillan, 627 Chapel Street, South Yarra, VIC 3141

College professors may order examination copies of Seven Stories Press titles for a free six-month trial period. To order, visit http://www.sevenstories.com/textbook or send a fax on school letterhead to (212) 226-1411.

Library of Congress Cataloging-in-Publication Data

Entekhabifard, Camelia, 1973-
   Camelia, save yourself by telling the truth : a memoir of Iran / by Camelia Entekhabifard ; translated from the Persian by George Murer.
   p. cm.
   ISBN-13: 978-1-58322-719-0 (hardcover : alk. paper)
   ISBN-10: 1-58322-719-9 (hardcover : alk. paper)
   1. Entekhabifard, Camelia, 1973- 2. Women journalists--Iran--Biography. 3. Journalists--Iran--Biography. 4. Iran--Politics and government--1979-1997. 5. Iran--Politics and government--1997-
I. Murer, George. II. Title.
PN5449.I68Z735 2007
070.92--dc22
[B]   2005028529

Book design by Jon Gilbert

Printed in the USA

9 8 7 6 5 4 3 2 1

To the memory of my father. To my brave and unique mother. To all those who have stayed in Iran.

Contents

Because this memoir is not a scholarly work, a distinction has not been made in the transliteration of the long a/*alif* and the short a/*fatha* sounds, with the exception of the word "Salaam." In constructions involving the Arabic definite article al-, the l has been assimilated to sun letters to reflect common pronunciation. Exceptions to the rule have been made for names of well-known individuals, which are spelled as they commonly appear in print media.

chapter one When the Shah Left, We Stayed

JANUARY 16, 1979

My mother sat dressed in black on the purple sofa in our salon, tears streaming down her face. Every so often, I'd peek out at her from my bedroom. Her ears were stuffed firmly with cotton, and at her side sat Mino Khanum, our close friend and neighbor whose hair was always dyed burgundy. She was also visibly upset.

My mother had covered her body in black to mourn my grandfather. I knew this because, two months before, we had all gone to Behesht-e Zahra, the largest cemetery in Tehran, and my parents had told my cousin Elham; my sister, Katayun; and me to wait in the car. I understood my grandfather had died. But of my mother's sobbing, I understood nothing.

The transistor radio sat playing at my mother's side, and from time to time she would take the cotton out of her ears to hear the voice of the radio announcer better. She wanted to hear the news, but at the same time, she lacked the strength to keep listening. With each news flash, her heavy sobbing intensified, and she jammed the cotton even harder back into her ears. It was Tuesday morning, and it was my birthday. At the age of six, nothing was more important to me than celebrating my birthday. I knew a party was out of the question; we were in mourning. But my mother had promised we would go downtown to pick out my present. The radio announcer started yelling at the top of his voice, "The Shah is gone! The Shah is gone!" Both my mother and Mino Khanum fainted.

◙   ◙   ◙

It had gotten dark, and with me clinging to my mother's black overcoat, we headed south on the downward incline of Khiaban-e Vali-ye Ahd. My mother was impatient, and she had been crying so much that her eyes and nose were red. I had not let her forget about buying that present. It was out of sheer helplessness that she had taken my hand in hers and set off for Mufid's, a store that was piled to the ceiling with Barbie dolls and colorful toys. Agha-ye Mufid, the owner, was always waiting for my sister, Kati, and me.

Our street, Kucheh-ye Omid, was enveloped in silence and total darkness. The avenue was quiet, too, but only a few streets before the main thoroughfare we were suddenly engulfed in a flood of cars with their horns blaring and headlights flashing. The street was filled with the sound of their joy, and my mother cursed them under her breath. Overwhelmed and bewildered, I clung even more tightly to my mother. She turned to me and said, "I told you it would be better not to go out tonight . . ." Her voice was lost in the din of car horns and people shouting. Everyone was congratulating one another and handing out sweets. They also congratulated us, but my mother kept her head down as we barreled straight ahead. After months of fighting between forces loyal to the Shah and the revolutionary masses, the Shah and his queen had left Iran for Cairo, and the people were pouring out onto the streets to celebrate.

In the midst of that frightful traffic and noise, a hand holding a giant stuffed cloth dog emerged from the window of a Peykan and danced, wiggling at us and no one and everyone at once. "The Shah is gone! The Shah is gone!" The man who danced the toy in front of us had whiskers down to his waist. His voice warbled, "*Tuleh sag-*

e Alashi, Bakhtiar-ra ja gozashti!" (You little Alashi dog, you left Bakhtiar behind!) He called the dog Alashi because the Shah's father, Reza Shah, was from the village of Alash in the north of Iran, and by Bakhtiar he meant the prime minister, Doctor Shahpur Bakhtiar. Bakhtiar was negotiating with various revolutionary groups, attempting to keep the country under control in the Shah's absence. He had even proposed going to Paris to negotiate with Ayatollah Khomeini. But when the people cried, *"Tuleh sag-e Alashi, Bakhtiar-ra ja gozashti!"* they also meant that they had driven the Shah out of their house—which is to say Iran—like an unclean dog.

At home in our house, we had neither listened to the personal communiqués from Ayatollah Khomeini who was arriving from Paris, nor did we join the throngs of revolutionaries burning tires in the streets. When revolutionaries tossed their manifestos into our courtyard at night, my father would throw them back out onto the street. We didn't want to know where they planned to gather, and we weren't interested in the mullahs or that surly old man with the crooked black eyebrows either. We liked to think that we could sit still and ignore all the commotion, and that if we did, the crisis would subside and the country would return to its regular old self.

When we had been in England for the summer holidays, my mother had gotten upset when she read the words "Death to the Shah" written in Persian on the wall in the London metro. In Hyde Park we'd seen young Iranian students standing on chairs, shouting slogans against the Shah amid a gathering crowd. On more than one occasion my mother yelled back at them, as she held Kati and me at her sides. "Come down from there you ungrateful brats! That poor Shah gave you money so you could go to school and now all that money has made you into wolves, and you stand up there howling away!" In London my mother hadn't been afraid to tell them she was a supporter of the Shah. She was proud of the Shah's pledge to safeguard the freedom and progress of the women of Iran, and of all the opportunities he had opened up for them. But today, in the middle of Khiaban-e Kennedy, besieged by the Shah's opponents, my mother just clamped her lips together in anger.

We finally reached the toy store, and it was closed. Every shop was closed. Afraid of looting, the shopkeepers had pulled down the shuttered gates at noon that day and hurried home. When I saw that the sign proclaiming "Mufid" in neon was turned off, tears started running down my cheeks. It was of no importance to me that the Shah had gone or that someone else would come to take his place or that the days ahead were bound to be completely unpredictable. I just wanted my present. My mother promised, "Tomorrow . . . tomorrow. . . ."

◙   ◙   ◙

Weeks before, a crowd of yelling students had flooded into the courtyard of my school, Ghafari, their faces almost laughably angry. Before the main entrance, a pretty young official with black hair stood guard. Her face was smothered in makeup, and she was wearing a button-down shirt and pants, a rifle slung across her back. I was in kindergarten, and my sister, Katayun, who was in third grade, marched around the courtyard with a group mimicking the older students. I tried to join in as best I could with this game, but an invisible hand—belonging to my sister—immediately took hold of me. She led me out of the ruckus to the wall at the edge of the courtyard. She was watching to make sure that I didn't get crushed. I kept trying, and the last time my sister drew me to the side, she put a cluster of pea pods in my hand and said, "Don't move. Stay here in this spot. Eat your peas until Maman comes to get us."

I couldn't play this game, but Kati sure was having fun. Every time the angry students rotated past the front of the main building, the older boys would lift chairs dragged from the classrooms above their heads and brandish them at the principal's office, chanting, "*Baroye hefz-e shishe, Madresseh bayad ta'til sh-e*" (For the sake of the windowpanes, the school must be closed). In the midst of all the protesters my sister waved at me and twirled her body in delight.

The principal of our school was a serious, fashionably dressed woman with long hair wrapped around her head like a hat and fancy necklaces draped around her neck. That day, she and the other teachers stayed timidly inside, glancing anxiously down at the revolt. Even Vice Principal Habashi's wooden meter stick, which she used to punish unruly boys at the front of the classroom every morning, was incapable of inspiring fear. The windows of the building shattered one by one, and there was nothing for the school authorities to do but close the schools and join the strike. That winter day was our last day of school in 1979.

The Shah's administration was faced with a mounting threat as the strikes swept across the country. Banks closed, the Abadan oil refinery went on strike, the electrical plants went on strike, and from time to time our homes were plunged into darkness. The government declared martial law and a nine o'clock curfew. But in the nighttime stillness people went up onto their roofs to cry out, "*Allahu Akbar*." Within minutes the few voices scattered here and there would grow to a chorus of hundreds.

We stayed home and watched TV and listened to the radio while my mother went back and forth to Mino Khanum's house to exchange the latest news. Mino Khanum's husband would go out to the demonstrations to gather firsthand information. But my father had warned us not to leave the house even to play because civilians were often randomly killed, caught in the cross fire of armed confrontations. We heard that police had opened fire at a large demonstration at Meidan Zhale, killing hundreds. Every morning we saw new slogans on the walls of our street, hastily scrawled in bright colors. "Hail Khomeini! They have struck down the martyrs. Death to the traitor Shah!" At first Kati and I would clean as much as we could reach off our walls, but eventually we had to content ourselves with making sure to remove the most dangerous of the slogans: "SAVAKi."

It was rumored that my father was an employee of the Shah's secret intelligence service. In those days, you'd hear terrifying stories about the crimes of the SAVAK and how they killed and tortured those opposed to the Shah's regime. We were not revolutionaries, and we did not participate in the demonstrations. And my father's cousins, tall men with shiny navy blue uniforms and dazzling shoulder decorations, would be seen going to and from our house. This was enough evidence to label us monarchists, SAVAKi, and *taghuti*. A few months earlier, in November, when the people first started taking to the streets, the Shah had appeared on television saying that he had gotten the message. To a certain extent, censorship of the press had been lifted, and in a show of combating corruption, he'd arrested and imprisoned about a 120 leading state officials, among them the head of the SAVAK, General Ne'matollah Nasiri, and Prime Minister Amir Abbas Hovida. But the people responded to these token gestures by repeating Khomeini's words: "The Shah must go." The people saw the SAVAKis as bloodthirsty traitors who deserved to be put to death.

But who could say this about my father? How could our neighbors hate us so much? During our summer holiday in England, we had spent a few weeks in the coastal city of Brighton with the Vaqadi family from next door. They drove a green Zhian and spoke Persian with a Kermanshahi accent. Kati and I used to go roller-skating with their young sons, Nima and Mani. But now they had joined the Islamic Revolution and were spending their days at the local mosque. Agha-ye Vaqadi was a poet with fine features, a bald head, and thick glasses—and of course a *tudeh-i*, a communist, as my mother would say. The *tudeh-i* were very active in the first months of the revolution, before Ayatollah Khomeini outlawed their activities, arrested their leaders, and executed large numbers of their members.

Nima and Mani had little glasses just like their father's and had become stars at their mosque. Mosques all over the country had become centers of resistance, the place to design placards and print propaganda, to plan demonstrations and disseminate Khomeini's communiqués. Passing by our house, Nima and Mani would stick their heads into our courtyard and cry out, "*Mardum chara neshastid? Nakone ke Shah parest id!*" (People, why do you just sit there? God forbid you're supporters of the Shah!) My mother would put on a scowl and shout back, "Dirt on the head of you *tudeh-i*! You've gobbled up all the country's money and gone mad! It would be nice if your father could come up with some better poetry!" My mother knew that just like the students in London, Agha-ye Vaqadi had studied abroad with the support of the Shah.

The worse things grew around the country, the bolder Nima and Mani got. They had made a banner almost ten feet long with a picture of Khomeini on it to carry at demonstrations. At night they would hang it on the terrace of their house in full view of our courtyard. In retaliation, my mother would fasten pictures of the Shah and his queen, Farah, to helium balloons to show off our loyalty. My sister and I would stand out on the terrace, each with a balloon in hand, making faces at one another. Before my father came home and caught the two of us with those balloons, we'd let them go. I really thought that they'd float all the way up to the moon to convey our greetings to the Shah and the Queen.

▣ ▣ ▣

My mother was madly in love with the Shah, and she was just as crazy about Reza, his oldest son. She carried around in her purse a picture that she had ripped out of a children's magazine of Reza sitting on a playing field in a soccer uniform. When the Queen gave birth to Reza, my mother, who was eight at the time, asked my grandmother if she could go to the hospital with a bouquet of flowers to congratulate Farah in person. She left the flowers with the guards at the door, singing the lullaby she had learned in school: "I'm a beautiful virgin, my name is Farah Diba, the third wife of the Shah . . . I will bear a crown prince, and I am going to call him Reza . . . La, la, la, my dear Reza, la, la, la, my dear Reza." I don't know whether this little bouquet ever got to the Queen, but for my mother the important thing was that Reza had come into the world and the royal line would survive.

My mother was one of many women of her generation who had been able to escape the traditional constraints of her birthplace thanks to the Shah's support for women's rights. She was independent and was, I believe, one of the first women in Jamaran who refused to wear the veil. My grandfather had died in an avalanche, and my grandmother—whom I called Mader-jan—was a widow. She was peaceful and kind, and she afforded her daughter every kind of freedom. But the other women in her family beat my mother severely in the streets, hoping to persuade her to put on the veil. She withstood all that pressure and attained a certain distinction for never wearing the *hejab*. New doors opened before her. She met my father at the progressive social club Kakh-e Javanan, and they grew to be friends before they married in 1969. This was in contrast to the customs of the day, where suitors would normally just show up, and families would be obliged to submit their daughters for marriage.

My mother's devoted love for the Shah was rooted in her childhood. Time and time again we'd heard her tell the same story of meeting him as a young girl in her hometown: "Jamaran was a village surrounded by wheat fields. Its roads were so quiet that if a car sometimes broke the silence, it was usually the Shah traveling between the palace in Sa'adabad and the palace in Saheb Gharaneyeh. Wherever I was, when I heard the sound of the Shah's motorcade far off in the distance, I would run so fast that my heart would almost burst out of my chest. I ran to where the desert began just so I could wave at him from the roadside, and the Shah would always wave back. One day, as I was coming home from school, I saw him driving alone. Suddenly taking leave of my senses, I ran in front of his car in a frenzy. It screeched to a halt, and he got out.

"I was afraid, but the Shah spoke kindly, running his hand across the top of my head, 'My dear girl, this time nothing happened, but you must never again run out in front of a car like that.'"

Then she'd stop, let out a sigh, and shake her head sadly. If my father happened to be passing within earshot, he'd pick up where she left off. "And then the Shah said he'd take a shit for you and tomorrow you should send him a plate so he can fill it up!" My father didn't care for the mullahs or the Shah, but he preferred the Shah's government to the mullahs. Naturally, Kati and I took our cues from our mother, and we didn't understand the riots and slogans. Why would people want the Shah to leave? My mother would say, "It comes from having everything they need or even too much of it." But it was we who lived content in the capital and had everything: water, electricity, telephones, modern streets, and highways. My father had a high-paying job that allowed us to spend all of our summer vacations in Europe. We rode around in a nice car and ate expensive food and bought our clothes in London from Harrods where my mother once tipped the salesclerk fifty pounds. We spent every summer in London and sometimes my mother would take me along on a winter trip just to shop at the Christmas sales. The price of oil had soared to the highest point in history, and the Iranians we knew were better and better off every day.

What did we know about the neighborhoods called Halabiyabad in south Tehran, where people lived in houses made of tin gas-cans? Or about the villages without drinking water? Many towns had neither electricity, nor proper roads, nor schools, nor hospitals, nor did they meet even the most basic standards of hygiene. The people were fed up with the excesses and wastefulness of the Shah and his family. How many people had been forced to spend years being beaten and tortured in prison as political detainees? We didn't know, and we didn't want to know.

◙ ◙ ◙

On one of those illusory days when it seemed that the chaos had quieted under the control of Doctor Shahpur Bakhtiar, Kati and I went with our mother to visit our grandmother in Jamaran. On our way back we stopped at Mumtaz, the fabric store. My mother was looking for some fabric to make a winter coat. Of course it had to be in black, because she was still mourning the death of my grandfather. Mumtaz had the best quality fabric. I remember how my mother would always look for crepe chiffon there and my aunt Turan, for silk.

The shopkeeper was busy unrolling the fabrics one by one across his counter when suddenly the earth trembled, and we heard a frightful noise. The Shahanshahi Guard was processing with pomp and circumstance along the main avenue from Sa'adabad Palace toward Meidan Tajrish. Soldiers were riding atop the tanks, covered in iron and armed to the teeth. My mother was drowning in patriotic joy. Then the sound of gunfire tore through the air. A revolutionary group had ambushed the parade, and the guard was returning their fire. The customers retreated to the back of the store in a huddle with a few disoriented people tumbling in from the street. I hid in my mother's arms, and we waited out the firestorm. When we finally emerged, someone told us that a man had been killed. Another man took a bunch of carnations from the vendor across the street and started placing the flowers on the pools of blood. People were chanting "Death to the Shah" and "Martyrs have been struck down." From then on, my mother decided we would stay at home and follow the revolution on the TV screen.

▣ ▣ ▣

FEBRUARY 1979

"Vay be halat-e Bakhtiar agar Imam farda nayad; moselselha birun miayad" (Woe to Bakhtiar: if tomorrow the Imam does not come, the machine guns are coming out). Doctor Shahpur Bakhtiar, the prime minister, had closed Mehrabad, the main airport, to prevent Khomeini's arrival. He even threatened to shoot his plane down. Khomeini said he'd take that risk. Bakhtiar gave his resignation and announced his intention to leave for France to prevent civil war and further bloodshed.

Ayatollah Khomeini, the leader of the revolution, landed in Iran on an Air France flight on the morning of the first of February. Millions of excited Iranians, women and men, had gathered at the airport to greet him. In response to a journalist who asked how it felt to be coming back to Iran after nearly fifteen years far away from his homeland, Khomeini replied that he didn't feel anything special, and this astonishing statement became a headline all over the world. Later, after the victory of the revolution, the image of him emerging from the plane, with a large entourage on the steps of the aircraft, became historic. It was shown year after year during the commemoration of the revolution. Every year the photo closed in, as his companions disappeared from official history, killed or pushed to the margins, until no one but Khomeini, his son Ahmad, and the pilot remained in the frame.

I remember well how the blue and white Chevrolet carrying Khomeini kept stopping to greet the millions who wanted to see him up close—their leader who had spent years in exile, first in Iraq and then in France. When Khomeini arrived in Tehran, he went straight to Behesht-e Zahra and proclaimed, "Mohammed Reza Shah has laid waste to the cities and populated the cemeteries." He sounded the glad tidings of freedom for the people of Iran—glad tidings of abundant water and electricity and the equal partitioning of oil revenue.

Only two weeks had passed since the Shah left Iran, and the military bases had not yet been surrendered. At first, loyalist soldiers put up resistance. But the air force was at the beck and call of the Imam, and the army bases were quickly secured. Most soldiers joined forces with the people and put flowers in the barrels of their rifles. The people would chant, "*Baradar-e arteshi, chara baradar kushi?*" (My brother in the army, why do you kill your brother?) Exactly ten days after Khomeini's arrival in Iran, the revolution was declared victorious. Iranian television proclaimed, "*Div chu birun ravad, fereshte dar ayad*" (When the devil goes out, the angel comes in).

My uncle Manuchehr (really my father's first cousin) was an officer in the Bureau of Investigation and worked at the Tehran Police Department. He was over at our house a few weeks after Khomeini arrived in Iran, and he pointed out that one of the men escorting Khomeini's Chevrolet was a thief, a fugitive with a long record. They'd been after him for months, and here he was on television, swerving on a motorcycle in front of the Imam. My sister and I were fascinated. Every time they showed a segment on Khomeini's reception we'd run up to the television screen and point out to everyone the notorious thief. Uncle Manuchehr later told us that this same thief had become a person of importance and visited police headquarters of his own accord. He proudly greeted the force, and no one had the courage to say a word, let alone arrest him.

◙ ◙ ◙

Ayatollah Khomeini was in the moon. In the evenings everyone turned their heads toward the sky. *We* couldn't see anything. I gazed at the spots on the surface of the moon and strained to make out Khomeini's frowning features, but I didn't see anything. My father said, "Isn't anyone going to ask these donkeys what that good-for-nothing is doing up there in the sky?" But Avid, my Uncle Bizhan's, and my older cousin Omid had started going to prayers. Omid wore a carnelian ring on his hand, and they could see Khomeini in the moon, too. When I stubbornly insisted that Khomeini was a donkey, Omid would bite his lip and hang his head. They had just moved to a new house in a desert area called Shahrak-e Gharb. Their yard was covered in shallow ditches filled with rainwater and tadpoles, and my father would bring a large stick when we visited to beat off stray dogs. The barking dogs would chase after our car for a long way as we drove off. My uncle said that this was soon to become the best neighborhood in all of Tehran.

It was a good time to settle old scores. The papers were filled with pictures of the victims of the firing squads swimming in blood. All you had to do was become a familiar face at your local mosque and then report that your neighbor was a SAVAKi. The first to be executed was the former head of the SAVAK, General Ne'matollah Nasiri. But all sorts of personal animosities and grudges were pretenses for taking revenge. Every day, people—some innocent, some bearing varying degrees of guilt—were delivered in groups to the revolutionary execution unit. There were neither courts nor defense attorneys; a council bearing the name Revolutionary Justice approved the executions on the spot. The name of one of Khomeini's disciples, Hojjat ul-Islam Sadeq Khalkhali, was enough to make your hair stand on end. It was even rumored that he personally executed former prime minister Amir Abbas Hovida.

We were at the mercy of the goodwill of our neighbors, the same neighbors who painted "SAVAKi" on our walls. We had yet to hear from many of my father's relatives. Many had fled, some had left the country, and the fate of still others was completely unknown. We passed our days and nights in worry and disquiet. My father took up a tile from the bedroom floor and dug out a cavity deep enough to hide a plastic bag filled with banknotes and our mother's gold jewelry. He brought home something we'd only seen in movies—a long, wide, double-edged sword called a *qama*. My father placed this fearsome weapon with its black leather sheath under his pillow, and he said to us, "If our house is attacked in the middle of the night, we will defend ourselves with this *qama*." When our father was at work, Kati and I would push aside his pillow to stare at it.

Instead of making me feel safer, the *qama* gave me nightmares. I had the same dream every night, a cartoonish vision in which soldiers with long spears would come to attack, riding on white horses, and there I would be on the ground trapped between their long legs. I would wake up with a start, remembering the sound of the slogans chanted by Nima and Mani, the two boys from next door who only six months before had been eating ice cream and laughing with us by the sea in Brighton. But instead of the revolutionaries, it was my young uncle, Ali, who came to our house late one night with a sandbag full of weapons and hid it in the closet where my mother kept her clothes. We listened to my father and my uncle identifying these weapons: Uzi, Kalashnikov . . .

The next day, my father called Katayun and I and softly told us, "Girls, be careful not to tell anyone that we have weapons in our house. You mustn't breathe a word of it even to your friends. And never go into your mother's closet." We both nodded, but from then on our greatest source of amusement was to go to the closet and look at all the different kinds of weapons, having no idea where they came from or what they might be used for. Years later I learned that they had been taken in raids on army bases during the climactic days of the revolution. Then one day, maybe in that same month, my uncle came back in the dark of night and carried away all those heavy weapons, putting in their place a Colt and a bag full of cartridges. The Colt took its place next to the double-edged sword. We were ready for anything.

◙   ◙   ◙

MARCH 21, 1979

That year, when Nouruz, the Iranian New Year, came it seemed most of the country was in great spirits—the people had resolved this was their first "spring in freedom." But my family was lost and confused. We had a piece of land in Karaj near the palace of the Shah-Dokht Shams Pahlavi, bought from the private office of the princess, and we planned to build a new home there. My father believed this neighborhood would come to be much more convenient and fashionable than the desert where my cousin Omid lived. The first Tehran metro line would run right by our house—assuming that we were allowed to hold onto our land. But we had to wait and see how the Imam would decide our future.

My extended family was split as their fortunes radically changed. Large quantities of money and property were being seized by the Revolutionary Courts. Those who participated in the revolution were reaping the benefits, but we, like many others, were slowly losing grip on our wealth. My mother's aunt Fakhri had her home repossessed for the crime that her husband had been Agha-ye Khan Malak Yazdi, the chief of the wealthy association, the Pious Department. In contrast, my maternal uncle Ali, by virtue of being with the Revolutionary Guard, ended up with a fine piece of land behind the Shah's palace on Niyavaran in Shemiran, and brought his young wife, Iran-Dokht, to live there.

He'd fallen in love with her a few years before, at the beginning of the revolution. He was fixing Mader-jan's rooftop in Jamaran, when he spied a green-eyed fair-skinned girl visiting a neighbor. Fair skin is very unusual in Iran and considered highly attractive. My mother and Mader-jan refused at first to go and ask for her hand. She wasn't Jamarani nor Tehrani, so she was a peasant to my mother. Finally the rest of "Jamaran" convinced them. At that time, it seemed everyone was related to each other in some way, so Iran-Dokht was literally marrying into the town, not just the family. The whole family followed tradition and went to propose to the northern people of Shahsavar. Everything was arranged quickly, maybe within a week, when usually even a fast wedding would take months (my sister's would later take a year). Iran-Dokht's stepmother immediately agreed to send this seventeen-year-old girl to marry—though she hadn't even finished high school. Her parents wholeheartedly gave their innocent daughter to one of the Imam's guards. I liked her as soon as I saw her; she was so beautiful, and I pitied her for not having a mother. Her beauty charmed us, and our prejudices turned to sympathy as the Jamaran family opened their arms to her. At first Ali and Iran-Dokht moved into a small room in my mother's cousin's apartment. They didn't mind the cramped conditions because they were so revolutionary. But then this attitude was rewarded with a splendid plot of land.

In contrast, my aunt Turan, my father's sister, was afraid to go out in her chic peach-colored Mercedes Benz with its royal plates. The Revolutionary Guard would stop expensive cars to check the identities of their owners. Usually, they'd seize the cars and take the drivers away to the Komité. My aunt's husband, Uncle Musayyeb, who was also my father's cousin, had been the highest-ranking member of our family under the Shah's government. He'd worked in the Shah's personal office as "His Majesty's Calligrapher." He would write His Majesty's letters in elegant script for the Shah to sign. The walls of my aunt's house on Khiaban-e Fereshteh were covered with her husband's calligraphic renderings from the *Ruba'yat* of Omar Khayyám, and with exquisite miniatures of their older daughter, Gita. Their second daughter, Mahta, had a beautiful face and was being groomed to be the wife of a man of distinction. In fact, it was even whispered among our family that perhaps one day she would make a fine wife for the crown prince, Reza. Only a few hours before the Shah fled Iran, the royal car came for Uncle Musayyeb. The Shah summoned him for one last private meeting. The subject of this conversation has always remained a secret.

My father's family took great pride in the notion that not only was their family's honor and history not less than that of the royal family, but was in fact even more distinguished. My paternal grandfather's cousin was Amujan Timsar, "Dearest Uncle the Major General." He had been the security chief of Tehran and would boast that he had had the title "His Majesty's Private Guard." We all knew his daughter Mahnavaz, who was the same age as my aunt Turan, had once been approached by Queen Turan, Reza Shah's third wife, for marriage with the Shah's half-brother, Shahpur Gholamreza. And we all knew that her family had declined this offer because Shahpur Gholamreza was a playboy and a philanderer and not worthy of their daughter.

Our proud family didn't go to the polls during the last two days of March to cast our votes on the new constitution of the Islamic Republic. But we heard on the first of April when the constitution was approved by a majority of the country, 99 percent to be precise, and Khomeini proclaimed it the "first day of God's government." Fresh waves of arrests swept the country and the executions continued. Our ever-present television constantly broadcast interrogations of those condemned to execution, exposing the "traitors to the nation." Then one night, we were shocked to see the image of my grandfather's cousin Agha-ye Sayf-Allah Shahandeh. He had been the editor in chief of a magazine now linked to the imperial government. He had gone into hiding, and we had heard that he had recently been arrested along with his daughter, Guli. My father, astounded, remarked harshly that he must have been severely beaten since his whole face was swollen. A dazed Agha-ye Shahandeh confessed like a parrot to treason, monarchist sympathies, and spying for foreign powers. They executed him and held his funeral at an undisclosed location.

My family became closer to his widow, Afsar Khanum. She never lost her sense of humor (and always had Smarties in her purse for me and my younger cousin Bita). And despite our sorrows, afterward I remember I also felt proud. Though many revolutionary families would be ashamed to have a relative executed, I was proud of my family's history because it showed strength and conviction. Two decades later, when I was taken to jail, I know my family was waiting anxiously to see if I would suddenly end up on national television. My uncle Bizhan later told me, with tears in his eyes, that he kept remembering the shock of that day and how afraid he'd been that they would lose me, too.

◙   ◙   ◙

FALL 1979

Concerned for our safety, my father sent us along with our mother to England for the summer. But we returned home to Iran to join him in the fall, following the construction of our villa in Karaj. My father wanted to stay close to his mother, and my parents were full of false hope for a coup d'état. The schools opened, and I went to my first class at Chista No. 1 elementary school, where Katayun was enrolled in the fourth grade.

There was no sign of boys in my class—the new Islamic government separated the sexes in school. The most revolutionary girl in our school was one of Katayun's classmates. Everyone called her by her last name, Torkan. Head coverings were not yet mandatory at elementary school (the law went into effect when I started 3rd grade) and no one wore the *hejab*, but this coarse, olive-skinned girl wore a long black veil. She had a mustache on her upper lip and a hoarse voice, and would read the Qur'an and start chanting slogans at the beginning of each day as we lined up in the courtyard before class. Her family had come from southern Tehran and lived in a rough-hewn house in a slum along the main road in Shahr Ara, across from the Bulvar-e Gulha. It had once been a wide, open area and seemed to have been settled by fiery revolutionaries overnight. My mother hated Torkan and would argue with her when she came to pick up Kati and me up after school. Her brother had died in the revolution, and years later, we heard that Torkan had gone to medical school on the compensation paid to her family for his martyrdom.

The mood of Iranians, regardless of group or faction, had heated to the boiling point. The burning and looting had come to an end, and the demonstrations against America weren't enough to quench the people's thirst. When my friends and I reached the front gate of our school one morning, we saw custodians with buckets and giant brushes in hand, painting something on the ground. Before we could take another step, they turned to us and said, "Go that way to go in. The painting is wet, it'll get ruined. *In sha'Allah*, tomorrow you'll be able to walk over it." I asked, "But what *is* it?" My friend Mozhgan Tokaldani answered quickly, "The American flag."

A few days before, the American embassy had been occupied by youths who called themselves Students Following in the Line of the Imam. They had taken sixty-six Americans hostage, demanding that America return the Shah to Iran. Ayatollah Khomeini announced on the radio that he supported their gesture. I gleefully clapped my hands, certain that we would have a special program before our lessons and that the first few hours of class would be canceled. The bell rang and we all lined up. Torkan had taken her place in front of the microphone and called out with great excitement, "Our motto of the day?" And we had to respond, "*Marg bar Amrika*" (Death to America or Down with America). And Torkan asked again, "The motto of the oppressed?" And we had to respond, "*Marg bar Amrika!*" She chanted, "*Marg bar Amrika!*" and we repeated it, *Marg bar Amrika*, our voices like a hammer hitting the courtyard.

Khanum Nuri, the faculty representative of Omur-e Tarbiyati, stepped up to the microphone. "Young ladies, you certainly must have heard that the 'nest of spying' was occupied by the Students Following in the Line of the Imam. We would like to go stand outside the spies' lair to show our solidarity. Those who want to come may, in an orderly fashion, get on the minibuses in front of the school when the morning program is finished. You have your teachers' permission, and we aren't having classes today. The rest of the students who aren't interested in participating in the demonstrations can call home and have their guardians pick them up or stay at school and go over their lessons."

The students burst out clapping and yelling with joy. I prayed that I would be allowed to go. I imagined the hostage takers as a bunch of young girls and boys dressed as commandos with guns standing in front of the embassy. We rushed to the minibuses. There were more of us than there were seats. Some of the girls had to stand and were hanging from leather hand straps. We pushed and shoved each other, as we knew if we couldn't find a spot, we'd have to stay back at the school. I leaped on window seats for me and my best friend, Delaram. We waved at our envious classmates who couldn't find seats as we departed. Beside ourselves with joy, we all just kept clapping our hands together.

For two hours, the caravan of Fiat minibuses from Chista No. 1 was stuck in record traffic on what had formerly been Bulvar-e Elizabeth and was now Bulvar-e Keshavar (Farmer's Boulevard). Inside we sang and clapped and generally misbehaved. The teacher scolded, "Children, we are not on our way to a wedding! Chant slogans! Give praise to Allah!" At about Khiaban-e Amir Abad, now Khiaban-e Korgar (Worker's Avenue), we faced a mass of people pressing eastward toward the American embassy, spilling into the streets. A riotous crowd of students and ordinary people seethed together, signs in their hands, struggling to make their way to the embassy. It was almost noon, and people were handing out tomato and hard-boiled egg sandwiches from the back of a pickup truck. We were getting cranky after sitting so long and complained, "*Yallah!* Why aren't we going anywhere?"

Khanum Nuri climbed into our minibus, holding a megaphone that now seemed completely useless. She shouted, "Children, quiet! Be quiet! Listen!" Our teachers never imagined we would be met with such pandemonium nor did they have the courage to take all three hundred schoolgirls out to continue toward the embassy on foot. They had decided to turn onto the nearest street and head back to the school. She told us, "It is enough that we've come this far to show our solidarity. The best thing to do now until we leave this street is to yell slogans out from our minibuses in an orderly fashion with clenched fists." Three or four girls stuck their heads out of each of the minibuses' windows. Khanum Nuri shouted into the megaphone, "*Daneshjuye Khat-e Imam! Bar tu darud, bar tu salaam!*" (Students of the Line of the Imam! Upon you praise, upon you peace!) Too tired to chant, we just clenched our fists in the air and screamed. You couldn't tell one voice from another, and we must have looked pretty funny to the demonstrators, as we certainly attracted their attention. A crowd of boys was marching in an organized formation shouting slogans, and our unharmonious voices clashed with their rhythm. One of them said, "Guys, will you look at that twerp?" The boys all turned their heads and burst into peals of laughter. Another one called out, "Look at that one's head! She looks like a monster!" They were making fun of Delaram, my best friend. She was an attractive girl with big frizzy hair like an afro, such as you rarely saw in Iran.

This was intolerable. We instantly changed our mission and went from chanting to waging war against these boys. We threw at them whatever we had left from lunch, from plastic bags to dry bread to wadded-up balls of paper. Khanum Nuri scolded us through the megaphone, "Girls! Girls! For shame! What's all this?" In tears, Delaram explained. Khanum Nuri climbed down to go talk with the custodian from the boys' school and again our chants changed from "*Marg bar Amrika!*" to clapping and cheering, "Khanum Nuri! Khanum Nuri!" Khanum Nuri tried to hush us from the middle of the frowning crowd. After that the teacher's assistant got on the bus with a pen and paper to write down the names of the unruly students whose marks for discipline would be penalized. We sat still. We were told that everyone's mark for conduct for the term would be lowered by one grade. As we drove away down a side street, there were still great crowds heading for the embassy. Exhausted, with lumps in our throats, we made faces at the demonstrators out on the street.

⊚　⊚　⊚

1980

That winter, my family still held out hope for a coup. Doctor Bani Sadr, who enjoyed the confidence and trust of Ayatollah Khomeini, was elected with twenty million votes as the first president of the Islamic Republic of Iran. Bani Sadr was a former classmate of my uncle Bizhan the dentist. Strangely, years later, he turned up again as a patient at my uncle's practice on Khiaban-e Sepeh near the parliament. Every time Uncle Bizhan saw us, he'd lower his voice and intimate that he had it on authority that in a certain month the regime would fall. And when that date had passed, another authority would give him a new date. The country was faced with a severe economic crisis. Fuel production had fallen drastically, and inflation had risen. Despite the new president and constitution, the country wasn't stabilizing. A few months after the revolution, the street assassinations began. A group by the name of Forqan took to killing prominent revolutionary figures. Their first bullets lodged in the heart of Doctor Mortaza Mutahari in May 1979, a university professor and one of Khomeini's beloved disciples. Khomeini was shown weeping on television, proclaiming Mutahari the apple of his eye. The day of Mutahari's assassination became known as teachers' day.

Khomeini had moved residences from the Madresseh-ye 'Alavi to the religious city of Qom but found it was too isolated from the capital. In April 1980, Imam Jamarani, who led prayers at the Jamaran mosque, suggested to Mr. Khomeini that he take up residence in Jamaran, the birthplace of my mother. How my mother's heart sank! The village lay among the foothills of the Elburz Mountains and could not be accessed from the north. It seemed like a safe place in the uncertain political atmosphere—quiet, unspoiled, with a pleasant climate. In the mornings, roosters crowed, and the scent of hot fresh bread wound its way through the earthy garden lanes. Crystal clear waters flowed from springs deep in the mountains into the little street canals. The local people were simple and fervently religious. Khomeini found the choice admirable, and he rented Imam Jamarani's house and cheerful garden. My mother was furious with Imam Jamarani, who was my grandmother's *rezai* brother. A *rezai* is like a foster sibling in Islam. When Imam Jamarani and *Mader-jan* were babies, my great-grandmother nursed them at the same time, so Imam Jamarani became *Mader-jan*'s *mahram*.

In Jamaran, many villagers took great pride in Khomeini's arrival, while others feared for their safety. The Pasdaran welded seven bolted iron gates along the street that led to Khomeini's home and issued special passes to local residents. Jamaran had become a restricted area. Though we luckily didn't need to pass through the seven gates to visit my grandmother, we still had to stop at the main checkpoint. When the guards would start questioning us, my mother would light up like a wild rue seed in a fire. Putting up her chin, she'd answer sharply, "To my mother's house, with your permission!"

Then we'd have to be searched. There'd be bearded men wearing the green uniforms of the Revolutionary Guard sticking their hands in our purses and handbags. We'd have to keep calm and call these provincial sentries "brother." Finally, they'd tell my mother to fix her *hejab* and wipe off her lipstick. This was all it took for my mother to explode. My sister and I would plead with her—we knew that being arrested by the Imam's guards was very dangerous and would be a serious headache. But she ignored us and would rain down a torrent of abuse on whichever guard had his turn that day. "If you just turned Muslim and just started going to prayer, we are from a long line of God-fearing Muslims! And if you are Muslim, why are you looking at my face? Lower your head and fill out the pass!" My heart would break into palpitations. Sometimes we'd drive off with her wailing and cursing all the way to my grandmother's courtyard. But sometimes the brothers would call headquarters on the wireless, planning to arrest us and send us to the

Komité. In the face of these threats, my mother's voice just grew louder and shriller.

Usually one of the local business owners with some clout would arrive on the scene to save us. He'd tell the brothers that my mother grew up there and that she had kids to look after and an aged mother sitting at home. Then he would turn to my mother and say, "Zahra Khanum, simply arrange your *hejab* a little bit. This brother was only looking out for your own good. Just offer your praise to Allah and Mohammed and Mohammed's line." By that time, the news would have reached *Mader-jan*, and we'd meet her walking up to the checkpoint in her white prayer chador. She would anxiously ask my mother, "What's all this fuss you're making? Keep your head down and come and go quietly. Do you want them to throw you in the corner of some prison somewhere?" My mother, still smoldering, would say under her breath, "I was fine. That stinking trash!"

I knew in my heart that the days of warmth that I remembered from before the revolution were never coming back. I didn't believe any longer in the tomorrows my uncle Bizhan and my parents kept promising.

chapter two My Commander

NOVEMBER 1999

I had arrived at the rendezvous half an hour early and sat in the courtyard of the offices of *Zan* looking at the flowers and the persimmon trees. It was autumn, and although it was only the middle of the day, the air was dark and moist after the heavy morning rain. Ashen clouds were spread across the Tehran sky. Water droplets, left over from the rain, dropped one by one from the points of the daisies' petals. I took a pack of Marlboro Menthols out of my purse and looked to make sure no one else was around. The first time I had officially bought a pack of cigarettes was three weeks before, the day after I was released from prison.

The café owner had smiled at me when I bought them. He hadn't seen me for a few months, and he shook his head in delight. He certainly would have read about my release in the morning edition of *Aftab-e Yazd*. My mother didn't know I'd started smoking—I would lock the door to my bedroom and secretly blow the smoke out the window. Majid, a co-worker of mine at *Zan*, once told me that I would meet all the requisites of a professional reporter if I added cigarette smoking to my repertoire. Fine, but today I had a cigarette in my hand, and I felt less like a newspaper reporter than ever.

I drew the tart Shemiran air into my lungs as I took deep drag after drag and slid the slimy leaves back and forth on the ground under my feet. *Zan*, my former workplace, was now shut down. No one else was in the courtyard. Not even Hossein Agha the gardener, who

37

was always rearranging the flowerpots, moving them this way and that. He was undoubtedly sitting in his room heating up his tea. He'd passed so many years in this courtyard that he'd grown old here. Early in the morning, he would transfer the blossoms from one bed to another with a trowel, or he would clip leaves and extra branches with his shears. At the start of the revolution, the owners entrusted all of it to him and fled. Maybe Hossein Agha hadn't been able to escape because he was lame in the left leg, or maybe he didn't want to run. The property was confiscated by Khomenini's new government and sold off at auction. The new owner had rented the building out to Faezeh Hashemi, the owner and editor in chief of *Zan*, with Hossein Agha in tow. When the newspaper was still running a few months back, he'd bring me a fistful of fresh, wet, white jasmine on a saucer nearly every morning and set it on the table, and I'd drop a handful of bonbons into an empty vase for him.

No trace remained of the previous summer's bustle. Everyone had left. After my release, I'd returned like a lost pigeon to stare in shock through the window at the old office with its overturned chairs. Now *Zan* had become my secret meeting place.

At least twice a week in the afternoon, I'd creep silently into the building like a shadow, and a few hours later, I'd go home.

My guest during these afternoons was a man in his thirties, medium height, with full-bodied, wheat-colored hair. He had a bony jaw, eyebrows that flowed into each other, and sparkling black eyes. To the guards, he was simply Agha-ye Muhandes (Mr. Engineer). Nothing more. In this way, I explained away the presence of this mysterious official appearing with a briefcase several times a week. When we were alone, I called him Farmandeh, which means Commander. He wouldn't tell me his real name.

With his eyes fixed on the stone walkway, he'd ring the bell of the guardhouse and enter with a "*Salaamu aleik.*" He wanted to be seen as little as possible. He'd place his black bag on the ground beside him, and I'd immediately motion for Farhod to bring us tea. Along with Hossein Agha the gardener, two guards also remained from when *Zan* was housed in the building: Farhad, an Afghan, and Ali, from Kermanshah. Both were my devoted friends and confidants. Whatever their feelings were about these comings and goings, they asked no questions, not even why I wore a chador. The usual procedure was that the day before a rendezvous, I would get in touch with Farhad to be sure the office would be empty. Agha-ye Muhandes always worried about an unexpected appearance by Faezeh. He said Faezeh knew him.

I sometimes thought about killing myself. I was tired. I didn't know what to do or whom to turn to for help. As I walked up the steps toward the editorial offices, I faced my own image in the glass window, a barrier between me and the old days. I felt no connection with the person I saw. It was not anyone I had ever known before.

The newspaper building was completely dark and silent. The great chandeliers were without power but I could see through the half-open slits in the dusty broken shutters. The crows in the courtyard were hard at work pecking at the orange persimmons. I was filled with regret, remembering my co-workers. Everyone had packed their things up quickly and left. But there was a drawing by our cartoonist, Nik Ahang Kowsar, still posted on the wall above my desk. It had been a joke for the benefit of the office, a caricature of me, extremely busy, talking on ten phones, with a hundred sheets of paper in my hand. Under it was written "*Al-hasood la yasood*" (Jealousy gets you nowhere).

Farhad opened the door of the public relations building across the courtyard and called to me. "Miss Entekhabi, Agha-ye Muhandes has arrived." A little shudder ran through my body.

I took my chador out of my bag.

The day after my release, my mother, my sister, and I had gone down to Khiaban-e Zartusht to pick out material for a chador. It wasn't a hard decision; I chose a light fabric, just thick enough. The shopkeeper who cut the piece congratulated me. With the cloth wrapped up in a bag, we took a taxi straight to my paternal grandmother's house. Her name was Parvin, so I called her Maman Bozorg or Maman Pari. She'd been a successful seamstress in the old days. Forty years ago, her tailoring school on Khiaban-e Amiriyeh was bustling with the most chicly dressed women in Tehran. When I was a child, I would often play there. There was a display case full of cloth flower decorations, handmade by my grandmother, and another with tiaras and bridal bouquets. Each flower was a masterwork of beauty and craftsmanship. And my grandmother's fine floral hand embroideries on tablecloths and cloth napkins were exquisite worlds unto themselves. There were wardrobes filled with evening gowns and jeweled and sequined dresses, and there were half-sewn wedding dresses on mannequins. We weren't allowed to touch anything. But on Fridays, after our elaborate noontime lunches, a general naptime was enforced. The pillows and bedsheets were brought out of the walk-in closet, and everyone had to rest until four. While everyone else was sound asleep, my cousin Elham and I would get up, quiet as mice, and creep upstairs to the tailoring shop. We'd open the wardrobes full of dresses . . . fabric . . . threads and needles . . . and the displays of flowers and bridal hair clips. . . . Time and time again, I pinned them to my hair and stood in front of the mirror looking at myself from behind and from the front, standing away and up close.

But that day I wasn't coming to my eighty-year-old grandmother, now living in a small apartment in the north of Tehran, for evening finery. I wanted her to fashion the piece of black cloth into that pyramid they call a chador. It was a simple matter. I stood at the table where she ate her lunch and draped the cloth over my head. My grandmother looked worried.

"Maman Pari, I've been swallowed by a black cone," I joked, hoping to cheer her up. She seemed to understand that if I needed a new chador for "official" visits, it meant that the Ministry had kept a hold on me—that I wasn't really free yet. My mother interrupted, "No, it's like people who have epilepsy. They draw a line around you to keep Satan away." Then we all laughed.

The cigarette fizzled on the soaking wet ground and went out. I murmured to myself, "May Satan keep away from me . . . ," and threw the black chador around myself and headed toward the public relations building. Agha-ye Muhandes was waiting.

◙ ◙ ◙

When I came to the prison, I chose names for the guards so I could tell them apart. Each group started their shift at nine in the morning and finished at nine in the morning the following day. They were employees of the Ministry of Intelligence and were not permitted to disclose their names to the prisoners. They referred to themselves as nameless soldiers for the Imam-e Zaman, the Imam of Time, who, according to the Shi'a faith, will reappear to guide the faithful at the apocalypse. I chose names that suited their shapes, appearances, and ages. The interesting thing was that they took a liking to my names and started calling each other by them. Zohreh and Monir and Taibeh were on one shift and Leila and Humaira and Hajiya Khanum were on another.

"Well! What do we have here? So at last it's come to the chador? There isn't a single proper chador in your whole house! What, now you're Muslims?" Leila mockingly held the hem of my chador to show off its fine knit to Humaira, the half-wit, and Hajiya

Khanum. It was a chador of fine black chiffon with raised velvet roses.

I had been in prison nearly two months. The day before, I had been moved from Towhid Prison to the Revolutionary Court for my first court appearance. All I had to cover my head was the black overcoat that I had thrown on when they came to arrest me. Taibeh Khanum, the plump guard with half-blond frizzy hair who specialized in dream interpretation, auxiliary prayers, and in all manner of irregular religious supplication, had lent me her black chador. She was a kind woman and had taught me a verse from the Qur'an to recite four times during interrogation and breathe at my interrogator to block his mind.

The women who guarded us, from the moment their shift started until the following morning, were locked in just like us. They sat all day eating and keeping the corridors under watch on closed-circuit television. They would take turns calmly checking on us in our cells every fifteen to thirty minutes through little peepholes but would only open our doors four times a day. The first for early morning prayers, then three more times for prayers, which also coincided with the three daily meals. Aside from that regulated cycle, under no circumstances would they come open the door; you couldn't even have unscheduled bathroom visits. But over the months I was in prison, they started talking about my good behavior, and I was allowed to have an occasional cup of tea or an extra bathroom visit.

The chador that Taibeh Khanum had lent me was thick and heavy, and the second I put it over my head, I was seized with a feeling of being pulled backward from behind. It weighed twelve or thirteen pounds, and I had to press my hands together under my chin like a vice so it wouldn't slip off. When I came back from court, my head ached and my wrists hurt so much I couldn't move them. I complained to Taibeh and asked her how she held it on her head every day. The three guards laughed. Taibeh Khanum lifted up my wrist and brought it next to her own. Her wrist was at least two times thicker than mine. They took a look at my petite form and said, "Who is going to marry such a weak and sickly girl!"

The next morning, before I was to be moved again to the courthouse, my interrogator visited my cell block with a plastic bag. My mother had sent me the most beautiful chador in our house. We had other chadors at home. We wore them to funerals at the Behesht-e Zahra or to government offices where "sisters without chadors will not be received." They were worn when we went with my mother to the *imamzadeh*s to pray and make votive offerings. But the exquisite chador with the velvet flowers was my sister Katayun's, bought during her wedding shopping. In Iran, it is customary for a black chador to be bought for the bride.

Now the chador was in the hands of Leila, the fat prison guard. Her sly eyes were fixed on the expensive, delicate fabric as she worked it vigorously. What did she understand of the message carried in the heart of that chador? I knew that my mother and Kati had sent me the best they could to tell me they loved me. I clenched my teeth together.

One after another, each guard said a little piece, using the chador to judge my family. I wanted to thrust out my hand and slash Leila's face with her deceitful little eyes. She was a lot younger than me, maybe twenty-two, and I knew what she wanted. She wanted to hear my cries swell until I'd have to be sent down to the basement to be whipped like the others I'd heard her drag across the floor.

I could bear their laughter. Leila's world was the world of her Revolutionary Guard husband. She would come and see my newly washed underwear, hung on a nail behind the cell door to dry, and would say in a loud voice filled with contempt, "But are you not a virgin? Aren't you ashamed to be wearing these? Who did you want to show them to anyway?" She was fascinated with my yellow ruf-fled Victoria's Secret underwear that I had bought in New York. And when my mother sent me underwear from home, she sent fine lingerie, and it became another source of jealousy for little Leila. On bathing days during Leila's shift, I'd wash myself and run out, even if I wasn't completely finished, because she'd secretly watch me. One time I shouted, "Oh, for the love of God!" and she turned her head away, and then she brought it back. She had been comparing her body to mine, it seemed, and took pleasure in my discomfort.

When they left me with Kati's chador, so I could dress to go to court, my tears poured forth. Inside my cell, I buried my face in the black fabric. The sweet smell of my sister's perfume rippled through the cloth. Kati was right there with me; I could pinpoint the moment she sprinkled the perfume on the chador for me, to give me the fresh scent of the freedom outside these walls. I shut my eyes. I threw my arms around my sister and wept with all my heart.

I had fallen in love with my interrogator—but the chador brought me painfully back to reality. In those two months alone in my cell, I'd tried to forget my life before. I was determined to find salvation by becoming a good Muslim, and being a good Muslim required sacrifice. So I sacrificed the memory of my family, believing that the only way to be released was to gain my interrogator's trust. My faith and my future were in his hands. I needed love and the power of love to change my desperate situation, and the person closest to me was the person I saw every day, my interrogator. I started loving him in my own way. First I began to trust him and believe that he truly could help me. Then I confessed to him, I told him about everything, from the way my parents had met and mar-ried to stories from my childhood and growing up, to my years as a poet and writer and a reformist reporter. I felt like a nun, I felt that I *needed* this confession.

In love, I concentrated only on him. I couldn't think about my beloved family outside. When I dreamed of him, it gave me peace and serenity, and I could forget his cruel treatment. I'd hear him coming down the hall for me, and I couldn't wait—I would imagine he wasn't coming to torture me but to love me. I needed this peace of mind to keep from going crazy and to store up energy to stay strong. How could I force him to love me, too? He thought of me as *mofsed*, deserving execution. I couldn't change him and I couldn't change the world. But I'd fallen in love, and I felt it, real love. I couldn't control my heart's beating when I heard him approaching.

With concentration and self-control I had cleared my family out of my mind, cleared out even my own existence. In order to win, I had to play a difficult part. We had never seen each other, as I always faced the wall in the interrogation room. I used my voice and my hands to draw him in—my voice soft and contrite as I confessed, and my hands dancing like swans. I could sense him changing slowly. I knew he couldn't wait for the moment he could turn me toward him, when we would face each other. I knew that to be able to do this, to ever have the chance, he would have to help me escape. Then my sister, with her scented chador, brought back to life my memories of the people I loved, of all the beauty outside the walls of the prison. The chador warned me that I had to hurry, that I couldn't lose any more time.

I also couldn't wait to see his face. I was confused, and I wondered—could seeing his face tell me whether I was really in love? My adventurous side, at least, wanted to see him, badly. His voice was strong, and at that vulnerable moment I desired a strong man to keep me safe. And he kept telling me that I was different. I believed that I was a smart and capable journalist who was different from others. I believed that he understood this about me, that he knew I was a person who could take risks that others wouldn't dare consider.

Sometimes, in the room together, he'd put photos in front of me, taken from the album the guards had seized from my room when they arrested me. Supposedly, they were used to illustrate some point, to have me explain an occasion or identify the foreigners I was with, to reveal secret information. In some of the images, I was made-up and posed at a party in a low-cut dress. He'd chosen some photos from my vacations, to Germany or southern France, where I was wearing a bikini, and he'd ask me, "Aren't you ashamed to be dressed like that!" I'd see beyond the harsh question and my meek answer, and would imagine a pious, religious man afraid of his forbidden love, battling with himself as he looked through my photos one by one.

chapter three Snapshots of the War

"Attention! Attention! The signal that you are now hearing, the signal that you are now hearing is a declaration of a state of red alert. This means that an air raid is imminent. Please leave your place of work and proceed to a shelter. Oooooooooooooooooooooooooooo . . ."

Whenever this emergency broadcast came over the airwaves of Radio Tehran, wherever we were, we froze in our tracks. "Feridun! Feridun! Kati! Camelia?" My mother would call for us during the sudden blackouts that followed.

"Maman, I'm here."

"Don't move."

When I saw the flashlight shining in my face, I knew that a minute later I'd find myself being carried upside down under my father's arm into the cellar under the courtyard of Maman Pari's old house on Khiaban-e Amiriyeh. We would descend the dark and narrow stairs two steps at a time. My father and I would be followed by my mother, who was three months pregnant with my brother Kai Khosrou, with Katayun, and behind them, my grandmother with my youngest uncle, Behzad. My grandmother had sewn a neck purse for everyone in the family, and we put our identity papers and a little bit of money in them. I don't know why—maybe so the rescue crew would be able to identify us in case we were found buried under debris? From the cellar we heard the sound of airplanes and the stammer of antiaircraft fire. My father and my

47

uncle usually left us women alone in the cellar and went up to watch from the roof.

We were homeless, temporarily living with my grandmother. My mother, sister, and I had recently returned to Tehran from Frankfurt, where we'd been waiting for my father to join us. We had gone to Germany after my parents finally realized that the situation in Iran for people like us, with our background, was only getting worse. The "tomorrow" we looked toward wasn't coming fast enough. But for a few weeks, while we waited in Frankfurt, my father had been dragging his heels. He had sold our house (our villa that we had so longed for, built right next to the princess's palace, and in which we had lived for only three months) for the cheapest price imaginable, and the buyers had moved in early, with our furniture still in the house, without paying the full amount. One day, after she had gotten off the phone with my father, my mother immediately called the airline and told us, "We have to go back so I can straighten things out with your father. He has thrown away not only our house, but also our brand new furniture." The plan was that we'd return to Germany with my father before the schools opened.

At Mehrabad airport in Tehran, my mother was very nervous as we lined up to be searched. She had hidden in her clothes the latest issue of *Paris Match* that had pictures of His and Her Royal Highness in Panama. "Excuse me, this lady is pregnant. Please let her to the front of the line," called out a woman's voice. Everyone moved aside for my mother. Three months pregnant, she made her way slowly to the front. The sisters, draped all in black with black gloves, stepped forward meekly. They fixed their eyes on my mother's, and seeing the cold indifference she wore on her face, they made a quick, cursory search of our things, and we were on our way. The next morning was September 22, 1980, and when we woke, the announcement came over the radio: "Respected citizens, Iraq has

attacked our southern borders and has bombed Mehrabad airport."
We all knew very well what that meant. Until further notice it
would not be possible to leave Iran.

At the beginning of the war, enemy planes were constantly
breaking the sound barrier with a dreadful sound, and my grandmother, along with everyone else in Tehran, had secured all the
windows of her house with an X of thick duct tape so that, in the
event of a nearby explosion, the shattered glass would not end up
strewn about inside our house. She also covered them with a dark-
colored blanket lest any light escape, alerting the Iraqi planes and
subjecting our neighborhood to bombardment. We'd try to finish
our supper quickly in the dim light, before seven o'clock, my grandmother warning, "Hurry! Hurry up and eat! The electricity will go
out soon."

The main topic of conversation at school in the morning was
the attacks of the night before and whether any of us had lost any
family or friends. There was also plenty of excitement whenever
the red alert sounded over the loudspeakers. My classroom was on
the third floor, and we'd drop our books and notebooks in a rush and
hurl ourselves out of the building, terrified we'd wind up buried
under falling debris. The stairwell was extremely narrow and a good
place for mischief. Everyone would start screaming, and from the
back, I would push the others. We'd get jumbled up, nearly all of us
stuck on the stairs with the sound of explosions above us. When we
finally poured outside, I'd wink at my classmate Farnaz to set things
in motion. "That was either Amirabad or Yusefabad."

Farnaz, nodding her head in agreement, would add, "Oh yeah,
THAT's right. Last night on Voice of Iraq, we heard them SAY
that they were going to strike those two neighborhoods today." The
handful of kids near us who had family and friends in those neighborhoods would start screaming and crying. The rumor spread
rapidly, and in no time half the school would be sobbing to be sent

home. The superintendents never could figure out where the rumors started and could only decry our wickedness over the loudspeakers after we were back to the white level of alert. They gave cups of sugar water to all those brats who were sitting in the school office almost passed out from crying.

But secretly, my heart would be about to explode, as I asked for permission to call my father's office at Shir-e Pak factory, near the heavily shelled Mehrabad airport. When the receptionist would answer, I'd start to calm down, then the weighty and measured voice of my father would ring clear, "*Befarma'id.*"

"Hello. *Salaam.* I wanted to make sure you were all right."

"Yes, you can see that I'm fine. Is there anything else?"

"No. Good-bye." As I left the office I looked around haughtily at the others, and under my breath so the teachers wouldn't hear, I'd hiss, "Babies! Fraidy cats!"

◙ ◙ ◙

We led a double life. Our homes were small islands of privacy, hidden from the Omur-e Tarbiyati, the eyes and ears of the new government. The moment you entered, you had to shut the door quickly behind you lest some stranger steal a glance inside. Many luxury items we considered indispensable to our lives were forbidden under the new government. Playing cards. Music cassettes. My father's bottles of vodka. All the forbidden books in our library. The VCR. Ali Agha, who we called "Agha-ye Movie," would come on his motorbike once a week with his black briefcase locked in his trunk. We had only a few minutes to tell him what we wanted. Kati and I wanted Indian movies while our parents wanted the old Nouruz specials from before the revolution, shows featuring Khanum Hayedeh and Mahasti from a time when they could watch the New Year turn over on TV with delight and excitement instead of fear and apprehension. Ali Agha would take back the movies from the previous week, set four new movies down on the dining table, close up his briefcase, put the rental fee—one hundred tomans—in his pocket, and go.

On the day Egyptian President Anwar Sadat was assassinated, a Hezbollah partisan extended a box of sweets to my father, trumpeting, "Anwar Sadat got what was coming to him." My father declined, saying, "I am not so thrilled when people are killed that I go around eating sweets." They brought my father from Shir-e Pak factory to prison for "examination of his beliefs." He was interrogated, blindfolded, for hours while the guards went through his wallet. As the director of the sales department, he was paid a handsome salary. In compensation for the wound he had inflicted on national revolutionary sentiment, he paid a "voluntary" settlement of six months' salary to the "Imam 100" account for veterans wounded in the war. He had no choice but to work six months without pay, cursing at the ground under his breath.

My father also put himself in danger by visiting the Behesht-e Zahra cemetery. If one of us two—Kati or I—didn't go with him, we'd spend the whole day worrying. One morning I woke early to be sure I didn't miss my chance—I felt it was impossible for me to allow him to leave without me.

"Baba, I'm coming with you."

My father's voice floated from the kitchen, "No, you sleep. Next time."

It was twilight, five in the morning on a wintry Friday in 1983. Fridays are the only days in Iran when everything is closed. My father wasn't going to work, and we didn't have school. I threw my nightclothes on the bed. Before my father could finish drinking his unsweetened tea, which he drank every morning, I was standing in front of him, carrying my coat and head scarf, my hands and face unwashed. My father was in a hurry to pick up Afsar Khanum before the traffic started, and we had a long drive ahead of us. When my mother snapped, "Do I have to do your homework for you?" I didn't answer, and I followed my father to the car with my mother still threatening in a cracked and sleepy voice. Tehran had been reduced to a pleasant dream in the clarity of the cold winter morning. Only a few cars stopped here and there at traffic lights, and occasionally a haggard street sweeper would push his worn-out old broom across the icy, tarnished pavement. Afsar Khanum's familiar figure, dressed in black with a bag in her hand, waited for us in front of her house. She got in the car and took one look at me napping in the backseat and said, "Feridun, why did you bring this innocent child? My dear Camelia, why aren't you at home resting on a Friday? Would you like to go sleep in our house?" I shook my head no and half-opened my eyes to read the scrawled slogans left over on Afsar Khamun's home from before the revolution. "100%—Bani Sadr," and further down, "Brother Rajavi." Rajavi's photo was still everywhere; he was the leader of the Mujahedin-e Khalgh party and had nominated himself for the presidential election. He had been popular at the beginning of the revolution when he led the Mujahedin's movement against the Shah, disseminating Khomeini's message throughout his networks across Iran. Without Rajavi, the revolution would never have succeeded, but just a few months after Khomeini's victory the Mujahedin turned in opposition to the Ayatollahs. The next slogan on the wall was illegible; someone had crossed it out with black spray paint and written beneath it, "It's traitors who run away. Death to the opponents of the *velayat-e faqih*." Rajavi had fled to Paris. But he led from exile, and his portrait printed on this cement wall was still in good shape.

Afsar Khanum was making a fuss, ceremoniously apologizing to my father for having inconvenienced him at such an early hour on his day off. In reply, my father joked that they could settle his payment later. Little by little we made our way from north Tehran to the outskirts. We drove around Meidan Shahyad (Shah's Remembrance Square), newly Meidan Azadi (Freedom Square), where travelers from the western terminal stood out in the street. Peykans and Fiat minibuses labeled "Azeri Junction—Meidan Azadi" frantically changed gears to pick them up and scattered lovely plumes of smoke around our car. The further south we traveled, the more the landscape changed. Around Meidan Bahman several hundred construction workers gathered, some sitting on the curbs. A pickup truck waited to carry them off to work, and everyone started trying to pile in, with the boss yelling, "Twenty people. No more than twenty needed." And he cursed in Turkish, saying anyone else had to walk. Work was so scarce these men lined up on a Friday. We reached Yaftabad and there was more hustle and bustle. People waiting outside a bakery in their pajamas and ragged flip-flops stared into our car as we drove past. Small children with their fingers up their noses played with trash in front of their doorways. The houses were wretched hovels. My father looked at me in the rearview mirror and said, "Take a good look and see how people are living and think about the value of the life you lead." As my father signaled to turn at the billboard that read, "Way of the Mausoleum. Entrance to Behesht-e Zahra," I thought about whom we were visiting.

◎　◎　◎

My mother burst into the house in a fit. She tossed her purse in a corner and collapsed on the sofa in the dining room. All afternoon, rather than focus on our homework, Kati and I had been watching anxiously out the window for our mother to return from Afsar Khanum's house.

"It's a good thing I didn't bring you two. It was no place for children. There were men in civilian clothes standing around on the street staring at everyone. They were keeping an eye on who was coming and going, and watching to make sure there wasn't any noise coming out of the house. The family didn't have permission to have a memorial, and we had to pretend we weren't coming to mourn. Your aunt and I had to go into the bathroom to put on our black clothing. You couldn't even cry, they would have come and taken us away." She started whimpering, "Oh, poor Afsar!"

Guli, Afsar Khanum's twenty-seven-year-old daughter, had gone to the firing squad four days before. Afsar was the widow of Agha-ye Shahandeh, my grandfather's cousin who we had been shocked to see confessing to spying on television some years before. He was the first member of my family to be executed. Guli had been in the middle of her graduate studies in England but had come back to Iran at the height of the revolution to marry her cousin, only to find her father on the run. The father and daughter arranged to see each other in a restaurant, and revolutionary secret police followed Guli to arrest her father then took them both. Guli was accused of conveying a message from a foreign agent to her father, and she was held in the dreaded Evin Prison for two years. But this fall we heard that she had been transferred to Ghezel Qal'eh Prison, and we all assumed that, sooner or later, she would be released.

That Thursday, my father had taken Afsar Khanum to the prison, as he often did on visiting days. But this time the guards announced, "Today you cannot see her." She asked them at least to accept the sack of food she had brought, but they handed it back. "Guli isn't here."

"Why? Where is she?" her mother asked.

"She hadn't been corrected. Hajj Davud moved her to Evin to be corrected!"

Afsar went home dazed with the sack in her hand. The next morning her telephone rang with the news that her daughter was buried in Behesht-e Zahra.

◙   ◙   ◙

My father gestured to me and said, "You go down there and sit on that bench till we get back." I waited in the Behesht-e Zahra's Rose Garden of the Martyrs with a bottle of rose water in my hand, wondering whether he would allow me into the forbidden area. A fine, stinging rain was falling. In the distance I watched Afsar Khanum's tiny body clad in black running in the wind, disappearing into the section designated for the executed. They called the grounds where Guli was buried the section of "infidels" or "atheists." There were neither proper tombstones nor proper names and addresses for the dead, just "six-month-old child" or "five-month-old newborn." And these small stones had been smashed and scattered about. Even the weeds and shrubs were burned day after day by vengeful hands, lest any blades of green grass appear on the graves of these nameless souls.

The Rose Garden of the Martyrs where I sat was covered in thousands of signs and plaques. "*Shahid qalb-e tarikh ast*" (The martyr is the heart of history). "*Shahidan zende and Allahu Akbar, Be khun ghalatide and Allahu Akbar*" (The martyrs live on—God is Great. They have been rolled in blood—God is Great). A photograph was fastened to each tombstone. "Martyr: Mohammed Ali . . . Soldier martyred for his homeland: Jevad . . . Martyred Pasdar: Mohammed." All the walkways had benches for the families of the martyrs to rest on. A few mothers and wives had spread prayer rugs over the tombstones and were reading from the Qur'an.

I watched the silhouette of my father as he stood guard on the main road, in case some revolutionary hard-liners appeared to harass his cousin-in-law as she sprinkled white *noql* (thrown to symbolize the deceased was of marriageable age) and wheat around her daughter's resting place, so that birds would gather there.

"Khanum? Khanum? Please, have some hot milk with cocoa."

A young boy of about seven with a tray in his hand called out to me. Steam rose high from the disposable plastic cups. His mother, a little behind him, held a newborn baby in one arm, and in her other hand she had a thermos from which she was filling some more cups.

"Please take. It's *kheirat*." The drink was to honor the dead, and I understood that they were relatives of a martyr.

"Thanks." I took a cup. He probed my face with his eyes.

"Is your father a martyr, too?"

"Huh?" I suddenly understood what he was asking. I was sitting facing the shrine of a martyr. I shook my head.

As we drove away, Afsar Khanum was in her own world, hunched over and crumpled up in the front seat. I gave her the cup of milk. It was still warm.

"Drink it, it's good for you." She took a small aspirator out of her purse and sprayed it into her mouth. I knew she had asthma.

We came to the gates leading out of the cemetery. In the large fountain, the spouting water had been colored red to represent the blood of the martyrs. Behesht-e Zahra was gradually coming to life. Cars filled with mourners and covered with wreaths of roses were driving in as we left.

On the way back my father drove much faster than he usually did. He turned on the radio to relieve the grieving, heartbroken atmosphere and asked Afsar Khanum to join our family for lunch. But she politely declined. "I have troubled you enough. It's Friday. You have things to do. I'll be very grateful if you would just drive me home." My father pulled up in front of the picture of Bani Sadr. To me, the former president's most distinctive feature was his glasses, which looked like the bottoms of little tea glasses. Afsar Khanum walked off with her slight limp.

Two years later, she, too, passed away. My mother said she suffocated in her sleep, but perhaps it would be better to say she died of grief. My sister, Kati, tells me that when she visits Behesht-e Zahra to pray, she asks her husband to watch out for her as she darts into the section of the "wrongly killed," as people call the section of the "infidels" now that the government has admitted, in some cases, to mistaken executions. She scatters rose petals in memory of Guli, her father and her mother, and all the others.

▣   ▣   ▣

1981

As the war continued, we heard the sirens and air-strike warnings so often that we became indifferent. The radio would announce a state of danger, and I would stay right where I was, sitting at the dining room table, doing my homework. When the windows rattled, I would step out into the courtyard and try to guess how close the explosion was by surveying the volume of smoke and in which direction it was blowing. But early one morning, I was woken by shots fired right past our house. My mother, overcome with excitement, exclaimed, "They're the Shah's supporters! It's a coup d'état! I told you that a reliable source indicated that, by the end of the month, they would . . ." Kati cut my mother off.

"Shhh! Shhh! Be quiet. Let's hear what they're saying over the loudspeaker."

Someone on the street with a megaphone announced, "Respected neighbors, kindly remain in your houses until further notice. A group of troublemakers is operating in your neighborhood, and our brothers in the armed forces are working hard to flush them out of their nest. You are in no danger." The Mujahedin-e Khalgh had turned against the government and were engaging in street warfare, bombings, and assassinations. The renegade *mujahedin* hid in residential neighborhoods in *timi* houses. We could hear machine guns and the megaphones asking the *munafiqin* to surrender. "The whole area is surrounded by our brothers in the army. Place your weapons outside on the ground and give yourselves up."

We went to the window and saw that all of our neighbors were at their windows watching, just like us. I waved at my Zoroastrian friends Nasim and Bahareh who lived across the street. Would the discovery of the *timi* house mean that we wouldn't have classes that afternoon? Our crowded schools now operated in two shifts. One week we'd go in the morning, the other in the afternoon. Every week we'd have new additions to our already-full class of nearly forty students, most of us sitting three to a bench. They'd be war-scarred girls from Ahvaz, Abadan, Khorramshahr, or elsewhere in the south. Our director would stand at the blackboard and present an olive-skinned girl with black eyes and dark eyebrows, looking from head to toe like a product of southern Iran. We all put on false smiles, but the girls sitting two to a bench would shoot daggers from their eyes, knowing they'd have to share their places with this new student, not knowing whether she'd be lazy or smart, or whether she'd have bad breath.

Since I was scheduled for the afternoon shift, I was happy when the sound of the clash intensified, as being forbidden to leave the house would mean there was no hurry for me to do my schoolwork. But it wasn't noon yet when the bearded man with the megaphone in his hand returned and pronounced, "Dear sisters and brothers, we are very grateful for your patience and cooperation. The area has been cleared of dangerous elements, and you are free to come out of your homes. *Allahu Akbar! Khomeini rahbar!* (God is great! Khomeini is the guide!) Death to the opponents of the *velayat-e faqih!*" We hurried down from the fourth floor, dying with curiosity. A neighbor who saw the whole thing was narrating the siege with great flair and bombast for an audience that had arrived on the scene before us. She described how the young men and women had been brought out of their hiding places in the house blindfolded with their hands tied behind their backs.

My own Uncle Ali had been accused of turning against the revolution and had disappeared. On June 28, 1981, his young wife, Iran-Dokht, called my father in tears. "For God's sake, come," she cried. "They've taken Ali . . ." He'd served in the Revolutionary Guard for less than two years when he was dismissed from the outfit. He told us that the conduct of the new government was incompatible with the Islam portrayed in their propaganda and that he was unable to serve in the ranks of thieves and liars. After that, Uncle Ali stayed home, absorbed by his wife and newborn baby. But that morning we'd heard on national radio that the office of the Islamic Republican Party had been bombed by *munafiqin*, and a group of government officials had been martyred. Had my uncle taken part in the bombing? I wondered.

My parents must have wondered the same thing. The Pasdaran searched my *mader-jan*'s house and my uncle's house and we expected them to show up at ours next. My father took my hand, and we stole out with the bag of cartridges Ali had given him in the early days of the revolution. We walked to a public phone booth at the end of the street, stuffed in the bag, and ran off. We took stock of whatever else we had in the house that was forbidden—bottles of liquor, playing cards, my mother's beloved issues of *Paris Match* with their pictures of the Shah and Farah, banned books, and finally my father's pistol. Late that night we took everything to the parking lot, and my mother buried it under old newspapers in an empty oil drum.

Every day my mother sat in fear by the radio, holding her breath as the announcer read the names of those executed. Each time she waited . . . but, no, they hadn't said his name. She could breathe again. My father worked all his connections, but the officials said they had never heard of Ali. My mother threw a chador over her head and went from standing at the gate of one prison to standing at the gate of another, my baby brother in her arms. She pleaded and got useless answers. After seven months we finally found him. He was in Evin and had been arrested for insulting the values of the clergy. On the morning of the bombing, Ali had been in line at the bakery, and a friend had asked him, "Did you hear that today they planted a bomb in the office of the Republican Party?" My uncle, who had nothing to do with the renegade mujahedin, was in good spirits at being newly released from the guard. He answered, "Tell it to my son's balls!" He hadn't yet made it to my grandmother's house with the warm bread when the Pasdaran stopped him. My grandmother spent that whole day sitting out on the balcony waiting for him.

◙　◙　◙

My mother had refused to speak to her brother since an incident in the early days of the revolution. As a zealous Revolutionary Guard, Uncle Ali had been charged with watching the houses of high-profile fugitives on Khiaban-e Sarlashgar Zahedi, a street parallel to my *mader-jan*'s in Jamaran. This was while relatives on my father's side, like Guli's father, were fleeing house to house. One night we stopped to visit Ali on the way to my grandmother's, and after passing through the security checkpoint, we came to a brown house with a graded roof. Someone called for my uncle, and he appeared at the entrance in the darkness in his special green uniform. He came right over and lifted me up in a single motion. The fingers of my kind uncle were adorned with gaudy carnelian rings. From his arms, I could see the house in disarray, trampled under the boots of my uncle and his friends. A rag doll lay ripped in half, dragged outside the front door, and peering in, I could see a wooden crib in a child's wrecked bedroom. I remembered how we used to take walks in the park with his girlfriends. Was it my same beloved uncle who had laid waste to the home of these children? My mother was upset and couldn't bear to see any more. I heard her say some nasty, indecent things to him under her breath. We turned the car around and sped down the hill, my mother crying in disbelief. The man whose house we had seen—Khusraudad—was pictured among the victims of the firing squad in the next day's newspaper.

Though my mother wouldn't speak to my uncle, we continued to visit Jamaran as always. In the summer of 1980, Khomeini, in observance of the birth of Mohammed, held a public meeting with the people. A screaming throng was advancing past my grandmother's house, where we'd gathered to celebrate the holiday. The women had tied their chadors at the waist to have their hands free in the crush of the crowd, and some of them were crying and beating their breasts. Everyone was supposed to gather in the *husseinya*, and Khomeini would speak from his terrace. But the adoring first had to line up, pushing and shoving, so the Pasdaran could issue them entry passes to see the Imam.

I was once blessed by Khomeini when my uncle Ali stole me from Mader-jan's home. My mother was away—perhaps to visit another relative in Jamaran. My uncle asked Mader-jan for a veil to put over my head and told me we were going to buy candy at the Mohsen Agha grocery store. I knew where he was really taking me, but I pretended that I was fooled, knowing how angry my mother would be when she found out. Uncle Ali ignored Mader-jan's warnings. With lots of "*Salaam aleikum Baradar*," we passed the gates into the Imam's courtyard. At my uncle's request, the Imam himself appeared in the courtyard and put his hand on my head and prayed.

Back at Mader-jan's house, my mother crouched on the terrace like a wounded tiger. As soon as we appeared, she tore into my uncle. Kati had been out with my mother, and in private she later told me she wished she could have met Khomeini, too. My mother cursed wildly at anyone and everyone around her that day, twisting my ears in a firm grasp, and promising that if I said a word to my father, he'd have our scalps—and we'd never be able to come back to Jamaran to visit Mader-jan again.

Since Khomeini had moved to Jamaran, the village had become "Khomeini's house." All day on the celebration of the birth of Mohammed, what my mother called "the idle masses" had been knocking on our door to use the bathroom, to take a drink of water, or to change their babies' diaper. It was impossible to refuse them. The strong smell of human waste rose from the far corner of the yard, where people lined up for the toilet. My uncle was in the Imam's special guard and brought by a stack of passes to Khomeini's rally. My mother shrugged her shoulders. She didn't need the passes. As people left our courtyard, they turned to her and said, "Hajj Khanum, how fortunate you are to be close to Agha-ye Khomeini. May you be rewarded by the Imam-e Zaman."

The neighboring garden had been taken over by revolutionary forces as a base for the units guarding Khomeini. These provincial soldiers with their green hats would sit up on the roof behind antiaircraft guns. But aside from keeping an eye on the skies and the Imam, they found something else to occupy their time, namely, peeping at my grandmother's house. Through the thick of the leaves of the walnut tree that stretched up toward the heavens, you'd see the face of a soldier hoping to catch a woman changing her clothes or something similarly exciting. But sadly, the house had only two old women living in it, my grandmother and her friend Nargess Khanum. And these were not the sort of women to venture out without a prayer chador. And if my mother ever glimpsed a shape turned toward the courtyard, she'd cry out, "Motherless bastards! Was the point of your revolution that you could come stand on the roof and look at women's bodies? Rotten pieces of shit!" Then they'd slip away like phantoms, scared off by her insults. But an hour later there'd be another shadowy figure on the roof. . . .

On the morning of the anniversary of Mohammed's birth, our courtyard was overflowing. As soon as it was announced that the Pasdaran would start issuing the required passes to the rally, people rushed forward like a herd of frightened sheep. A group went by carrying something I couldn't see, wailing and crying, "Ya Hussein!" The Imam Hussein was one of the sons of Ali, the first Shi'a imam; he had been killed in an ambush at Karbala, and the Shi'a forever repented his death, often punishing themselves publicly. Dust rose off the ground in clouds, and my mother picked me up under her arm and shut us in the house. The sound of shrieking and moaning swelled from every direction. Men, women, and children were being trampled underfoot. As the crowds retreated, hundreds were left lying bloody on the ground. People busied themselves attending to the wounded and the dead. My uncle, a brawny, athletic man, showed up every fifteen minutes with a corpse over his shoulder, carried from who knows how far away, and lay the motionless body out behind our back wall. We brought out white sheets. My uncle murmured in Arabic, "*Enna l'illah wa enna aleihi raja'un*" (Verily, we come to God and to God we return) and drew the sheets over the faces of the dead. At one point, he emerged from the bewildered crowd shouting, "Move aside! Make way!" But the young girl draped over his shoulder gave a violent twitch and hung lifeless. When he put her down, I saw the stain down his back. Afraid to die, the helpless girl had peed on my uncle's shoulder.

It took several hours for ambulances to arrive and the tens of thousands of people to disperse. The sound of wailing and weeping continued. "*Ya Hussien! Ya Imam-e Zaman!*" (Oh Hussein! Oh Imam of Time!) Families that had gotten separated in the confusion came first to peek under the white sheets. They uncovered the faces of the dead and then either went on their way or else started moaning. And again they were knocking on the door of our house. They wanted to know where their loved ones had been taken. My mother would say, "To either the Reza Pahlavi or Manzaria Hospital." And my uncle would growl under his breath, "Say Martyrs' Hospital. Pahlavi is dead!"

◙ ◙ ◙

"Ali, Ali, Ali, dear Ali . . ." My mother held her brother tightly and cried uncontrollably in front of Ghezel Qal'eh Prison. After seven months without word of his fate, four more months passed before she agreed to visit him for the first time. He was half alive after being tortured in Evin. Luckily, he had been moved. At least at Ghezel Qal'eh you could ask for a lawyer to look into your case. Kati and I, too, had wrapped our arms around our uncle's legs and were crying. For the entire visit we were kept outside, and we sat on a piece of cardboard we'd laid down. In my mother's hand was a bag full of underwear and *qand*. My mother had a blue voile chador with bright roses all over it, and we tried, like the dozens of other families that had come for visits, to stay composed and look unemotional and revolutionary. My uncle was too ashamed to kiss his wife, but when he saw the picture of his nine-month-old son, he broke down and wept bitterly.

My uncle had bought a Kit Kat and Smarties from the prison store for Kati and me. Hoping that homemade food would restore her brother's health, my mother started packing him a little bundle of meat sandwiches and other food, clothes, and pocket money every week. I remembered how at the Ashura holiday he used to march, holding high an almost two hundred pound metal tree with sixteen branches, with the crowd cheering him on in one voice, "Ya Ali..." Now he was thin and wounded. He told my mother at length about how he had nearly been executed for being a *mujahed*—

how they had put him in a cell for those awaiting execution until a friend in the Pasdaran had recognized him and moved him. They had beat his stomach until it had been torn to pieces. He had to be brought twice to the prison hospital to have his ruptures stitched up.

A year passed since his arrest, and after much discussion, everyone agreed on a plan to bribe the prison director. "In order to free your uncle we need hard cash," my mother explained, as she moved nuts, one by one, from a set of engraved antique silver dishes into an empty porcelain bowl. When the plates were empty, she took out a handkerchief and wrapped them. Bowls, plates, spoons, and decorated trays disappeared from our dining table. Aunt Mahin, an old friend of my mother's, arrived.

"Mahin, put this gold in your bag as well. By the way, did you bring your chador?"

Aunt Mahin recited, "*Bismillah ar-Rahman ar-Rahim*" (In the name of God the Merciful and the Compassionate) as she put the jewelry in her handbag. I recognized my grandmother's bracelets; my mother's long necklace with the portrait of the first Shi'a imam, Hazrat-e Ali; her enameled bracelet from Kuwait; her other bracelet embedded with Pahlavi royal coins; and my uncle's wife's wedding ring. My mother called out, "Camelia, are you ready?"

"Where are we going?"

"To the bazaar."

Aunt Mahin and my mother had put on black chadors so they could hide the valuables underneath as well as conceal the money they collected. Being so short, I felt trapped in the congestion of the bazaar. I couldn't see anything, and I couldn't breathe in the thicket of women in black chadors. I held my mother's hand tightly to make sure I didn't get lost, and we went from shop to shop. My mother sold everything, and the complicated negotiations began. Again and again, my father was brought to the prison to negotiate for Ali, blindfolded so he couldn't recognize any of the interrogators or secret prison officials. He acted as the guarantor for my uncle's bond, giving up to the Ministry of Intelligence his own passport and therefore his ability to travel outside the country, along with hefty bribes, so that my uncle would be released.

Before, my uncle had been a robust, athletic man, but my new uncle was broken and tormented. All year round, in the snow and freezing cold, or in the unbearable heat of the summer, he'd sit on the roof and play with the pigeons. I'd go up to watch the neighbors with my uncle's field glasses.

"*Salaam*, Uncle!"

Coo, coo, coo, coo . . . Sunburned and defeated, my uncle watched his birds with his head tilted back, emitting faint noises from his throat and scattering handfuls of millet. The birds would flutter over to eat. Another man, Akbar, an emaciated *taryaki*, sat across from my uncle. A tray lay between them, with two empty tea glasses and a little bowl of *qand*. My uncle stuck his head out and called, "Iran! Iran!"

And the voice of his wife rose from the vent, "Yes?"

"Give two teas to Fatima to bring up."

I had heard Aunt Iran voice her heartache many times to my mother. "Zari Khanum, when will it end? From morning to night he's up on that roof calling those pigeons! And he has every two-bit hoodlum up there with him!" She'd pour the tea, mumbling under her breath, "Snake venom for all I care!"

"Fatima, take these up and bring down the old tray. For the love of God, Zari Khanum, do you see what kind of life we have here?" And she'd wipe the tears from her eyes with the corner of her informal cotton chador. As my cousin brought up the fresh tea, my mother followed on her heels. My uncle's guest, upon seeing my mother, put his tail between his legs and quickly ran off. She had war written all over her face.

"Ali!"

My uncle mumbled a greeting as he slurped the hot tea from the saucer. He was an old man at thirty-five. His long hair had gone completely white; his moustache hung down from both sides of his mouth like a dervish's. I looked at my uncle, orbiting around another world; was he alive or did he just bear a striking resemblance to a living being?

"Your wife and children are ashamed! Why don't you put a stop to all this? You're up here on this roof shooing birds around from morning to night. You stare at the sun so much your pupils are yellow! Comb your hair at least. Cut your beard. These people are ashamed! Your wife is young!"

Aunt Iran hid in the space behind the half-open door to the roof, but we could hear her crying. My uncle raised his face to the sun. He didn't answer but tears streamed down his face. . . . He hadn't said a single word. My mother cried, "Ali, speak. Say something. Do you want to see a doctor?"

I couldn't bear to be there any longer. I ran down the stairs to the floor below and found my chubby cousin Fatima, delighted at this rare opportunity to be left alone with the box of sweets my mother had bought for them, trying to eat them quickly before her mother came down. I started to quarrel with her. "Don't you have any manners? Leave some for your brothers!" I went into the bathroom so I wouldn't be able to hear the sound of my uncle's agony and his wife's heartrending sobbing. My mother's voice drifted down the stairs. "I don't know what they've done to this poor creature. It's like talking to a wall."

◙   ◙   ◙

"They're not worthy of you. May they bring you good fortune." With these words, my mother placed a pair of brown leather shoes in front of my uncle Musayyeb. She had recently visited London and brought back this gift. "Try them on and see if they fit," she added. He said, "Zari dear, they're super. I'll save them for when I go to meet His Majesty at Mehrabad airport." It was the winter of 1980 and they both still believed the Shah would return. My aunt's courtier husband, "His Majesty's personal calligrapher," had worked in the Shah's private office. Worried about being arrested in the months after the revolution, Uncle Musayyeb spent most of his time in his pomegranate groves in the village of Nurabad. He always assured my mother, with extreme optimism, that "next month" the mullahs' government would fall. But the months kept passing, and the Shah died in exile on a hospital bed in Cairo that July.

Among our family and neighbors, the only person to publicly mourn for forty days and nights after the Shah's death was my mother. She dressed from head to toe in black and wore a black chiffon veil and gloves. Local business owners advised her to stop with this useless business to avoid any harm that might befall her or her family. She'd shrug her shoulders and say that it wasn't a crime to wear black.

JANUARY 1985

The Iranian revolution had entered its fifth year, and I was in the fifth grade at elementary school. That week my classes were on the morning shift, and I came home to the surprise of an empty house. I stood ringing the doorbell, kicking at the frozen snow on the doorstep.

"Camelia! Camelia!"

Our kind neighbor Menizhe Khanum called to me. She was always keeping watch from her kitchen on the third floor of the apartment across our street. She and my mother were friends, and we'd visit often. She could turn your cup of coffee over onto a saucer and read your *fal* in the grounds. Menizhe Khanum would always see wedding proposals, money, and news coming by telephone. She'd look at me slyly and say, "You little devil, who is this boy in your cup?" I'd put on a big frown and shrug my shoulders, my mother watching me like a hawk.

"Dear Camelia, come up," she beckoned. "Your mother went out, and she said you and Katayun should stay at our house."

"Where did she go?"

"I'm not sure. I think she had to go to your aunt Turan's house."

To Niyavaran in the middle of the day? I was afraid but didn't ask any more questions. Menizhe Khanum was Zoroastrian. Above her wall clock, a piece of paper read, "Good words, good thoughts, good deeds." My mother said that they were much better than Muslims, since they weren't liars or hypocrites, and they minded their own affairs. Their prophet was a man named Zartusht, and I had gone to their temple on Khiaban-e Qavvam-e Sultaneh many times and savored the scent of aloe wood and frankincense burning. I was busy compiling a list of guests to invite to my birthday party, so I brought the list up to discuss with Menizhe Khanum's children, Nasim and Bahareh. Katayun came home and joined us for dinner.

It was after nine when the doorbell rang. I saw my mother, facing away from me, and she was dressed exactly as she had been four years earlier. Black coat and skirt, black festooned lace veil, and a black snakeskin handbag in her hand. A gentle snow had started to fall and was swirling around her, landing softly on the ground. I was afraid to come any closer, but when she heard my footsteps she turned. Her eyes were blood red. She gazed at me and burst into tears.

I didn't have any black clothes in my wardrobe for Uncle Mussayeb's memorial, so I wore dark blue. In my aunt Turan's house, there was an undulating sea of people dressed in black. It was the sixth day after my uncle's death, and this gathering marked the eve of the final day in the weeklong funeral. My mother, Kati, and I had visited the home every day for the past week, as is traditional in Iran. My father was staying over with his sister for the whole month, to keep her company in her grief.

A photograph of my uncle Musayyeb smoking a pipe had been placed in front of the door in the middle of a wreath of roses. He had died of heart failure in Nurabad. My uncle's royal colleagues were there, the ones who hadn't fled and who'd been spared from the vengeful wrath of the revolutionaries. The whole family. Those we knew and those we didn't know. A dignified old man with a cane and formal dress was standing next to my father and my uncle's brothers, greeting the guests. "Who is that?" I asked. My sister whispered into my ear, "That's Agha-ye Vaziri, Uncle Musayyeb's old colleague. He hasn't been paid his salary in five years, and he's waiting to get it from the crown prince."

My cousins, Mahta and Gita, were two perfect ladies, greeting and kissing the mourners with solemn faces. Gita had been married the year before, and Mahta had just finished high school. They knew how to delicately salt a cucumber and how to descend the stairs in style and how to gracefully cross their legs. They had practiced walking with books balanced on their heads. They were raised to be courtly, but courtly days were gone. Mahta, with her white face, used to always say as a child that she'd marry the Shah's son. But where was Reza, the Shah's son, today? Was he thinking of us? Mahta kissed Kati and me, and then she said, "Children in the back room."

Every day that we visited for the past week, the children were all stuck in the same back room. When I had ventured out to talk to my mother or father, Mahta or Gita had stopped me and brought me back again. I was tired and bored as I watched Bita, my aunt's youngest daughter, playing with a toy that looked to me like a makeup kit for Barbie. When I was her age, I would also carry my

Barbie dolls from room to room in a blue basket, happily telling myself stories. My fat cousin Omid, with his drooping stomach, had been kept content with all the meals coming from the restaurant Sarv. Sinking his teeth into some chicken, he asked us skinny girls to give him our leftovers.

Then I suddenly remembered something and snuck out once more to the front. All the lights were off and a *rowzekhan* was singing in anticipation of the seventh day after the passing of my uncle. I stumbled through the commotion, tripping over the feet of weeping women.

"Today is my birthday."

"What?" my grandmother asked softly.

Straining my voice, I said again, "It's my birthday."

When the singer came to sensitive verses and sang "father" or "orphaned children," the sobbing would swell. It was January 16th, and everyone had forgotten me, again. My grandmother blew her nose and whispered, "Happy birthday, but you see, your uncle is dead."

◙   ◙   ◙

"Zari dear, these are Musayyeb's things. I don't know anyone who could use them. If you know someone in need of them, take them as a *kheirat* for Musayyeb." My widowed aunt was packing up the house to move to a smaller apartment on Kucheh-ye Mahmudiya. Their large old house on Khiaban-e Fereshteh had a warm, carpeted basement that made a perfect hiding place when we'd play and an old courtyard with jasmine bushes clustered around the trunk of a pine tree. But I didn't like their salon. It was dimly lit with thick velvet curtains. Even thinking of it gave me nightmares.

After Friday dinners, my aunt would summon the spirits. My father called her "Turan, the ghostbuster." She said that on Friday evenings the spirits were free. She'd lay a sheet of paper covered with drawings and inscriptions flat on a small table. It must have been some kind of conjuring spell. Then she'd turn off the lamps and light a candle, and Mahta would send the children to the back room. We could hear my aunt's calm, strong voice. "Oh spirit who art here in this room, we greet you in peace. Oh spirit who art here in this room, kindly give us a sign."

We would sneak out to watch from behind the door of the salon, but when the tea glasses started to quiver on the table, my blood would freeze, and I'd run back before the spirit could appear in front of our eyes.

My father told us that my aunt was moving because the house wasn't safe without Uncle Musayyeb—that they were afraid of thieves. But my aunt told my mother and me that she'd heard the sound of the hooves of djinn and that at night they'd hear the rattling of glass cases coming from the salon.

I swallowed hard.

"Why? Are the spirits you called still in the house?" I asked. My aunt narrowed her eyes and said, "Evil spirits dwell in houses. Haven't you heard of evil spirits? You can't reason with them. And besides, this house has a very long history."

My eyes popped out of their sockets. What if a spirit should seize me one night by the neck when I went to use the toilet or get a drink of water? Then what would I do?

My aunt turned to my mother. "Zari, that old pine tree in the courtyard? Thirty years ago a little boy hung himself from it. He lived here with his grandmother."

"Who told you that?" my mother asked casually.

"I've heard the sound of weeping and moaning coming from the courtyard at night for years. My next-door neighbor Khanum Tasheyyud will back me up. She knows!"

I asked, "The tree with the jasmine sprouting up around it? A kid . . ."

My aunt interrupted me. "That is precisely why spirits are attracted to this house." She pointed out a thick book on the table with the title *Speaking with the Spirit World* and a ghostly figure on the cover. "I want to establish contact." My aunt went on with excitement. "For thirty nights you must grip a pen and press its point onto a sheet of paper and close your eyes and concentrate. Then you can ask questions, and your hand will start to move by itself, guided by the spirits, and they will answer." Then she winked at me and said, "Your little cousin Bita is reading the book, too." She smiled, and I could see her sharp silver-plated teeth.

When we got home, my mother began sorting through my uncle's things. I asked her, "Maman, is Aunt Turan telling the truth?"

"About what?"

"About the spirits in the sideboards of their house . . ."

My mother interrupted me. "Your aunt is a little cuckoo." She pulled a pair of leather shoes out of some yellow tissue and stared at them. "These shoes, they're the shoes that . . ."

SPRING 1999

"Did you know my uncle? Agha-ye Musayyeb Vafa'i? He was your father's personal calligrapher."

I was in the United States, in Virginia, interviewing Reza Pahlavi. For me this was the most important question in the world. As a child, I had stood in front of his photograph at the museum at the palace at Sa'adabad and asked, "Do you remember us?" In the picture, Reza was a little boy in shorts standing in front of his toy car in the gardens. Today a young man in a white button-down shirt sat across from me. I had waited years and traveled a long way for this moment. I had waited ages for his answer. Shouldn't there be someone who hadn't forgotten us?

Reza politely stared at his hands and tried to give a sincere answer. "Yes, yes, I do remember something. But I don't remember his face very well."

I pressed the button on my tape recorder and started the interview for my newspaper. The next day in New York I put a new photograph of Reza Pahlavi in an envelope for my mother and wrote: "To all those who have waited. To Uncle Musayyeb and his waiting brown shoes. To my father who sleeps peacefully in section seventy of Behesht-e Zahra, waiting for the mullahs to fall. To my uncle who died suffering on the staircase up to the roof, his eyes burned by the sun. To those who were never able to tell us when these dark days would pass. To my childhood spent in hope and longing. And Mother, to your youth, full of regret. This is Reza Pahlavi today."

chapter four Cool Summers of the Peach

FALL 1999

In otaq sahm-e tu nabud
Ke penjereh ra va gunjeshkan ra
Asheq budi
Dar tabestanha-ye khonuk az halu.

Sahm-e tu az mordad, sayeh-i ast
Ba ketabi be ruye zanuvan-e kudaki.

This room was not your fate
When you were in love
With the window and the sparrows
In the cool summers of the peach.

Your fate in August is a shadow
With a book on your childhood knees.

—Mandana Sadeqi

I stood at the mirror murmuring a poem by my friend Mandana. She had written "Camelia in Chains" for me while I was in prison and had mailed it to my mother about two months ago. It was the first thing my mother handed to me when I came home. Throughout our adolescence, Mandana and I went together to poetry festivals in cities around Iran. She was from Abadan, in southern Iran, and we had met in 1990 at the poetry and short story evenings held by the Club for Creative Literature and the Intellectual Development of Children and Young Adults in Mashhad. I applied a thick layer of green eye shadow. The color suited me, and I opened the Chanel rouge case. My face was pale. I put mascara on my eyelashes and lipstick on my lips. I recited her poem to myself: *Sahm-e tu az mordad, sayeh-i ast / Ba ketabi be ruye zanuvan-e kudaki . . .* (Your fate in August is a shadow / With a book on your childhood knees . . .).

In my heart I said to Mandana, "I remember that child with the book on her knees. And today, again, I am going to the Club for Creative Literature . . ." But my appointment was not to read poetry. That morning, the phone had rung, and I'd picked up the receiver. A familiar, firm, and measured voice had said, "*Salaam aleikum.* Don't forget—one o'clock this afternoon, at the club." Then a dial tone had emanated from the phone in my hand.

I had left prison only yesterday, looking like a hairy monster— my eyebrows had grown together like when I was in grade school, while I lost half the hair on my head. My face was covered with red splotches, and none of my clothes fit. I'd actually gained weight as I lost muscle, sitting alone every day in my cell. I went directly to the hairdresser with my mother. She didn't want to show me in that state to any guests who might stop by. The staff of the beauty salon shrieked when they saw me but then tried to pretend I hadn't changed all that much. They wept with both happiness and disbelief, and the other customers couldn't understand this emotional outburst. But after two hours of frantic effort by experts, I looked only a little better.

The day before my release my interrogator had come to set our "appointments" on the outside. And to deliver his ultimatum: I would be released on the condition that I sign my *tak nevesi* and begin spying for the Ministry of Intelligence. It seemed that he'd made me scrawl my signature thousands of times. As he reminded me of our dates, I just nodded my head. I was burning inside. As always, I was seated facing away from him, my eyes blindfolded. But he could see my hands as I signed.

"Good. I'll see you the day after tomorrow. Bear in mind that you must observe your *hejab* well and definitely come wearing a chador."

"At the ministry who shall I say I am coming to see?"

In a mocking tone, he said, "Who said anything about the Ministry of Intelligence?"

Meekly I answered, "Anywhere you say." I kept my tone quiet, acting as if I were confused. And I honestly was confused—I expected I would be made to prove myself and that the first place I'd report would be the central office of the Ministry of Intelligence. I'd written a role for myself to play, and I told myself that I would have to keep it up until I was truly free. My freedom meant more than a conditional release from Towhid Prison. I believed I could somehow keep playing the role until I was a free journalist again, until I could live free from threats to my safety and to the safety of my family. And pretending I was in love had inspired real love. In my heart, I wasn't ready to give up the role. I didn't want to become a spy, to criticize and investigate my colleagues. My stomach turned at the thought, yet I agreed to everything. I had entered into an agreement not to be "me." I melted at the sound of my interrogator's voice. I let him mold me into a new person, the person he wished me to be: a soldier waiting on the orders of her commander.

He smirked. "Is the Club for Creative Literature building good?"

Was he making fun of me? I knew he wanted to hear my voice again on the outside, to see my attitude toward him after I'd been released. And I knew both of us couldn't wait to face each other for the first time, to look into each other's eyes. My desire mixed with my fear. I was afraid of what the future held, of how far and where

I could go with this man, and how I could control the situation. But though I felt these fears, I didn't want to consider them. I pushed them away.

"At the club, come to the guard post and say that you are Khanum Zarafshan. Keep your face covered tightly. They will show you the way. Good-bye. Be a smart girl, and when you're out of here, always think about that blindfold."

It was the building where I had spent all my teenage years . . . The office of the literature teachers . . . Our poetry readings . . . How was it possible that this was the secret location of the Ministry of Intelligence?

The taxi I had called stood waiting. The girl that looked at me from the mirror today was not the girl I had been yesterday. It was a new face, but I did not want it. I took one last look at myself, then took a deep breath, and tucked the chador in my bag. I couldn't go out with a black chador in front of my neighbors. Drowning in perfume, I got into the Peykan. At Khiaban-e Vozara, took the chador out and muttered an explanation to the driver—"The hassle of government offices"—and put it on so tightly that only my eyes peeked out. I shuddered at the idea of running into any of the fine poets who had been my literature teachers—Agha-ye Sha'abani or Agha-ye Ebrahimi. If I met their eyes, I wouldn't be able to keep up my performance.

I crossed the avenue and stopped in front of the guard post. "My name is Zarafshan. I have a one o'clock appointment." With total surprise I realized that even the guards were expecting me. They directed me toward the building and the security office inside, but I could have found my way with my eyes closed; I had walked this path hundreds of times on my way to classes. But what was I doing here today? In the security office, a young man with a beard scanned my face, as I kept my head down and wondered at his plastic sandals. I could only think of the lost pleasant evenings when I'd crossed this hall before.

"Please go in."

I closed the door behind me. It was heavily padded with leather on both sides, so no sound could escape or enter. My heart was beating furiously. He was standing facing the window with his back to me. I said, "*Salaam*," and he turned.

I had uncovered my face. The chador was still on my head, and I was wearing a black silk head scarf and an ash-colored overcoat, the top two buttons of which I had undone. Without a word he stared at me in shock. Suddenly, he started screaming at me. "Aren't you ashamed to come here made up like that? I thought you had become a human being! Out! Satan out!" Still yelling, he continued, "Oh God, the man outside, what will he think about all the makeup this one is wearing?"

I was stunned. He marched behind me and opened the door and said something to the little man with the sandals. Furious, he barked at me to go and wash my face.

In the bathroom I turned on the cold, sweet, refreshing water, and watching myself in the mirror, I cried for my foolish mistake. I wiped away the green eye shadow with a paper towel. It wouldn't come off, and there was green up to my eyebrows. But I scrubbed my face the best I could and pulled the chador back on. As I passed the sentry again, I felt that maybe he was laughing. But I didn't look—I told myself I didn't care.

I knocked cautiously before turning the door handle. He had opened the window and was fanning the air with a newspaper. He said he was suffocating from the nasty smell of my perfume, that it had contaminated the whole building with its syphilitic smell. Angrily, he motioned for me to sit. I didn't know how I should react—this was not the scene I had imagined. I kept apologizing, saying I was sorry for not knowing how I should be dressed. I told him I'd wanted to look fresh and cheerful, not like someone depressed to see him. But my excuses weren't enough to calm him down. He was so angry, he said, "For a minute, I thought it was the devil at the door. I thought I had trained you well. But you've failed."

Both of us were left with a bitter taste in our mouths. It was a terrible start; I was crying and begging his forgiveness. He told me, impatiently, "It's enough for today, you'd better go. Just go! I will call you tomorrow. And never show up like that again. Is that clear?" I nodded my head and jumped up nervously like a rabbit, then went home to plan my next move.

chapter five Madame Camelia

1982–1986

We were at war. Iran had been declared an outlaw state. Imports from many places were prohibited, and domestic production was not sufficient. There was a shortage of everything from food to clothing, fuel, and even stationery. Many goods were rationed, and the government distributed a small booklet with white pages to be stamped to every family in every neighborhood. Stationery was available only on the black market, but students could present their Basij booklet to the cooperative and receive notebooks, pens, pencils, and erasers for a set government price. The cooperative notebooks had thin paper covers, and the pages were coarse. Our handwriting looked smeared and crowded between the lines. In a word, they were ugly, and I could not awaken any desire within myself to write in them. But a look from my father was all it took—the important thing was to pay attention to schoolwork. "Lots of other children can't afford even these notebooks," my father would say.

As soon as new coupons were issued, everyone rushed to stand in a long line. Even with the rationing, provisions were scarce, and if the cooperative ran out, you'd have to go to the black market. But in one respect our family was very lucky: Shir-e Pak factory where my father worked was a dairy producer. To get a bottle of milk, people lined up at five in the morning, and even then it was reserved for the very young or the very old. Butter was considered a luxury, and most people never even saw its color for months. We had as much butter, cream, and milk as our hearts desired. Our neighbors would come to depend on my father, and a few extra sticks of butter or packets of milk were enough to keep us popular.

My friends and I would stand in the bakery line after school. Bread wasn't rationed, but the first duty of bakeries was to produce enough bread to send to the soldiers at the front. Civilians would wait hours to be sold no more than twenty pieces of thin *lavash* each. Iranian food is almost always served with *lavash*, so that was enough for only a few days for a typical family of four. Normally, several members of the same family would wait together to buy enough bread to last the week. My friend Mahtab would hold my place while I ran home to warn both our mothers when our turn was coming up. My mother would give me a twenty-toman bill (two hundred rials) in case she didn't get there in time. We'd read our textbooks in line and ravenously eat the *aluche-ye kisa'i* we had bought from passing vendors, which, in the words of my mother, was "the dirtiest food in the world." We listened to the other people in line whispering carelessly about the eminent demise of the regime and the numbers of war dead and the news from the Persian-language services of foreign radio stations. Gossip ranged from the rising prices of sugar and *qand* to the rumored illnesses of government leaders.

People used nicknames for all the leaders. Akbar Hashemi Rafsanjani was known as Akbar Kuseh (Akbar the Shark) since he didn't have much of a beard, and Ayatollah Montazeri, who was expected to succeed Khomeini was Gorbeh Nareh (the Tomcat), and Khomeini's son was Ahmad-e Gerian (Crying Ahmad) because on days when Khomeini met with the people, he'd stand off to the side with a sad face. Ali Khamene'i had lost the use of one hand when the offices of the Republican Party were bombed, so he was named Ali Yekdast (One-Hand Ali) or Ali Geda (Ali the Beggar) for how he'd gesture with only one arm, his palm upturned like he was asking for pocket change. But people only complained in the bread line, keeping their grievances among friends. When they wrapped their hot bread in their handkerchiefs and turned into the twists and turns of the alleys, they'd look nervously around to make sure the unsympathetic ears of the "sisters" and the "Komité-lings" hadn't been listening.

They kept an eye on us alley after alley, everywhere we went, and could appear suddenly in shopping centers, in front of girls' and boys' schools, and even at private parties and family affairs. The government jammed the Persian-language foreign radio with ear-splitting noise, but the internal Iranian radio was a pack of lies and propaganda, so ignoring the static, we'd turn our ears every night at eight o'clock to Radio Israel. We would go cautiously into the salon, the room from which the least sound would leak outside. Everyone would squat by the radio listening intently. But there were other ears at work in the dead of night, listening for the familiar music through cracked windows and doors, and suddenly shadows would fall on the walls of the courtyard.

When we had parties, my father would check the street outside every half hour to make sure the Sisters of Zeinab and the brothers weren't about to stage a raid on our house. My mother, my sister, and I would keep our head scarves and overcoats close to our chairs so we could put them on immediately if needed. The words "they're here" would throw a party into disarray, as guests ran for the door. Anyone who'd been drinking would swish cologne around in their mouth, and women and men would quickly separate. But there was never enough time to get rid of corroborating evidence. The armed Pasdars would burst inside and the Sisters of Zeinab would round up the women before they could throw away the pro-hibited playing cards, alcohol, music cassettes, videotapes—any-thing that would boost the severity of charges in court. Family gatherings were routinely broken up, but it was especially bad if mixed groups of young people were caught. Teens caught drinking were in some cases publicly flogged, and girls could be sent to the government hospital for verification of their virginity. Girls who failed the exam were forced into an engagement with whichever boy they'd been caught with. Anyone arrested could be kicked out of their high school or university, and for an extra measure of humiliation, the boys had their heads shaved to the scalp with an electric razor.

It became obligatory for women to wear the *hejab* in the middle of 1981. Shopkeepers put signs in their windows that read, "We reserve the right to refuse service to women without *hejab.*" And menacing jeeps appeared roving around Tehran, monitoring public decency. My father would say, "If you touch your head scarves in front of them, you'll catch their eye. Pretend you don't see them when you're in the street." I called them "Tripods." *The Tripods* was a series of science fiction novels—*The White Mountains*, *The City of Gold and Lead*, and *The Pool of Fire*. As a child and as a teenager, I must have read this trilogy a hundred times. Tripods were fearsome three-legged beings that would lay waste to Earth. In the books, these metallic overlords enslaved humans by putting caps on their heads that would make them instruments under the tripods' control. These books inspired me during the gray years of Khomeini's rule. I can still shut my eyes and lose myself in the story, as the hero, a fourteen-year-old boy, escapes and finds his way to other freedom fighters in the white mountains of the north. I'd put the book down on the couch and stare out the sitting-room window at the white Elburz Mountains to the north of Tehran, and I'd ask myself, "Are there freedom fighters waiting up there for me?"

The official names for the Tripods would change over the years, but in essence they remained the same. The squads were first called *Ya Sar-e Allah!*, then their name changed to the Authority for the

Detection and Prevention of Vice, then the Vice Squad, the Guidance, and so forth. My mother tells me that today they're called the Thunder. On the back of their jeeps, "4WD" was written for "four wheel drive," but they'd say this stood for four slobs (w for *velgard*) whose wives are sleeping around (D for *dawyus*). Two armed Pasdars sat in the front of the jeep and two women in the backseat. One of the Pasdars was the driver, and the other was the guardian of the sisters. When men resisted arrest, the escorting brother would get to shine, dragging the captive into the car and kicking him in the process. In accordance with Islamic law, the sisters couldn't lay their hands on an unrelated man.

We rarely left home except for simple outings to the restaurant Eskan, the arcades of Meidan Argentine, the Surkheh bazaar, and Khiaban-e Jordan. When the ominous white cars appeared, our hearts would throb in our breasts, and despite my father's warning, our hands would unconsciously gravitate to our head scarves. If we were wearing colorful clothing, we'd try to hide behind one another. The sisters, wrapped in chadors, veils, and black gloves, would come crashing down on your head like a nightmare. It was possible that they'd let a glimpse of exposed hair slide, but nail polish and makeup, never. Sometimes they contented themselves with our tears and pleading as long as they didn't find anything in our handbags like cassette tapes or "obscene" pictures of Hollywood movie stars or expatriate Iranian singers, like Fataneh, Moeen, or Andy and Kouros from Los Angeles. We'd beg for forgiveness and put ourselves down a thousand times while listening to their speeches about the fires of hell and how letting one strand of hair show implied disrespect to the blood of martyrs. And if they took you with them . . . The booming voice of my father rang in my ears, "If any of you go with them, you won't ever be coming home."

When I was twelve and thirteen, we all wanted to be punks. To be a punk, I needed pants with their cuffs rolled up and crazy-colored socks. Our punk rock spiritual leader was my sister's friend Kristian, an Armenian girl. Her mother made the homemade vodka that my father and his friends bought and called by the code name Sabaquz (a made-up word). Kristian could dance like Michael Jackson and told us all about having a real boyfriend, like the enticing secret behind "kissing like the French people." She wrote "Madonna" and "UB14" (for UB40) on my yellow binder, and I'd parade around the schoolyard with the English facing out. I made a fake gold bracelet from the strap of my mother's handbag and wore it next to my big round watch. It was everything to me to be "with it" and to be seen by the boys cruising past my school.

My favorite way to spend Thursday afternoons, when school let out early for the Friday holiday, was to visit my uncle Manuchehr, because he lived in the coolest district of Tehran. Gisha was lined with stores, and boys would drive their sports cars back and forth down the avenue. As soon as our father buried his head in his backgammon game with my uncle, Kati and I would poke my mother in the ribs. "Say it!" "Say it!" was our way of asking permission to go out and stroll past the shops. My mother would escort us out and then she'd turn executioner: "Fix your head scarves! I'm in no mood to deal with you being arrested! Get in front of me!"

One Thursday in Gisha I had rolled up the cuffs of my pants to show off the bright striped socks that my cousin Fariba had knitted for me. And I'd pushed up my sleeves and undone the top buttons of my overcoat, flashing the color of my blouse. Young people walked through the crowded streets checking each other out, sometimes exchanging phone numbers. That day, my mother remembered something she needed at Kayhan's Pharmacy, and she pulled us all in with her. I was restless and poked my head out to watch a traffic jam under the overpass, and I accidentally made eye contact with a woman in a black chador, then lowered my eyes to read "Guidance Patrol" on the side of her car. I quickly retreated back to sit with my sister and brother in the back of the drugstore, but within moments someone tapped me on the shoulder. I thought at first that she was just asking directions. "Excuse me, please speak louder," I said. Then I turned and looked at her. Chador, veil, black gloves! She commanded, "Come outside with me."

I whimpered for my mother. It was too late for me to arrange my head scarf, unroll my pants, or anything else. My mother followed, protesting, "WHY do we have to go outside?" The Guidance Patrol vehicle was pulled up right in front of the door. A second woman had gotten out and was opening the car door so they could put me inside. "Why? What have we done?" my mother asked. The bitch pointed and said, "Do you not see the state in which your daughter has brought herself out in public?" She pointed at my socks and said, "Could she have gone out wearing anything more vulgar than this?" People stopped around us to watch, but we knew no one would intercede on our behalf.

Suddenly Mother turned to me and screamed, "You! You went out looking like this when I wasn't looking?" She started beating me, yelling over her shoulder, "This girl is killing me! It'll be good for my nerves when you take her away. I know her father will shut her up after that!" As her blows rained down on my head and back, the Sisters of Zeinab changed gears to rescue me from her abuse and calm her down. My mother wept while the women asked me if I wasn't ashamed to go out looking like a punk when I had such a good mother and if I knew that "punk" was just another word for trash. They searched my purse, but all I had was a handful of change and a pocket mirror. I kept nodding, my head and eyes down, as I fixed my clothes and scarf. I was stinging with shame with dozens of people watching me. "Now you're a lady." Finally, they left. "Idiot!" my mother and Kati said in unison. I started crying and complained bitterly about the beating. My mother pinched my arm hard and said, "It worked, didn't it?"

◙ ◙ ◙

The ancient tradition of Chaharshanbeh-ye Suri was forbidden. The new government wanted to replace Iranian culture with Islamic culture as Iranian culture was considered imperial. They wanted to erase the connections people felt to their past. For centuries, Iranians would build fires on the last Wednesday before Nouruz, the New Year, and jump over them to cast their bad fortunes into the flames. Then they could start the new year with a clean heart and an abundance of hope for the future. At sunset on Chaharshanbeh-ye Suri, the Tripods would roll out from their bases to take control of Tehran, but nothing could deter people. Our neighborhood held the largest celebrations. Kati and I would go through the alleys of Gisha to find the hawkers who hissed, "Bottle rockets! Firecrackers!" The guy would scan behind him for plainclothes police, then quickly ask, "How many?" We'd buy sparklers and handmade "grenades," plastic bags of gravel and combustible powders. You'd have to throw these grenades really hard for them to explode. The next day, the local newspaper's accident blotter would be filled with reports of people who were blinded, had their hands blown off, or were even killed.

To scare us, the boys would throw grenades at our feet, and to show that we weren't scared, we'd take grenades out of our purses and throw them right back. The hot gravel would strike my hands and cheeks. My cheeks would be burned, but I had no choice; Chaharshanbeh-ye Suri was a battle, and we had to keep it going. At sunset the inner lanes filled up with so much smoke that the Tripods didn't dare enter the dense clouds. They parked and waited to strike. One year, a boy named Farid blew up a one-pound grenade that rattled the guts of the mobile patrol unit waiting at the mouth of Kucheh-ye Zanbaq, our little street. As our fireworks flared higher, their backup arrived from headquarters, and they attacked. Everyone quickly flew into the nearest house with an open door. The Tripods were left stranded among the bonfires and smoking heaps of ash. Only a few spectators from outside the neighborhood fell into their clutches. In the courtyards we stayed up till after midnight, eating nuts and setting off the rest of the sparklers and hurling the grenades over the wall onto the street. As we jumped over the bonfires, my sister and I would sing: *"Dunya mal-e mas', Dib geleh dareh . . . Siyah-I ru-siyas', Dib geleh dareh"* (The world is ours, the devil is unhappy . . . The darkness is ashamed, the devil is unhappy).

◉ ◉ ◉

Mother's Day was observed on the birthday of Mohammed's daughter, Fatima Zahra, and at school they gave prizes to girls named Fatima, Zahra, and Sadiqa (another name by which the Prophet's daughter is known). On Nurse's Day, the birthday of the sister of Imam Hussein, the Zeinabs of the school got prizes. News programs broadcast on Seda va Sima started inventing terms such as "Zeinab-like" or "Yasser-esque." The government was encouraging Islamic names against popular taste, but they remained unusual in my generation. In the modern and well-to-do Tehran of the 1970s, someone's name demonstrated their level of education, cultural sophistication, and beliefs. Arabic and religious names had long been out of fashion, especially in big cities. Even if someone had a traditional name, they would often go by modern names instead. They all had pretty much the same story: on the night before they were born, their mother or father or some relative had dreamed of a *masum* or *imamzadeh*, and in reverence the family decided to use that name on their child's identity card. But they still called their child by whatever name had been chosen before the blessed dream. My classmate Fatima called herself Helga, and my cousin Fatima was called Maryam. Our downstairs neighbor was Raqia, but her husband called her Shahla, and my co-worker Farnaz burst into tears when it was accidentally revealed that the name on her identity card was Sadiqa.

In 1979, the new Islamic government decided to change the culture by propaganda and by force. It became forbidden to choose certain names for newborns. Among them was Camelia. I smiled to myself at the thought that there wouldn't be any more girls named Camelia. For once, I took pleasure in these extreme measures. My little brother was born in March 1982, and my father had to fill the official's pockets with one-thousand-toman banknotes before he would make out an identity card in the name of Kai Khosrou Entekhabifard. Kai Khosrou was a Shah of ancient Iran. As Kai Khosrou grew up, he really did look like one of the ancient rulers from the portraits in the *Shahnameh*. With his thick eyebrows, which grew together in the middle, and his black eyes and olive skin, he had that somber, proud look of a king.

God knows how many times Kati and I were chased by Kai Khosrou with his toy plastic sword. He'd stand on a chair or the table, yelling, "King Kai Khosrou banishes you little girls!" Following that announcement he'd pose dramatically, brandishing his sword before jumping down to run after us. I was nine years older than him and Kati twelve years older, but we were rendered defenseless by the stroke of his plastic sword. We ran around the living room calling for our mother to "stop that crazy king!" As he grew older, many of Kai Khosrou's friends called him "Khosrou" for short, but my family always called him by his full royal name. We wanted people to recognize my father's brave choice at the registry office.

In my third grade classroom at the Nehzat-e Islami girls' school, there were two students who the Omur-e Tarbiyati loved to torture: Camelia Entekhabifard and Satgin Yaghmai. My sin was the Westerness of my name and Satgin's was the un-Islamic meaning of hers. At the beginning of the school year, the teachers from the Omur-e Tarbiyati opened their attendance books to introduce each student and remind them about the observance of *hejab* and prayer. Group prayer was mandatory in schools, and they lowered our marks in discipline and religious education whenever we were absent or misbehaved during prayers. I lied along with the others, bending down and getting up and going through the motions of reciting the prayers. Affectation and lying were the first things we learned in school, along with great caution in the questions we asked and the answers we gave. My last name begins with an *alif*, so was listed at the beginning of the role call. I braced myself as the teacher would raise her voice and ask, "What—what–elia Entekhabifard? Who is that?" Everyone laughed loudly, and I stood up. I held my chin up and said, "Camelia. Camelia Entekhabifard." She would mockingly reply, "And where are we from? Are we Armenian?"

She knew that I wasn't Armenian. Religious minorities were permitted to leave before the Qur'an and Islamic education hour began. Besides which, the Omur-e Tarbiyati were well informed about their students and their families' beliefs before school started. Anything they asked that first day was just to ridicule us. I answered, "No, Camelia is the name of a flower, and we are Muslim."

She had been waiting for me to say that we were Muslim to launch into a rehearsed speech. "There are hundreds of beautiful, expressive names to be found within Mohammed's family, and we have to go and choose an infidel's name for our Muslim child?" She concluded by suggesting I volunteer to turn in my identity card and pick out a new Islamic name. I silently sat back down, my classmates gaping at me. I was petrified with worry that when the new regime issued identity cards, I would be forced to change my name. But Satgin was in a much more difficult situation. Her father, Kurush Yaghmai, was a famous pop singer before the revolution.

When the teachers questioned her name, she'd quickly say, "It's Persian, meaning 'Kurush's wine cup.'" They'd cast their faces up toward the sky, as if in total incomprehension. Her name had gone from bad to worse. Wine from the cup of the great Persian king Kurush! Satgin would always sit back down in tears and say stubbornly that she loved her name and would never change it.

Then, in the fourth grade, Khanum Arablu, my religious instruction teacher, said in front of the thirty students in our class, "Camelia was the name of a depraved Western woman, and it doesn't befit you, a Muslim girl, to have the name of a disreputable woman. Certainly, your family didn't know anything about where this name came from." I looked at her wide-eyed. She was very pale, and the black veil she wore under her black chador covered her whole forehead down to her eyebrows and both of her cheeks. She told me to change my name with the ease she might ask me to close the curtains, saying, "Somayeh. The name Somayeh is becoming of a smart, bold, and articulate girl like you. Somayeh is the name of a woman worthy of Islam, a woman who, because of her unshakeable faith and devotion, is ready to sacrifice herself for the noble cause of all Muslims and freedom-loving people of the world. *In sha' Allah*, with the blessing of this name, you will become one of the women who struggle for Islam as *mujahedin*." She picked up her pen and crossed out "Camelia" and wrote above it "Somayeh." "I personally will call you Somayeh from now on."

My eyes burned like two little balls of fire. The tears wouldn't come. When the bell rang for recess, you'd have thought it was a special alarm to spread the news of my humiliation. Mournful sympathizers came to our classroom in droves to stare at me and peek at the attendance book. My name meant so much to me, and it was well known in our school. I was Camelia, the drama star, who performed in the morning assembly and the chorus. I had won prizes every year at the festivities commemorating the revolution. But I didn't have the courage to fix the attendance book.

The next period, our regular teacher returned, a woman dressed in a green, instead of a black, chador. She frowned, creasing her eyebrows together, and said that people's names are their personal responsibility and that she would speak with the director. But early the next morning, my father burst into the director's office like an erupting volcano. He asked to meet personally with this "chaste" woman who had disrespected his family, so he could impress upon *her* what it means to be depraved and disreputable. "Tell this woman that if she's unlucky enough to have a name like Sughra or Sakina, she should think first of all about solving her own problems and go change her own name!" Sughra and Sakina were old-fashioned Arabic names, chosen typically by poor laborers or peasants. Simply put, they were ugly and difficult to pronounce, and not the sort of name any urban woman would want to be called. Apologizing profusely, the director just repeated, "The Omur-e Tarbiyati did not mean it this way, they were merely joking around with Camelia."

This time when the first recess bell rang, everyone flocked to hear the story of my father's valor. The director gave our class a new attendance book, and my heartache could be forgotten. Khanum Arablu came to class without any acknowledgment of what had happened. But when it came time to demonstrate our lessons, she called on me in a shrill, wavering voice. "*Madame* Camelia, if it's not too much trouble, please go to the blackboard."

It was Maman Pari who'd named me after a flower when I was born on the cold and snowy afternoon of January 16, 1973. My father had been looking for a name that started with a k sound to match my older sister Katayun and was immediately pleased with Camelia. At home, my mother sometimes called me Kameli or Kamel. And

I hated the nickname Kami, so of course that's what I was called at school. Kami was short for the boy's name Kamran. But to my grandmother and my father, I was always Camelia.

Even now, when I dream about the past, it is my Mader Pari's home I see, the old building with its red rose bushes and grand old persimmon tree. When her tailoring school and studio were bustling with fashionably dressed clients, we weren't allowed to go upstairs or play in the courtyard before four. I'd be waiting in my swimsuit for the moment of deliverance when I could run to Mader Pari's "pool." The three of us—Kati, my cousin Elham, and I— wearing bikinis, would jump into the water and paddle around for hours. When I got older, I'd gaze at my grandmother's six by nine feet wide, one and a half feet deep garden pool in wonder. I couldn't believe that the three of us had been able to swim in it or that I had called this little basin a pool. A small wooden platform would be brought up from the cellar in the summertime and placed at the edge of the garden, and after hosing down the courtyard and watering the garden, my grandmother would place bowls of sherbet, lettuce, and oxymel on the platform and turn on the sprinkler.

When my grandmother heard about all the upset with the Omur-e Tarbiyati over my name, she took it as a direct insult. "She was wrong, that stupid cow! What does she know about *Lady of the Camelias*? You should have told her she can name her own daughter anything she likes. It is an honor to be Camelia." And that was how I discovered there was a book with my name in the title. I excitedly asked my mother for the book about Madame Camelia. We were all avid readers, and our best birthday presents were when my mother would let us pick out any book we wanted from the local bookseller. Our bedtime was nine o'clock, but I'd curl up and secretly read with a flashlight under the covers. But my mother looked at me and said, "That book is not suitable for a girl your age!"

Being denied permission made me want to read it more than

ever. But *La Dame aux Camélias* was also banned. After the revolution, many Persian and foreign books were only available on the black market. Every bookshop around the University of Tehran had a sign out front saying, "We will buy the books from your library." They'd sell second-, third-, fourth-hand books for ten times their original price. For several weeks I saved my allowance rather than spend it on chips and cheese puffs, and ordered the book from my neighborhood bookseller. When it arrived, it was a little pocket-sized edition. It looked to me about thirty years old. On the cover was a washed-out picture of young woman holding a white flower; the title read "Alexandre Dumas, *fils'* masterpiece, *La Dame aux Camélias.*" The bookseller wrapped it up in newspaper and gave it to me in a bag. At home, I had to keep the book in my underwear drawer or under the mattress, and read it secretly, hiding in the parking lot. As I remember, the book wasn't easy for me to understand. I hid that prohibited book for many years before I had the courage to put it on our shelves. But I remember how hard I cried on the day when I got to the final pages where Marguerite dies. I was forlorn for weeks. Marguerite Gauthier was with me everywhere I went.

chapter six The Basement of Towhid Prison

"They will beat the soles of your feet so badly that you won't be able to walk. You filthy bunch of saboteurs and anarchists, now have yourselves a good excuse: President Khatami! Did you think that Agha-ye Khatami is of the same ilk as you troublemakers? Or did you think that now that Khatami is here, you could just throw away the government? Well, you were blind. The eyes of those who give their lives for the Imam and the revolution and the eyes of the soldiers of the Imam-e Zaman are open. They'll teach you. I will teach you a lesson that your friends seem to have forgotten. There are many ways to make you talk, you animal! I will hang you. Do you understand? For spying and treason. It'll be easy for me. I've signed execution orders many times for girls and boys much younger than you. Blasphemers and traitors both get mandatory death sentences. You understand? Have you been to Behesht-e Zahra? Have you seen the section for the godless, Khavaran? They'll bury you like a dog, and then your mother can sit and cry over you. Do you understand what I'm saying?"

A stream of sweat was running down my spine. The waistband of my pants was completely soaked. How many hours had I been sitting there on that wooden chair with my face to the wall? Ten hours? Five hours? A tight blindfold covered half my face. A prolonged, strange noise would interrupt the interrogator's threats, and then he'd start again. It was a buzz like insects hovering around me

97

or like a bell being hit over and over. His horrible voice and all the sounds gyrated in my head into a howl. Where was I? I didn't know. The yelling and the insults made it impossible for me to think. I told myself I had to stay strong. No, I didn't want to meet a fate like Guli's. I wanted to stay alive and return home to my mother. My mother . . . She must have been doing something to help me. I thought of all my well-connected friends, of Khatami himself, who I had campaigned for a few years earlier. I had worked for the reformist papers, for the very movement that he'd given license to in taking power. Wouldn't he notice the news of my arrest and come to support me? I thought of Faezeh. Surely someone must be coming to save me.

When they forced me out of the car, someone put a metal object in my hand and said that it was a radio antenna and that I had to hold it to follow them. The men couldn't touch me themselves. I was pulled along with shaking and uncertain steps, like a blind person. I knew that every minute I was in more and more danger, and I kept telling myself to stay rational and calm. We stopped for the men guarding me to exchange some papers with the prison officials, and then we kept going. I heard a buzzer, and a woman's hand took hold of mine and led me forward until an iron door slammed shut.

"Lift your blindfold a little so you can see your feet and you don't trip," the woman said. "Now take off your blindfold."

She was young and slight with an olive complexion. Frowning, she gestured for me to undress. On a table lay a pair of white cotton pajamas with blue stripes, a polyester chador with a gray and violet floral pattern, and a pair of cheap men's slippers.

"Put on the pajamas and keep on your scarf and black socks." My pink shirt, my jeans, my mother's black overcoat, and my green cotton sash—one by one, they all went into a plastic bag.

"Put your watch and purse on the table, too." She took my shoes.

"Put the sandals on, fix your blindfold, and move along behind me."
She led me into a cell and bolted the metal latch shut. "Keep quiet.
Don't bang on the door. Understood?"

I understood. Less than ten minutes later she came back. She
threw the chador at me. "Get ready quick. You're going for interrogation."

What was in store for me? I acted calm, but my beating heart was
making a dreadful sound. A man's soft, nasal voice said to the olive-
toned woman, whom I later named Humaira, "Follow me."

I was allowed again to raise my blindfold only to the point where
I could see the ground in front of my feet. I followed the pair of
brown shoes two steps ahead of me. I clasped the chador tightly
under my chin with one hand and held the front seams together
with the other. The sound of my plastic slippers gave me goose
bumps. They were opentoed, and the right slipper was torn and
slapped my foot with each step. Its chilling sound was the sound of
my downfall—the sound my mother called low class, the steps of
"laborers."

"Come in here. There is a chair. Sit facing the wall, keep your
hands away from your blindfold, and don't turn around."

"You creature from hell, this will be your grave. I've had my eye on
you for years. I know how you throw yourself around, and I know
how you like to play. You've fallen into the wrong hands now. I
haven't been to a prison for an interrogation in ten years, but I knew,
you animal, that you'd play games with the others. I had to come after
you myself. You can't play games here, you Israeli spy. Who is your
contact in Israel? Tell me! You're going to come clean about all your
spying. Don't worry, the memories will come back to you. You're
going to get such a beating that you'll remember the milk you drank
when you were a child!"

What memory came back to me above all else? The ten days of

the Fajr International Film Festival. Ten days when my sole desire was to watch every film shown, knowing that I might never get to see them uncensored in a public movie theater. I would have given anything to see those films. It was winter, but I lined up at seven in the morning despite the cold in front of the Azadi Cinema to buy tickets for Mohsen Makhmalbaf's films *Naseredin Shah Actor e Cinema* (Once Upon a Time, Cinema) and *Nobat-e Asheqi* (Time of Love), and Bahram Beza'i's *Mosaferan* (Travelers). In desperation, as the lines slowly moved, I flashed a big smile at the provincial soldiers who had gotten there perhaps before dawn and were now minutes from the ticket window. They made room for this delicate little girl, and in order to get those precious tickets, I endured the revulsion of their legs pressing against mine, their dry, empty smiles, and their hands running over my back. I was stifled by the swelling crowd and the deadly pressure of uncouth, opportunistic hands, but I stood my ground in hopes of getting into the theater.

How had I found myself yet again in such a precarious and compromising situation? What might I give up to this man in Towhid so that he would allow me ahead of him? Hours seemed to pass in the ten minutes my interrogator left the room to pray. I could sense that the whole time there was a third person with us, a sinister presence behind me writing, taking careful notes. I trembled at the return of the interrogator's footsteps as he moved close to yell in my ear. I was terrified he'd kill me. He paced about the room, coming up to me suddenly, smashing a book or a rolled-up newspaper into my head. When he drew near, I'd freeze with fear. I was waiting for a terrible blow or for something sharp to stab my head or back. The beatings and abuse were awful, but my fear was even more exacting. But I kept silent facing the wall, afraid in the darkness behind the blindfold. I didn't want to lose hope. Had there ever been a day in my life when I didn't have some hope?

I collapsed in my cell after the hours of interrogation. A guard brought me a cold copper bowl full of rice with stew on top. "That's your lunch. You missed lunchtime, so it was refrigerated. In two hours, they'll give you dinner. If you haven't done your noon and evening prayers, you can go do your ablutions."

"Oh. Yes, prayers. Definitely. What time is it?" I stood up, exhausted and dizzy. It was five in the afternoon. Had I really been up there all day? With that polyester chador over my head, I faced the *qibleh* and knelt and stood a few times, cursing inside.

My throat was like lead, so tense and stiff I couldn't even swallow water. I didn't want dinner. I wanted to be alone. My cell was like an empty crypt with white walls and a blue iron door. There was nothing in the room. The floor was covered with moist gray carpet, and above me a bright light bulb lit up the room like a spotlight. "Turning it off is out of the question!"

I began the "homework" my interrogator had given me—several sheets of paper marked "Ministry of Intelligence, Interrogation Form." They wanted to know how many boyfriends I'd had and what we had done together, how religious my parents were, whether I had ever drunk alcohol, what I believed about God. An expression in Arabic was printed in bold black ink at the top of each page: *an-Najat fi Sidq* (Deliverance lies in honesty). Below the Arabic, the Persian translation read, "*Nejat-e shoma dar rastgui ast*" (Save yourself by telling the truth). I spread the papers over the rough, damp carpet and lay down on them.

I couldn't sleep. That first night seemed it would never come to an end, as I shivered, listening to the moaning and crying throughout the prison. When they opened my cell at daybreak, I picked up the pages scattered beneath me. They glistened with the moisture they had absorbed from the floor. I performed my ablutions numbly. I had forgotten how to pray, but it didn't matter. What mattered was that I went through the motions, as unseen eyes were watching me and would report my every move to the interrogator. When I finished, the bitch on duty barked, "Get ready. Your interrogator is waiting outside."

In those plastic slippers three sizes too big, I shuffled along noisily behind him up the stairs, this time more calmly. The ill-fitting, stinking polyester chador was fastened firmly to my head by the blindfold. I watched his feet, and in a self-assured Islamic tone I greeted him, "*Salaamu aleikum.*"

"*Aleikum as-salaam.*"

His shoes marked him as different from the other guards. They were formal brown shoes and were always neatly polished. I could see his white socks and the sharp crease in his pressed khaki pants. He must not usually work in this building to be able to come in so neat and clean. I remembered how the day before he had said that he hadn't come in for an interrogation in ten years. He must be a person of higher stature, perhaps a departmental chief in the Ministry of Intelligence. I put the puzzle off to one side but kept it in mind.

The future would prove me right. To be saved from this mess, I needed someone strong, someone with influence. He would be my savior.

◙   ◙   ◙

The days passed, dragged on like a thousand years, without a glimmer of hope in the darkness. It was as if I had disappeared. When I was sent to the court on the second day of my detention with two intelligence agents, they required the usual formalities. I lay blindfolded in the back of a van with tinted windows, with a sheet over my head so I wouldn't be identified in the Tehran traffic. Our vehicle drove down the congested avenues and sometimes stopped at red lights. In the parking lot at the Revolutionary Courts, they said that I could sit up and take off the blindfold. The city was there before my eyes. I was alive and surging with energy. But I was a prisoner. I was tied up. As I was escorted through the courthouse parking lot, I felt like the criminals I had seen time after time on television or when I was on assignment, brought to the courts in the same detestable prison clothes that I was wearing. Did passersby think I was a female smuggler? Or a woman who had stabbed her abusive husband with a dainty little dagger? I hung my head in shame. Who was I?

I was thrust into a room before the judge appointed to my case to hear the charges against me. The middle-aged judge with gray hair at the tip of his beard was the same man who, at the request of the Ministry of Intelligence, had issued the warrants for my arrest and the search of my home. Judge Yadegarfar looked at me and said, "Are you a human being or a monster? Understand that an execution order is waiting for you." He opened the file and read, "Having Israeli contacts and spying for the State of Israel. Engaging in activities for American spy organizations and for those with interests in harming the Islamic Republic. Working for foreign media outlets by means of transmitting intelligence, research, and published reports fabricated for the purpose of harming the rule of and inflicting wounds upon the Islamic Revolution."

"Believe me, none of these accusations are true. Hajj Agha, you have made a mistake. I am a writer. I am a reporter. You have made a mistake. In what way have I been a spy? Let me go home. We are a respectable family, and I really don't understand what you are talking about. I don't know anyone in Israel, and I am not working for any American organization and . . ." And like a cloud in early spring, I burst into tears.

Yadegarfar pointed at the file and said, "It's all documented clearly in here. The brothers have conducted the necessary investigations, and you will not escape easily from Islamic justice. The punishment for spies is death. Your crimes are very serious. Relations with an Israeli spy . . ." He shook his head sadly and said, "This is a court of justice. It is the Revolutionary Court, and no one is brought here without reason. Confess. Ask forgiveness. Your crimes will be lessened, and God will have mercy on you."

◎ ◎ ◎

With the total composure with which he might have asked someone to sample a pastry or to write an essay on springtime, the interrogator asked me, "OK, tell me how many people you've slept with so far."

I couldn't believe my ears.

"Don't play innocent. I know you've even been with the local butcher—I have his testimony in my hand. Why don't you say anything, you whore? Don't tell me you're a virgin, that you've kept yourself hidden from the sun and the moon. Talk. Tell me, you spy. Fine, so now you're dumb. Well, I'm going to make you tell me about the first time you gave it up, play-by-play. In the name of God, you will tell me or you're going to the basement!"

I knew where the basement was. The basement was where they took the other prisoners. The woman who had made herself crazy or maybe had just gone crazy. All night she screamed, "Nafisaaaaa!" and banged on the door of her cell, shouting that her sister Nafisa was waiting for her on the other side of the door. The sisters called the brothers, and they dragged the helpless woman across the floor, saying they would show her Nafisa. Her screams echoed in the distance, and later I could hear her throwing up in pain and crying out to God. My heart flew about, battering my chest like a wild bird.

I asked Hajiya Khanum as they brought me to my cell, "What happens to the lady who calls for her sister when you take her to the basement?"

"The basement? You really want to see it?" she asked. Leila, standing next to her, chewing a big wad of gum, winked and said, "*In sha' Allah*, you'll get a chance to go to the basement, too!" Laughing, she slammed the door and closed the latch.

And Leila's wish came true. . . . On the way to the basement I cried, "I'll tell you! Let's go back up! I swear to God I'll tell you!" My knees were shaking, and the guards grabbed my arms before I collapsed. They pulled me up, half off the ground, and it was as if I was flying through the air back to the interrogation room. I'll say whatever he wants, I told myself. I'll make up whatever he's asking for, I'll find something to tell him. I won't let myself be tortured, and I won't stay in prison. I'm getting out of here, I told myself and clenched my teeth. "I swear to God I'll tell you."

"Shut up, you idiot—don't bring God's name into this! Now you're being a sensible girl. When I ask you nicely to talk, you talk. In the name of God, sit down and let's hear what you have to say. . . . I have a list of sixty-seven men who've been with you. Start from the beginning, the beginning of the beginning . . ."

I lied and made up stories to answer all the names on his ridiculous list. But to begin at the beginning . . . that meant beginning with a name well known in Iran. And in that first confession, I told the truth.

◙　◙　◙

FALL 1997

It was twilight when we turned the corner in our blue Renault and almost hit a late model car speeding around the corner. "Maman, watch out!" Before I could finish, my mother swerved expertly and slammed on the brakes. The guy driving the other car lowered his window, and my mother aggressively stuck her head out hers to tell him off. All three of us fell silent for a second. The young man got out, and my mother's angry tone turned reverent. I tried to hide my exhilaration as I stepped out to meet him. That morning, more than ten hours ago, I had managed to lose my celebrity admirer at Mehrabad airport, and now, by chance, here I was face-to-face with him in my own neighborhood.

"I waited for you. I looked all over so I could give you a hand. Where did you go?" A big smile had spread across his face.

"Forgive me," I answered. "You had a lot on your mind. I didn't want to trouble you."

I had first seen him at the Frankfurt airport, when I was shopping at the duty-free store. I was wearing a dark blue coat and skirt, and I had my head scarf handy to put on before I boarded Iran Air. As I compared chocolates and perfume, I noticed a young man following my every step. He looked Iranian and very familiar. But I just couldn't place him. On the plane, business class was practically empty, and he sat down in my row. He got up a dozen times to shift his luggage around in the overhead compartments, and all at once I recognized him. He had been a guest of a newspaper I wrote for, *Aftabgardan*, at our press booth at the international book fair. I had interviewed him. He was Ali Daei, the soccer champion.

"Excuse me, would you care for some chocolate?" I thanked him and reminded him that we'd met before. He laughed.

"You've done some serious shopping!" he said, pointing at the baby seat that I had carried onto the plane and stored in the cabin with some effort. Alert to the question politely concealed in this comment, I answered, "It's for my sister, for her baby shower. She has a little girl on the way. And no, I'm not married." He was charming, and I had to make myself sleep the rest of the flight so I wouldn't keep talking to him. When we arrived in Tehran, he found the slightest pretenses to help me with my bags.

"Don't go anywhere. Wait at the gate, and I'll come and help you." At arrivals, hundreds of fans were waiting to receive him with flowers and posters. They rushed forward and devoured him like a crashing wave. A full head taller than everyone else, he raised his eyebrows and signaled to me to wait for him. Overwhelmed by the crowd, I grabbed my luggage and made my way to where my mother was standing behind the glass divider, waving at me. I had been in Germany for almost a month, and I couldn't wait to see her and Katayun.

My mother kissed me and said, "Did you see Ali Daei? He was on your flight. I was praying to myself, thinking how nice it would be if you met him."

"Oh my God! You're too much, Maman. Come on, let's go before he shows up again. I just got rid of him, and now you say how nice it would be if I had met him! What did he do, what's with the huge crowd?"

I found out the answer when we almost crashed into Ali Daei's car. He was home for an important game. In the next few days, the Iranian national team would play Australia in Tehran. If Iran beat Australia, our team would go to the World Cup. Ali smiled. "Where do you live?"

My mother answered for me. "At the end of this street, in building number four."

Ali hastily pointed at a large white house behind him. "That's my house. Isn't it nice that we are neighbors! Why don't you take my number and give me yours while we're at it." He jotted his number down on a scrap of paper, and my mother gave him ours. "I gotta get down to the television studio for an interview. I'll see you in the morning!"

My mother was in seventh heaven. "Camelia, Khanum, you are very lucky."

Ali Daei was the most eligible bachelor in Iran. The captain of the Iranian national soccer team, he had a degree in engineering from Daneshgah-e Sharif University and a contract with one of the biggest soccer clubs in the world. The next morning our doorbell rang, and he was sitting in my living room. He was shy and very polite. He could tell immediately that there was no father presiding over our home. In Iran, most families hang an oversized photo of their beloved deceased in their salons, so as soon as he walked in, Ali faced my father's photo. My father had died suddenly when I was a teenager, and I was still reeling from the loss. When he was young, he'd been a champion player of table tennis and volleyball, and he'd coached at the Shir-e Pak sports club. He had just finished a game of table tennis when he died of a heart attack in the shower. My mother pointed his photo out to Ali and said, "Camelia's father was also athletic—he lost his life at the sport club."

My mother couldn't hide her joy at having a celebrity in the house, and Kai Khosrou was in paradise. He was fifteen at the time and soccer obsessed. He couldn't believe he had such a hot story to tell his friends—the Iranian national team's captain was dating his sister! If we got married, he'd have a guaranteed seat at the Persepolis soccer club. He couldn't stop grinning, his face one big smile. My mother served us tea and quizzed Ali about his parents, where they lived, and when he'd bought the house nearby. She showed him my watercolors hanging on the wall and bragged about my writing talent. She completely ignored me when I raised my eyebrows to signal that she was going too far and that she had to stop the Q & A session.

In the space of five minutes the news spread throughout the building, and our neighbors had gathered on the front steps with hand-held cameras to take videos and get his autograph. In the blink of an eye, it seemed the whole town knew we were an item. As we started seeing each other regularly, we found that it was impossible to meet at home. Uninvited guests rang our bell continuously. People just wore us out. So he'd come pick me up in his car, and we'd set off for some unspecified destination in Tehran. We would drive to a quiet area and park under the shadows of a big tree to hide and talk. Or he'd take me with him to run various errands; we'd chat along the way, and then he'd leave me in the car to sit and wait for him until he'd finished up and would drive me back home. Our star-crazed neighbors were monitoring my house so closely it was difficult for him even to walk me up to the front door, so he'd drop me off outside. He started making vague promises. "What I want is to get married. But I've got a problem to take care of, and until then you have to keep our secret and wait." I'd nod, but at home, I knew my mother's news headquarters were in full swing. Also, everyone from *Zan-e Ruz*, where I worked, had found out, as one of the secretaries lived across the street from us in one of the houses built for employees by the weekly's corporate owners. (It was still some years before *Zan* would make its appearance in Tehran. Despite their similar titles, the two publications were unrelated.) It seemed like the only person who didn't know about Ali and me was Hafez of Shiraz, the fourteenth-century Persian poet.

Iran tied with Australia, one-to-one, which was a big victory for Iran. I was the first person Ali called from the stadium. "We did a perfect job, darling! I love you. I'll come home to you in an hour." Wild with excitement, Tehran had burst into celebration, and I listened from our terrace to the cheering in the streets. Ali bounded up the steps to our apartment, took my hands in his, and kissed them. And then he left for Australia for the rematch.

He was a star, and I was only a small-time writer. My destiny was in his hands. And I think, even more than me, my mom was the one in love with him. The phone kept ringing, and my mother cold bloodedly insisted that I answer it. She wanted the whole world to call and convince me to follow Ali. But they all expected to hear that he had proposed.

"Hello, Camelia, *salaam*. What's new?" Everyone started with this question.

"Nothing—the only news is that you're still calling about him!"

And then my friends and family would start in. "Don't be such an ass. Try your luck. Opportunity knocks only once. You'll be a star. You'll travel. He's a millionaire. All of Iran is after this boy, and he's in love with you—and you play hard to get?"

When he asked me, I agreed to fly to Germany. The hawk of good fortune was sitting on my shoulder. My family would normally have been scandalized by my living with a man I wasn't married to, yet now they were thrilled. I thought he was a good candidate: famous, rich, gentle. I liked that he called me from anywhere in the world to share a sweet moment—just to say goodnight and that he couldn't wait to have me in his home. It was the first time that, from the bottom of my heart, I'd really wanted to marry a man. And, of course, who he was made a difference—everyone was attracted to him. I was also highly manipulated by my mother, who was really pushing for the relationship. She wanted to be able to proudly tell everyone that I was marrying Ali Daei. My family was sure that if I went to Germany, we'd get married there.

I got off the train in Bielefeld, and Ali stood waiting for me at the station. He waved at me. I jumped up, almost out of my shoes, to embrace him.

"Whoa! Whoa! What are you doing? You'll ruin my reputation. Everyone here knows me. Quick, get in the car!" This was our first encounter since he'd left Tehran a month earlier. He had my heart, and I wasn't myself.

Karim Bagheri, a teammate, lived in a cozy unit next door to Ali's apartment with his young wife, Leila, and Ali had no choice but to introduce them to me. In my honor, he invited them out to dinner, but he told them that I was a friend of his cousin's, and that I'd come to Germany to wait for an interview at the embassy for an American visa. They seemed to believe him—at least they didn't ask me any questions. I was mortified, but I also didn't contradict him.

Leila was a provincial girl from Tabriz, where she'd lived her whole life until good fortune alighted on *her* shoulders, and she'd married a famous player from her hometown. To go out to the Italian restaurant, she'd put on a pink satin evening gown and fasten a tiara laden with paste jewels to her wavy black hair. Ali and I would sit in the car laughing at her together until our sides split.

But though we ridiculed Leila together, he treated me like a personal secretary. In the evenings, when he got back from the soccer club, he'd plop a big sack of faxes and letters on the ground for me to sort through. They were always full of letters from young women, accompanied by their pictures, entreating him to marry them. Some wrote that they had wealthy fathers, and some wrote that they observed *hejab* and were good homemakers. Still more asked him to send them money or gifts. I crumpled up the letters and sat miserably with my arms wrapped around my knees. I had no idea why I'd followed him so easily to Germany or why I would now trudge through the snow to the supermarket every day without fail, just so I could make him *khoresht-e badamjan* or *fesanjun* for dinner. I spent hours on the phone with my mother, asking about recipes for *kuku-ye sabzi* and *khoresht-e qorma sabzi*. Was I supposed to be happy with this life? I had expected to have the life of a celebrity, like the stars who appeared in *Okay* or *Hello* magazine. I thought we'd go out together every night and have a fancy, romantic lifestyle. But nothing was romantic—he hadn't bought me a single gift or even taken me out to the movies. In my mind, I'd become his housemaid as well as his lover.

We weren't made for each other. We desired different worlds. He expected me to be an obedient Eastern woman whose greatest thrills in her married life were making her husband's dinner and cleaning the house. Though "marriage" or even "engagement" weren't things he spoke about often. He hated my job and asked me never to return to newspaper reporting. He wanted to turn my world into washing and ironing his practice uniform. He would fight with me over burned eggplant *kuku*, saying, "What kind of strange food is this? Why couldn't you have made something better?"

I wept when I told him I wanted to go home to Iran, but he barely responded. At the train station he tried to put a wad of money in my hand.

"No, really, I don't need it. Thank you for your hospitality. *Khoda hafez.*"

My mother finally changed her tune. "Camelia, Ali Daei called here yesterday and asked after you. I didn't give him your number."

"What did you say to him?"

"Nothing. I said you weren't here. And then he said who does she think she is, this daughter of yours? That he has thousands of girls chasing him. And then I told him that you weren't one of these girls, that he should go after the girls that are after him."

◎ ◎ ◎

As I told my story, I could hear my interrogator marching back and forth behind me. When I finished, he spoke in a sad voice. "Dust on the head of your mother for sending her daughter to Germany and shame on Ali Daei, who is a respected man and acts so pious."

The list of sixty-seven men sat in front of me, a heavy file of sin, and I was amused to see the names of my uncles Bizhan and Manuchechr listed along with some of my father's old friends. Apparently they had simply gathered the names of any and every man listed in my phone book, regardless of whether we were related or remotely close in age. I said, " I am very sorry, but I have to tell you, even my own uncle is on this list!" He coldly responded, " So what? Anything is possible from you."

chapter seven Tulips Sprouted from the Blood of the Young

THE LATE 1980S

We were standing in front of the Shaqayeq pastry shop in Shahr Ara, when Kristian's mother happened along. She teased me, asking, "Do your chicks have beaks?" She wanted to know if my breasts were growing. I crinkled my eyebrows and acted like I didn't hear her. She turned to my mother and said, "When did she start getting her period?" My mother responded with a pointed look. All our relatives and friends buzzed with this question. In Iran, like so many other Middle Eastern countries, this is a big issue. When a girl gets her first period, she's no longer a child and must behave like a woman. It's not an easy process. They don't educate you at all about it at school, but it's openly discussed among women in the family, though an embarrassing topic for girls to raise themselves. My mother, however, simply didn't know the answer—I refused to tell her.

I was fourteen, and we fought constantly. For whatever reason, my mother had never been able to speak honestly with me about entering the world of womanhood. When I got my period, I was caught off guard, bewildered and angry, like a child whose mother has let go of her hand in the street and run off. I felt fragile and emotional, and she didn't seem to understand me, or if she understood, she just shrugged her shoulders and said to herself, "She'll say something about it when she's ready." And the longer we didn't talk about it, the more the distance between us grew. I'd hear the chatter of all the women in the kitchen. Frowning and sour-faced, I wouldn't answer anyone, not even Kati, when they asked, "Did you get it yet?" My cousin Elham was sent on a mission to ask me in private, but I lied, "No, and don't ask me again." I knew it was my mother who really wanted to know.

I didn't have to share a room with Kati anymore, and in my own private bedroom, I'd write poetry, paint, and read novels by Daphne du Maurier. Having my own room also meant that it was no longer a hassle for me to dispose of my sanitary napkins every month. I hid most of them in a box in my wardrobe. My mother and Kati kept a stock of pads in the bathroom, but I wouldn't use them. I'd ask my friends to buy them for me instead, and they would shake their heads with sympathy. And sometimes I'd use tissues, sticking the dirty ones in my schoolbag and discreetly tossing them with my soiled underwear into piles of trash on my way to school. Even washing my underwear might have exposed my secret. The cold war of my puberty seemed endless. Eventually, my mother stopped prying, but what was I supposed to do with a giant carton of used pads?

One day I was welcomed home, as usual, with the sound of my mother's shouting. But that day she didn't greet me by telling me to wash my hands and face. Mohammed Agha, our weekly housekeeper, was sitting in the kitchen eating his lunch. "You filthy girl, aren't you ashamed? You know how to do everything except this one thing?" I was clueless as my mother yelled. She grabbed my hands and pulled me toward my bedroom. At first I thought she must have read my poetry notebooks and inferred something of my secret infatuations. In the doorway, I froze. All the bloody tissues I'd hidden were piled in the middle of the room. They looked different in broad daylight. They'd changed color. My skin was crawling, as if I were standing naked with everyone laughing at me. "Mohammed Agha opened the wardrobe to clean it with a rag, and he called me and said that it smelled like a dead animal and that maybe there was a dead mouse in there. Fine, *you* have no decency! But *I* melted with shame in front of Mohammed Agha!"

Still carrying my schoolbag and wearing my uniform, I went and sat in the courtyard, angry as a wounded tiger in a trap. I dreamed of running away. But where? What should I have said? And why should I have said anything? For hours I sat miserably alone while the gossip spread throughout our building. From Jinus's mother, Khanum Bayat, it reached my father and Agha-ye Bayat. They decided they couldn't put the box in the trash out front, since people would certainly come rummaging and stumble upon its contents, and the reputation of the entire building would be ruined. After nightfall, my father and Agha-ye Bayat dug a pit out back and buried it. And so not only my mother, but our housekeeper and our whole building found out my secret.

◙   ◙   ◙

Tired of war and the high cost of living, we looked back fondly on the days before the revolution. Once-common items were now coveted as luxuries—chocolate, bananas, pineapples, chewing gum. I'd ask Kati, "Remember when they'd bring the poppy cart to our street?" We'd pluck the green tips off the flowers, drop their tiny pearly seeds in a bowl, add a spoonful of sugar, and eat them. Our mouths watered at the memory. I conjured up flavors in my mind that I hadn't tasted in years, just so I wouldn't forget them. Kai Khosrou was born too late to remember these delicacies himself, but he would see my drooling mouth and say, "I want some!"

Kai Khosrou had discovered the taste of bananas thanks to the gifts of our former neighbor Agha-ye Qarekhanian, who was a flight engineer at Iran Air. He always brought something colorful back from his trips—boxes of Swiss chocolate, fashion magazines and perfume from Paris for my mother, and Chiquita bananas for Kai

Khosrou. We were forced to ration the small bunch so Kai Khosrou wouldn't start nagging Agha-ye Qarekhanian before his next trip. He'd cry and beg my parents for bananas. "Don't mention them by name," my father would say. "He'll start crying." Years went by when you couldn't find bananas in any of the shops. The U.S. navy blockaded the ports in the Persian Gulf; no cargo ships were allowed to dock at Iran's ports. More importantly, the government preferred to spend money on basic goods instead of bananas or other luxury items. Iran was politically and economically isolated, and we thanked God when we able to garner our daily necessities.

Then, one snowy day, I saw a vendor holding bananas at a stoplight at an intersection on Parkway. Kati and I started bouncing up and down in the back, yelling, "Bananas! Bananas!" until my father pulled over to the side of the highway and called the vendor boy. The boy said he had brought them from Pakistan. They were small, scrawny, black, and astronomically expensive at twenty tomans for one little banana. But after that we were regular customers for the boy at the intersection.

The anarchy of the revolution and the war that followed had filled our childhoods with misfortunes and regrets. My generation, by the age of twelve, was sharp witted and cynical—we had had to grow up too fast. As teenagers, we put the days of brainwashing behind us. We "children of the revolution" unfortunately turned out to be not all that revolutionary. We had learned the hard way how to live under Islamic law.

Of all the do's and don'ts and taboos, the hardest thing to accept were those ghastly school uniforms. The overcoats were so long they fell below the knee, the matching pants had to cover the tops of our shoes, and we wore long veils that reached down to the elbow. We'd have to roll up our pant legs for the vice principal's inspection. If by accident we wore white or even cream-colored socks, we'd be sternly reprimanded, and our grade for conduct would be penalized. Our socks had to match our dark uniforms, which were always brown or navy blue. I prayed every year that the school would choose a new color. Even black was too much to hope for. They knew black was chic and attractive. You couldn't wear black even if you were in mourning.

The Omur-e Tarbiyati would regularly barge into the middle of a class and make us lift up our veils, checking whether we'd plucked our eyebrows or dyed our hair. I'd be the first to be summoned to the office for insubordination. I had shiny brown hair, and they never believed that this was its natural color. My mother would be called in to the principal's office, and she'd angrily tell them to look carefully at the roots of my hair. Then I'd go back to class, and a few months later they'd forget, and the whole ritual would start all over again. We weren't allowed to bring pictures of our families to school; we couldn't even have portraits of our parents in our wallets. We couldn't wear brightly colored shoes. Having beauty products or cosmetic mirrors was forbidden. Our schoolmates who belonged to the Islamic Association would search us daily. These spies for the Omur-e Tarbiyati hung a heavy tarp just inside the school's front entrance, and every morning five or six of them would be stationed there with two more flanking the tarp to catch anyone sneaking by. They'd look in our purses and through our notebooks and in our plastic lunch bags and our pockets and under our veils and in our shoes, and finally they'd search our bodies to be absolutely certain that we didn't have anything dangerous like a tube of lipstick. They confiscated anything they'd found and would read the covers of our notebooks, always with a crooked smile, to be sure we didn't give them a false name. However obsessively the girls at the door went through our purses, I'd always find a new way to conceal my forbidden items, such as photos of family birthday parties or weddings, or pictures cut out of magazines of Western celebrities like

Madonna or Michael Jackson. Under these conditions, how could I be bothered with my studies?

My father would write all my compositions for me. Always. And my grades always oscillated between 17 and 18 out of 20. Then one night in my second year of junior high school, I was waiting for my father to come home so he could write my assignment as he had been doing for years. But it turned out that he had to stay late at work. For half an hour, I paced around my room. Finally, I came to the conclusion that I'd have to write it myself. I was an avid reader; I had read almost the entire school library, and I was a good student of grammar and Persian. I loved reading. All summer I read novels and books of poetry, but I hadn't yet discovered how reading inspires better writing.

In composition class, we'd have to bring our notebooks up to the blackboard and read aloud. For the first time, I read my own work, and everyone in the class clapped for me. My teacher, Khanum Allahyari, gave me a 19. She was suspicious, and it was decided that the following week I'd write my assignment in front of her. I wrote it and I got a 20! "Thank God I don't have to write your compositions anymore," my father said.

After I found the confidence to write for myself, I started composing poetry. One day, at the beginning of the school year, our wonderful literature teacher, Khanum Shahrudi, handed me a postage-paid envelope addressed to a post office box in Tehran. "Camelia, I think that if you had a good instructor, you could be a fine writer and poet in the future. At the Club for Creative Literature and Intellectual Development of Children and Young Adults, there is a center called Afarineshha-ye Adabi where they look at the creative writing of young people and provide them with feedback and guidance. You should write to them and tell me how it goes." The envelope glowed in my hand like a winning ticket. For me, it was a ticket that could take me to the other side of the world.

I was so happy I couldn't contain myself. At home, I picked out dozens of pieces from my poetry notebook and copied them onto nice paper to mail. They were poems about love and the beauty of nature, about the sky and the sea and the forest, about my love for God, much inspired by the poetry of the well-known contemporary Iranian poets Forugh Farrokhzad and Sohrab Sepehri.

At first, my correspondence wasn't taken very seriously at home. But with keen deliberation, I'd write two letters a week to the center. They would read my new work and send it back in a white envelope with a critique. Two months of this and my parents issued a serious ultimatum: "We are going to tear up any letters that come from the center on the spot. Poetry time is over. You need to spend your free time on your studies. You have final exams this year." I was astonished to receive a 20 for my final exam essay, and the principal commended my writing to my parents. "You should take you daughter's talents seriously." But my mother sniffed and said, "But what good is it when she got a 17 in science!"

That summer I had more time for my clandestine letter writing. My bedroom window faced the courtyard, and I'd keep my ears open, waiting for sound of the postman. As soon as I heard his motorcycle, I'd find an excuse to go outside, and I'd take the letter from him and stuff it in my underwear. As the months passed, the letters from the center were joined with correspondence with new writer friends I'd met through the center, which put us in touch with each other to read and review the work of our peers. I didn't have enough room in my clothes to hide them all. Over the next couple of years, the letters from my wonderful friend Mandana, who was from Abadan, the oil city in southern Iran, were sometimes sixteen to twenty pages long, although my replies were never as long as her shortest letters. To keep the letters out of my mother's claws, I would jump from my window down into the courtyard, grab the letters, and quickly climb back up to my room.

"No more literature!" My mother threatened to divorce my father if he allowed me to attend the Dabirestan-e Olum-e Insani, the High School for the Humanities. So I reluctantly agreed to the Dabirestan-e Olum-e Tajrubi, the High School for Applied Science, called Fayazbaksh. But when I was asked in class what field I planned to pursue in the future, I answered, "Journalism." I'd fallen in love with reading the newspaper. I'd read the daily paper from *alif* to *yeh*, even the classifieds and the obituaries.

During the war, we had a limited number of newspapers to choose from, most of them conservative government papers: *Kayhan, Etela'at, Jumhuri-ye Islami, Abrar,* and *Resalat.* We subscribed to *Kayhan.* The front-page headlines were devoted to the latest update from the front: a tally of the advances of the Army of Islam and the retreats of the outlaw enemy, the numbers of Iraqi soldiers killed and the numbers of Ba'athists captured, the funerals of martyrs after Friday prayers in front of the University of Tehran. Then they would fill the rest of the pages by regurgitating yesterday's news, while other events were never reported—there was no news about the taking of Karbala. The war seemed endless, and the newspapers never predicted the defeat of the enemy or mentioned peace.

There were two State-run networks on TV. It didn't make a difference what channel you turned to—both invariably featured a mullah droning on about Islam or Ahangran, the famous rhapsodist of the frontlines of the war, wailing away. Behind him a group dressed in black would be crying, "Hussein!" and beating their chests, while he sang:

> *Bahr-e azadi-ye Qods az Karbala bayad guzasht*
> *Az kenar-e marqad-e an sar juda bayad guzasht.*
> *Pish ay rasmandeh shir!*
> *Khane az dushman begir!*

For Jerusalem to be free we must cross through Karbala,
Through the resting place of that severed head.
Onward, O lion warrior!
Wrest your home from the enemy!

My father would turn off the television and curse the world that had confined us to two black-and-white channels. He said it was because turbans came in only two colors. "Either they are black or they are white." On Fridays, as my father fanned kebabs on the grill in the empty courtyard with a cigarette in his mouth, he'd yell, "Camelia, turn up the radio!" We all listened carefully to the sermons of the Friday prayers. The food would appear on the table amid the *Allahu Akbar*s of the "Minister of Chanting" (as my father called whoever was chanting at the Friday prayers). I'd tell Kati to pass me the quarter-pound hunk of butter, and I would put a large slab of it under my white rice. Rafsanjani, speaker of the Majilis (and later the president of Iran), would talk about world arrogance. Ignoring my mother's glare, I'd pick a large clump of basil leaves out of the other greens. A thousand times she'd said, "They're 'edible greens,' not 'pickable greens.' Put a handful on your plate and eat them all."

We'd eat our *chelow kebabs* in silence and listen to the speech. As soon as they started with *Allahu Akbar* again, we'd turn off the radio and try to guess the truth behind the proclamations of the mullahs. We might guess a portion was a series of excuses for the high price of gas, or we might have gathered that there were secret behind-the-scenes talks in progress with the United States, the government wasn't going into decline, and that the war was going to continue as before. If there were any mention of poorly covered women, we knew that the next day there'd be Basijis on motorcycles armed with clubs making surprise sweeps in shopping centers and restaurants. The leader of Friday prayers would give them the necessary justification to attack.

Many years passed since the war had broken out with Iraq when in addition to the now-familiar language of "war-stricken refugees" and "martyrs," a new phrase was added to our vocabulary: "the victims of chemical weapons." Our hearts gasped at harrowing images of victims killed or horribly disfigured by Saddam Hussein in the 1988 chemical attacks in Halabja. And it wasn't only Iranian soldiers that were targeted. We were afraid. How could we defend ourselves if we were attacked? We listened anxiously for radio warnings. And we knew mustard gas had a pleasant odor, so if we ever detected a sweet smell, we had to cover our mouth and nose with a damp towel and rush around shutting the windows and doors and plugging all the vents and cracks to save ourselves. In Tehran, we had a way to deal with everything.

Families sent their sons out of the country any way they could. The Pasdaran would stop young men in the street to check their identity cards, searching for draft dodgers. Some parents sent their sons over the border legally before they came of age. Others were smuggled out. They'd travel from hideout to hideout in the mountains and plains, disguised as rams in herds of sheep, until they reached Turkish soil. My cousin Omid was sent to England before he reached sixteen, and Mino Khanum's son Ali, most of my friends from school, and our old leftist neighbors, Nima and Mani Vaqadi, all safely made it outside Iran's borders. But not everyone was so lucky. Some were killed in the cross fire between border police and the smugglers, while others were taken alive and sent to prison and then pressed into military service.

Another way to avoid military service was to enroll immediately in university. But Shahryar Nakha'i, my third cousin, was in his final year at high school and not very studious. The year before, he had used a *tak madeh*, a special allowance to drop your lowest grade, to gain entrance to Arabic class. You could use a *tak madeh* only once. The vice principal suggested that he volunteer to go to the front.

Volunteers enjoyed particular privileges in their education, so Shahryar went to war to compensate for his low marks in Arabic.

"Don't go! Son, don't go!" His mother went crazy. Shahryar's father, Sarahang Iraj Nakha'i, had been a commander in the gendarmerie in western Iran. He sadly failed to convince his son that it would better to fail out of school than to gamble away his life. Shahryar was a tall boy with broad shoulders. In 1986 we heard that he had shipped out, and then the next month the news came that he had been wounded. In an operation at Fav, a rocket hit his troop's boat, and everyone fell into the marshes around the island. He was hit in the back, and the marsh water led to an infection. Shahryar lost both of his legs. One had been amputated above his thigh, the other a little lower. It was terrifying. All of us, even those he didn't know by name, cried for him.

I didn't see him again until years later at a family gathering at my uncle Manuchehr's house. Shahryar had a beard and was wearing the kind of green overcoat usually worn by the Basij and the Pasdaran. He was walking without a cane. My uncle told us that they'd attached prosthetic legs and that he was getting payments from the martyrs' foundation. When Shahryar sat in his seat, I could see bright red plastic in the gap between his pant legs and his socks. My mind struggled with what it meant to be crippled. I asked myself how one event could alter a person's life forever.

Then my father told us that it seemed that, in order to hold onto his job, he would have to spend a few months at the front. He started attending the firearms training classes set up by the Islamic association of Shir-e Pak factory. I found the class manual, and as I read the descriptions of locking and loading guns, my heart sank. I was fed up with the manuals and the war and death. Why should my father fight? He wasn't a part of all this death, he didn't belong to Khomeini's revolution.

"Baba, come, let's run away," I said. Startled, my father asked,

"Run away from what?" and he looked at me in wonder. I was ashamed to look in his eyes and say, "Let's run away for your sake, so you don't go to war and get killed." Instead I pleaded, "What I mean is let's leave Iran." My father stared off into the distance and replied, "What would we do anywhere else? This is our country. Where would we go?" Luckily, he was never called to the front.

The bombing of Tehran stopped for several years in the middle of the war, though the red alert still sounded at school. Then construction workers appeared and dug a giant hole in the middle of the school's large courtyard. This was turned into an underground shelter with a thick concrete ceiling. It had four stairways leading into it, and we'd sneak down to poke around. "Don't go in under any circumstance," my mother would say. "If a shell hits, you'll all be buried under the rubble. It doesn't have any ventilation. You'll all suffocate."

The shelter was a harbinger of worse times to come. Seven years into the war, in early March 1987, only three weeks before the Nouruz holidays, Tehran was once again targeted. We were jolted awake by the sound of a monstrous missile exploding. Voice of Iraq warned that they would keep attacking until they toppled the mullahs' regime. As soon as the missiles showed up on the radar screen, the Ministry of Defense would announce a general state of emergency, but we never knew where they might hit. With the intervention of the United Nations, all the schools were again closed, until almost the end of the year, when the Department of Education blundered through a poor excuse for end-of-the-year exams and gave everyone a passing grade. Kati needed to pass to graduate, and she got her diploma without a hitch.

My aunt Turan was visiting her old neighborhood by the Hesabi intersection when a missile exploded in the vicinity. When we heard the news, my father came home quickly to take us to see her. She was lying stretched out on the sofa with a hot water bottle. My cousin Bita was in better shape, but they were both faint. My aunt had cut her hand on broken glass, and it was wrapped in bandages. We listened breathlessly as she described the attack. "Bita went to see her friend while I was shopping for groceries. When I was finished and Bita still hadn't come back, I went to a public phone to call her . . . and I heard the air-raid sirens sounding, and I saw that everyone was looking at the sky. I looked up and saw something bright the size of an oil tanker coming straight at us, the sound of its jets drowning everything else out. Everyone was stunned, nailed to the spot. It landed a few dozen meters from me, and after an instant all the windows came crashing down, and there was the sound of an explosion." My aunt raised her wounded hand. "Thick smoke poured out from the next street. I wanted to run, but it was like my feet were stuck to the ground and I couldn't move. Bita was right there where it landed."

Bita broke in. "When I saw it, Morwarid and I just froze. Then I automatically turned my back to the window, and there was a huge shock wave. The door and the window and the glass all came down, and we were thrown on the bed. . . . I thought I was dead. I lifted my head and saw that the window frames and the curtains had fallen on top of us. And there, where the neighbor's house had been, there was nothing. The sky was on fire, and there was ringing in my ears. We got up and automatically started running and screaming."

We turned to my aunt. "Everyone was running away, and I came to my senses. 'Bita! Bita!' I screamed and ran like crazy. My shoes came off, but I kept running. I could hear the ambulance's siren in the distance. I was screaming and running. I couldn't feel my heart beating. No more sound would come out. I sat down right there on the ground. It was impossible to tell which house had been struck, and I just sat and cried."

We let out all the air that had been trapped in our chests as Bita finished. "My ears were burning as I ran . . . I found Maman sitting on the ground like a gypsy, beating her head."

"I don't know how we got out of that inferno," my aunt wailed. "When I saw Bita, I started shaking. Like my soul was leaving my body right there . . ."

As missiles hailed down on Tehran, people left in droves—not for the Nouruz holidays, but for safety. Several acquaintances of ours had been killed, and we, too, fled for a villa in Karaj belonging to our close family friend, Aunt Mahin. Her garden was in disarray, and the house was packed with other refugees. Amid all the traffic, there wasn't enough room to drop a needle. We slept next to each other on the ground. When the air-raid siren sounded, most of us crowded into a corner while a few stepped outside to watch the missiles soar over Tehran. Afterward, everyone would sit by the radio and listen to the foreign Persian-language broadcasts on Radio Iraq, the Voice of America, or the BBC.

We stayed in Karaj through the critical peak of the war. Then we returned home, and the hot summer descended. On July 18, 1988, I heard our neighbor screaming uncontrollably from the hallway. As usual, the door was unlocked, and Khanum Bayat had entered without knocking. "It's over! It's over! Khanum Entekhabi, the war is over!" My father stood shocked, still in his underwear. We turned on the television. Khomeini had, in his own words, "drank the cup of poison" and agreed to the United Nations Security Council Resolution 598. We all cried, "The war is over!" It was hard to believe, but it was finally over. All afternoon, people handed out sweets in the streets. We didn't have to worry anymore about my little brother, and soon the soldiers would be coming home.

Then, only a few days after this joyous occasion, we heard about a massive attack on the border town of Islamabad Gharb carried out by the Mujahedin-e Khalgh, who had regrouped under the leader-ship of Rajavi in Iraq. With the protection of Saddam Hussein, the *mujahedin* had organized their own radio station and television net-work and carried out acts of terrorism. Now they had taken advan-tage of the cease-fire agreement and captured Islamabad and advanced to Hassanabad, moving toward Bakhtaran (also called Kermanshah). Four days later the air force and an army of Basijis and Pasdars crushed them, and thousands of *mujaheds* were killed on Iranian soil. The TV showed the images of the young men and women who'd died. The *mujahedin* called the operation Forogh-e Javidan (The Eternal Radiance) and the Iranian authorities called it Mersad (Ambush). Khomeini's wrathful response was a massacre of political prisoners, atheists, *mujaheds*, and *tudeh-is*—all burned in the fire of his vengeance. Once again, we had family members who sat sobbing in mourning for a loved one who'd been executed with-out even being allowed a proper memorial. My father's cousin's hus-band, who'd been a *tudeh* officer, was among those executed, after seven years in prison.

We were not aware of the extent of these executions until years later, when human rights organizations released information about the silent murder of thousands of political prisoners. At the time, confusion reigned. One day national radio broadcast that Khome-ini had disinherited his successor Ayatollah Montazeri, who I later discovered (via his online memoir) had written a letter to the Imam about the massacre. That very morning, when we passed Meidan Fatemi, we noticed with utter disbelief that the giant mural of Montazeri had simply disappeared.

◙　◙　◙

"Not a chance. Don't even bring it up. You father will skin all of us alive." My mother was washing dishes in the sink, and I was whining incessantly.

"I said don't talk about it." Then she shouted, "Get out of the kitchen!"

Once my father said no, it was impossible to change his mind. Everyone said it was unthinkable that my hardheaded father would give his daughter permission to go to Mashhad by herself on a two-week-long bus trip. I had been invited to the National Youth Festival of Writers and Poets. Students from all over Iran would gather in Mashhad to listen to one another read their work. My school surprisingly hadn't said a word, not one. They, in fact, were quite pleased. The Club for Creative Literature had promised constant supervision and secure dormitories, and that boys and girls would be kept strictly separate, except during the public readings.

That left my father, and I had only three days left to get the consent letter signed. A light bulb went off in my head—Uncle Manuchehr! He was the only one who spoke my father's language. I went to the phone booth with a two-rial coin and invited him over. My father was closer to Manuchehr than to his own brothers. Manuchehr was about five years older, and they had been friends since childhood. When all my father's family was opposed to his marriage with my mother, Manuchehr was the one who went to my grandmother's home to propose on his favorite cousin's behalf, and ever since then he and my father had always stood behind each other.

Though my father wasn't religious, he was traditional, and he didn't trust the new ruling social class. He didn't want me, his daughter, out alone in the world with these kind of people. He believed that all the urbanized, educated, intellectual people had fled or been killed and that the nouveaux riches of the postrevolution society were disgusting poseurs. They were unknown to him, and he didn't want us to fraternize with them. "There is no more respect for women in this country," he would say. "You have to stay away from these kinds of people." But I wanted so much to meet other writers my own age, to make new friends, and have the chance to learn from them. And my uncle Manuchehr knew exactly how to lead into the subject when he visited. Then I presented the invitation, and incredibly, my father consented.

How lucky I was! My father began looking at me with new pride and respect in his eyes. "My daughter, bring your book of poems!" he would ask in front of our guests. Nervous and embarrassed, I'd rush through a broken and unintelligible delivery. "Bah, bah, bah, bah, bah, bah, bah," my father would murmur with approval. The bemused audience, not having understood a thing, would have no choice but to nod their heads appreciatively.

Then once, when we were alone, he asked again, "Bring your notebook." My father was sitting in the just-watered courtyard smoking a cigarette.

"Read." I read the poem haltingly.

"Dear daughter, a good poet must have good delivery. The way you read, no one is going to take you seriously. Poetry must be read calmly and with great feeling. It must be read with conviction. Try again." His words stayed with me as I practiced diligently and memorized my poems, and my shyness turned into self-confidence.

With a thousand good-byes and *salvats*, I boarded the bus and set off with my face to Mashhad and my back to Tehran. We passed through Feiruz Kuh, Gunbad-e Kavus, Shahrud, and Quchan, stopping to sleep in a different city every night. My father had advised me to sit in the last row of the bus, so I did. And he had advised me not to eat meat on the road, so all I ate was bread and yogurt or cheese. In the end I caught a cold, but as night fell and we drove into Mashhad, I was full of energy. It was after midnight by the time the driver told us to stand up to greet Imam Reza, the eighth Shi'a imam. In the distance the dome of his shrine shone bathed in spotlights.

"*As-salaamu aleik ya Musa bin Reza!*" (Praise to you, Imam Reza, son of Imam Musa!) we called out to the golden dome.

Our instructor, Azar Fakhri, who had held my hand and let me rest my feverish head on her shoulder, said, "After we have supper, we'll go to the shrine at three o'clock in the morning."

Our dormitory was enormous; girls were spread across the floor, asleep, with a few whispering softly to one another. They gave each of us newcomers a blanket and a pillow. Designed to receive caravans of pilgrims, the house, like others in Mashhad, had a large salon, a fully equipped kitchen, and multiple bathrooms. The boys were housed elsewhere, far enough away that there couldn't be a chance for contact between us. I picked a spot in the corner and pulled the blanket over my head. At three o'clock, when Azar called me to go to the shrine, I couldn't get up. A girl with big black eyes and dark skin looked up at Azar and with a south Iranian accent said, "Don't worry about her. You go. We'll look after her." And then she turned and smiled at me.

And so I met Mandana from Abadan. Mandana was a victim of the war, and she lived in a refugee camp in Bandar-e Abbas. She introduced me at breakfast to dozens of others, including Vida from Shiraz and Nasrin from Azerbaijan. With my pink valise full of clothes, I felt I'd turned overnight into the spoiled little rich girl from Tehran. The rest had nothing. I gave the pocket money my father had given me to the group leader for safekeeping and kept my suitcase hidden behind a cushion. No one had any money, and I looked completely out of place in my modern blue jeans and yellow tunic blouse. I refused for days to change that outfit and draw attention to my packed valise.

On the way from the dormitory, we cheered when we saw flags hanging from streetlamps announcing our program: "The First Annual Nights of Poetry and Short Stories Series—Fall 1987, Ferdowsi Hall, Mashhad." Our beloved mentors, distinguished poets Asadullah Sha'abani and Ja'far Ebrahimi, introduced us one by one. I read my poetry with increasing feeling, my voice rising—until I saw my friends in the audience pointing behind me. My veil had gotten stuck on a lit candle and was now smoking. One of the instructors came up and put out both the candle and my veil. We all laughed long and hard for the rest of the night. My veil had a hole in it bigger than a two-toman coin. Nasrin later sent me a letter from Azerbaijan with a caricature of me reciting with a headdress trailing smoke.

When I came home, my mother took one whiff and said, "Ayeesh! Your clothes stink! Why didn't you change your shirt?"

"It just wouldn't have done!" I called out from under the shower.

When Mandana and I began writing to each other, she came to know everyone in my family. She sent a card for my mother's birthday and comforted us when my father died. When Kati was getting married, it was Mandana who took my hand and said, "You're tired, sit down. I'll help in your place."

Mandana wrote me horrifying accounts of the refugee camps in Bandar-e Abbas. Of a girl who'd become pregnant by her father-in-law. Of the poverty and decay and displacement. Of Khorramshahr and Abadan. Of the siege of Abadan when her brother Bahman was lost, and she and her mother searched the drawers of all the morgues one by one. Of her memories of her neighborhood in Abadan and her longing for the war to be over so she could return to Kucheh-ye Parvaneh.

On the day she returned, she wrote me that her house had been hit by mortars and bullets, and their furniture had been looted. "This is a burned city. Like our hearts. We have been welcomed back by a burned city." My father had come home late, and we sat around him so he wouldn't have to eat dinner alone. I had been crying for Mandana, and he told me to bring the letter and read it to him.

"Camelia, I am writing you from Kucheh-ye Parvaneh. From a

street deserted by all signs of life. I am writing you from Abadan. From the city of the suffering, of those who sit in the blood and the dirt. My heart is swollen and decayed like the corpses cast out into the windswept lifeless desert. Our house is a ruin with three walls. My childhood bike still stands in a corner of the basement after being burned a thousand times." My father listened with his eyes fixed on the television, but he was looking at Mandana and her burned city. His throat was choked with sobs.

Everyone was silent, mourning Iran's scorched earth. "The people of Abadan defended the city with empty hands, and our sons and brothers fell to the ground like flowers in the fall. My friend, believe me, today the date palms are broken. Tell me, when will our youth, our date palms, when will they be green again?"

◎   ◎   ◎

WINTER 1989

Seda va Sima, the television station, appeared on our doorstep about a week before the February memorial celebrations for the revolution. They asked to see "Khanum Camelia Entekhabifard." It was a Friday. We had eaten our *chelow kebabs*, and my father was sleeping in his bedroom downstairs. My mother brought out tea and pastries, and they explained that they were producing a program for the commemoration that featured the country's successful and distinguished teenagers. The Club for Creative Literature had recommended me, Camelia, girl poet and painter.

Then they asked, "Do you have any poetry about the revolution or the Imam?" I immediately answered, "Yes, of course. I have a poem written for the Imam." There was no way I'd pass up this opportunity. That settled it, and they toured my bedroom to decide whether they should shoot there or at the studio.

Later, I opened my poetry notebook. Which of these were for Khomeini? None of them. But was there any other way to grow up in Iranian society? Everyone lied and so I lied, too. When my father woke up from his nap and heard what had happened, he was beside himself with joy. We didn't tell him that they had wanted poetry glorifying the Imam. He was only given a one-sentence summary: "They want to do a show on Camelia."

At the studio, there were other teenagers like me sitting and waiting with their parents for their chance to record their spots. We each had ten minutes to present whatever talent we possessed in front of the camera. The boys in front of me started by rehearsing, but when Seda va Sima started shooting, they slipped up dozens of times. The director, Khanum Parvin Shemshaki, would cut and have them start over from the beginning. When my turn came, I decided to pull out all the stops. "Would you like to run a test?" they asked me. I shook my head. I had a few of my watercolor paintings in one hand and my poetry notebook in the other. I had picked out one of the poems I most loved reading. They pulled my veil as far forward as they could. The director had sharp eyes. "Please take off your bracelets," she said. I took them off. "Ready . . . Begin!"

I read my poem carefully, introducing it as "for the Imam . . ."

Man tura
Ta nehayat-e sepidehdam,
Az faraz-e shakhehaye purtavan-e bid,
Asheq o sarseporde am.

Man tura
Chun zolal-e cheshmeh sar-e deh,
Az miyan-e kuhsar o meh, asheqaneh dide am.

Man tura
Chun sedaye parandeha

Me to you
til the dawn's end
From atop the strong branches of a willow tree
I am in love, devoted to you

Me to you
like the limpid waters of a pure village stream
Lovestruck, I caught a glimpse of you
Between the hills and the fog.

Me to you
Like the singing of birds . . .

Then I showed my paintings to the camera one after another. I spoke for ten whole minutes without a glitch. Khanum Shemshaki said, "You were terrific, kiddo. That was great. Great delivery. Confident. You're a born newscaster."

At sundown on one of the ten days of the Bahman celebrations, the program was broadcast, and quite accidentally everyone happened to be home. My father was sleeping, and I ran to wake him up. We quickly stuffed the blank video cassette we had bought to record the occasion into the VCR. My little family watched the screen attentively as my ten-minute segment was shown all over the country. Out of the corner of my eye, I looked at my father. He seemed thoroughly engrossed in the program and was beaming with pride. I knew that winning this celebrity had required deception on my part, and that I would never have been accepted in the popular crowd and on television without lying. I learned this well in school, faking my prayers in front of the Omur-e Tarbiyati each morning, pretending in order to get through the day. Yet, seeing my father's face, I was satisfied.

▣ ▣ ▣

SPRING 1989

When Khomeini got sick, he was shown on television in a private hospital that had been built near his house in Jamaran, and it seemed that he would recover quickly. Our relatives in Jamaran, who'd assembled at the *husseinya* to pray for the Imam's health, reported faithfully the rumors that he was recovering. On the evening of June 2, 1989, my mother had hosed down the courtyard like she did every evening, and we were sitting pleasantly on the grass, eating dinner. Our upstairs neighbor Shabnam, a girl from my school, had joined us. We had our end-of-the-term English exam the next day, and I was mindlessly hoping that it would somehow be canceled. As we said goodnight on the steps, I said to Shabnam, "I'll come get you in the morning at seven. That is, of course, unless Khomeini dies!"

The next morning at 6:45, my mother called me from the top of the stairs. I came sleepily into the kitchen. The radio was on. They were broadcasting the Qur'an. I perked up my ears. There was something odd about hearing the Qur'an on the radio at that time of day. The radio sounded three chimes for the start of the seven o'clock news, and then the announcer's voice came back on. "*Enna l'illah wa enna aleihi raja'un*" (Verily, we come to God and to God we return). He followed with his report in Persian. "Oh great and martyr-yielding nation of Iran, the Spirit of God has rejoined with God." I didn't even have the decency to listen to the rest of the announcement. I let out a shout and sprung up and down, yelling, "Khomeini died! Khomeini died!" And then my mother started raining blows down onto my head and shoulders. I escaped and ran outside. "Shabnam! Shabnam!" She opened the door. "He died! He died! Khomeini died!" Shabnam's sleepyheaded mother, Khanum Mir Eskandari, appeared behind her and quickly followed me downstairs to our apartment. My shoulders stung. My mother sat dumbfounded by the radio. When she saw me, she started going crazy all over again. She was completely hysterical. To this day I still don't know why, with news like this, on a day such as this, I needed to get a beating.

Khanum Mir Eskandari asked, "Now what are we going to do?" The war had come to an end, but the economic and social situation in Iran showed no sign of improvement. Was there going to be another revolution? Would Iraq attack us again? Would mobs pour into the streets? Would the mullahs in line to succeed Khomeini start fighting? Would civil war break out?

To me, the first important thing that happened was that the schools were closed for a week, and the final exams were postponed. A period of national mourning was announced. A council of experts elected the president, Hojjat ul-Islam Ali Khamene'i, as the successor to Ayatollah Khomeini in his position as supreme leader. New presidential elections were rapidly scheduled, and Hashemi Rafsanjani was elected president, an office he would hold for two terms.

Tehran sunk into an uncharacteristic calm over these heaven-sent holidays. Khomeini's funeral was held at Tehran's large *musala* and was broadcast live. My family didn't budge from our places in front of the television the whole day. We weren't going to miss a second of Iran's most historic moment. We ate breakfast, lunch, and dinner in front of the television. Everyone would just dart into the kitchen to fetch their own food.

Khomeini's glass casket was carried vertically so people could see him. He was covered all over with white gardenias. Millions of mourners had come from all over Iran, men and women, all of them crying and beating their heads and faces. And Khomeini, up there in that glass coffin, was sleeping peacefully. From the *musala*, where the mobs bid farewell to the leader of the revolution and the founder of the Islamic Republic, the funeral procession wound its way to Behesht-e Zahra for the burial.

Millions more waited for Khomeini at Behesht-e Zahra, and thousands had climbed up on top of huge rectangular containers, which reminded me of those a movie crew might have, that had been set out to hold back the crowd. The grave had been dug, and there were piles of dirt surrounding it. When the procession arrived, the people rushed forward, breaking through the police lines. The mounds of earth reserved for covering the corpse vanished in the blink of an eye. Everyone grabbed the blessed dirt as Khomeini's body bobbed through the crowd, passed from one set of hands to another. Everyone wanted to touch the body or make off with a piece of his shroud. We watched in astonishment as his shroud was torn off, and his naked body fell out of it. The photographers seized on this unique moment, and the cover of next week's *Time* magazine showed the leader of the revolution with his shroud falling to expose his bare chest and arms.

The corpse was rescued from the clutches of the screaming, surging mob and put in a helicopter. According to Uncle Ali, they flew him back to the Manzeria clinic to be wrapped up in a new shroud. Soldiers drove the people back, and more troops arrived on the scene. I can't recall exactly how much later the helicopter returned with the body, but when it did, they quickly buried him and blocked the grave so the crazed mourners couldn't dig up his final resting place and steal the soil.

The rumors we heard later told another story. People said that, among the mourners, it was *mujahedin* and family members of victims executed by the regime who were tugging wildly at Khomeini's body and who ripped his shroud to pieces.

◙   ◙   ◙

Little by little, my poems and *ghazals* were starting to get published in newspapers and magazines. When I won first prize in a poetry competition for our province, my reward was to join with a group of other distinguished students to meet the new supreme leader, Khamene'i, and then visit Khomeini's tomb. The magnificent mausoleum was fashioned after the Al-Aqsa Mosque in Jerusalem, and the building had progressed with unbelievable efficiency. It would be completed sometime around the first anniversary of his death. I carried in my purse a black chador and the letter of permission from my mother (my father didn't know anything about the field trip, and we didn't say a word to him).

At the entrance to the mausoleum, we took off our shoes. The construction still wasn't quite finished, and there were men at work on the exterior. We approached the gold-encased grave, and the teacher with us from the Omur-e Tarbiyati kissed the railings and tossed an envelope of money into the tomb. The interior of the tomb was full of coins, women's gold jewelry, and envelopes that people had thrown as votive offerings. On the white marble floor in front of me, there was a ghostly image of a red tulip. I looked up, and above the grave I saw stained-glass windows decorated with pictures of tulips. A line of poetry that had been written on doors and walls around the city came to mind: *Az khun-e javanan vatan laleh damideh* (From the blood of the young, the nation has sprouted tulips).

Tulips had sprouted here, too.

chapter eight I Will Plant My Hands in the Garden

"Tell me, you whore, who is your Israeli contact! How many times a year did you meet with him? I'll have them beat you like a dog! Do you need me to tell you the name of your contact in Israel? I'll tell you. Yaqub!"

I racked my brain. Yaqub . . . Yaqub . . . Nothing came to mind. They must have known I'd met George Soros in America . . . maybe that's what he was talking about.

"I swear to God I don't know. I swear on the Qur'an you're mistaken."

"Dirty little rat! Our intelligence is very accurate. Yaqub came with you from Jordan to Dubai so the two of you could sleep together, and then you left for Tehran. Tell me what information you exchanged with him! Tell me, or I'll let you rot in your cell until you put your vile ways behind you."

I had made that trip as a reporter for *Zan*. His shouting was lost as that strange horrible buzzing tore through the room again. My head was filled with its insect sound. And it surprised me into remembering Yaqub, as my interrogator's voice drifted further away.

I'd been exhausted by my trip to Jordan but so excited to tell Faezeh and my friends at *Zan* everything about it that I'd gone home from the airport only to drop off my bag before heading over to the paper. I hadn't even taken a shower. When the funeral of King Hussein had been announced, I had made the decision overnight to report on the event and had bothered the Jordanian ambassador in Tehran at his home late in the evening in order to get a visa on the spot. Now I was back home, jet lagged and thrilled that my article had made the front page.

"And you are? Let me see if she's in the office."

My co-worker Farnaz fixed her big green eyes on me. She covered the receiver and said, "What a voice . . . Who is this guy? He said he's Yaqub from Dubai."

I jumped up and grabbed the handset. "*Salaam* . . . Yes, I made it back fine . . . Thanks for calling . . . Bye."

The biggest charge I faced in prison was spying for the Israeli government. The sick paranoia of the Ministry of Intelligence could not accept that I had merely drunk a cup of tea with Yaqub, that I had met him and his friends accidentally, with no idea where they were from or where they were going. I had stopped in Dubai for only eight hours to transfer to my flight home to Tehran. With a transit visa I went to a hotel in the city to shower and have breakfast. And with the hospitality I was raised to display, I introduced myself as soon as I noticed that the strangers seated next to me were speaking in Persian. "*Salaam*," I said. "I'm Iranian, too." Typically, all Iranians outside of Iran will do this. Regardless of how the stranger looks, they'll great each other with a warm, "Are you Iranian? I heard you speaking Persian!" (I should say that my attitude has changed. Since I left Iran the last time, if anyone asks me if I'm Iranian, I curtly answer, "Yes, I am," and avoid further conversation.)

I told Yaqub and his friends about King Hussein's funeral in Jordan. They explained that they were on a trip to buy antiques; one of them was from Tehran and the other two had a shop in London. Yaqub was wearing a fancy chain around his neck. I looked at the pendant and asked, "You have a Faravahar—are you Zoroastrian?"

"This is the sign of a commander in the Israeli armed forces. We are Jewish. That's not a problem, is it?" I shook my head. He explained that like many other Iranian Jews, he had left Iran at the beginning of the revolution. He'd gone to Israel and served in the military, though now he was living in London. They walked me to a taxi, and we exchanged business cards, and I promised to stop by their store someday on my travels, if possible. That was all.

My interrogator kept asking me about a pendant I used to have, a *chai* I always wore, shining under my thin head scarf. Several girls in my office had asked to see it, wanting to know about the Hebrew word. I told them it meant "life" and that the charm was a gift from a Jewish friend in Germany. Then I'd joke with them, making my eyes wild and saying, "Didn't you know, I'm Jewish!" and laughing at their shocked faces. But I didn't have the *chai* anymore—I'd given it away to a lovely woman from the United Nations whom I'd met in Bosnia. She'd invited me for her birthday, and all I had with me to give her was my necklace. Since I had nothing to show my interrogator, I swore to him that it never existed.

Yet now that it had been settled that I would confess to sleeping with sixty-seven people, I threw Yaqub's name in there, too. And so I confessed that Yaqub had followed me up to my room and that we had slept together and had kept in touch by phone after that, but that I never knew he was a spy. If it was a sin to have sex outside of marriage, the sin was raised to the sky to sleep with a Jewish man. I talked about Yaqub like I'd known him for years. They wanted so many details, I began to think that maybe Yaqub really was a spy sent by Israel to Dubai to contact me. . . . Or maybe he was double agent, and the Iranian government had told him, "Camelia seems too easygoing, check that girl out for us." I was frustrated and confused to the point where I couldn't concentrate on anything beyond giving my interrogator what he wanted. I promised him I was terribly sorry, that I'd never speak to strangers again in my life. He asked me, "How could you sleep with him?" And I answered, "I wasn't educated properly, I wasn't a good Muslim, I was addicted to sex. I'm full of sin, you should punish me however you decide . . ." I was so tired. I told him I had wanted to find someone to marry and that I'd tried out anyone who seemed interested in me, but I'd failed, and now I wanted to become clean, to become a good Muslim and beg God for forgiveness.

Seda va Sima regularly broadcasted interviews with young people who had been arrested in the student strikes. They'd bring the helpless captives in tied up, and they'd confess to ties with the monarchists and agitators against the government and to accepting money from various groups to undermine the Islamic Republic. I'd seen Manuchehr Mohammadi and Qolamreza Mohajeri Nezhad, two leaders among the student activists, brought before the camera. In the glorious dawn of the reform movement, Mohammadi had been on fire. He was outspoken and brave and toured the globe, from East to West and even to the America. He lectured Iranians in exile, inviting them back to Iran to witness a new era, proclaiming an "Iran for all Iranians," the message of Khatami's campaign. Iranians in exile had never heard someone speaking out so boldly against the government. Now as I lay on the hard, smelly carpet, I could sometimes hear what I recognized as Manuchehr Mohammadi's sickly voice somewhere above me. He cried like he was out of his mind and begged God for help.

My whole body hurt. I had waited days in a vacuum, through the harsh interrogations, imagining Faezeh or Golriz, my friend from a human rights organization, appearing like angels to save me. And now, from among all the voices that surrounded me, the strongest voice came from inside me, saying that if I ever wanted to get out of here, I had better help myself.

I buried my head in my hands and had a conversation with

myself. I was a good actress. I had starred in leading roles in plays in high school. I loved the theater, but drama wasn't an acceptable pursuit to my parents. I had always told myself that I'd get another chance to prove my brilliance on the stage and that it would be the greatest performance of my life. I knew that building up my focus would take days or months, and I resolved myself. I took a deep breath and plunged into my role.

Every night and every morning, when I was alone in my cell, I'd close my eyes and meditate. My painting instructor, Feiruzeh Gul Mohammadi, had taught me this invaluable art of gathering energy and channeling it toward a specific goal. I was focusing my energy to work on the mind of my interrogator. Feiruzeh was a dervish, and steeped in those principles, she channeled her overflowing energy and light into the creation of her art. At the end of her watercolors class, we would sit cross-legged and meditate as Feiruzeh asked us to find a point within ourselves and concentrate. "Your eyes will open themselves to the images that will be embodied in your paintings." She inspired me, and over the New Year's holidays I even went to find the dervish in the main Tehran bazaar who sat from the first twilight till dawn writing Sharaf ash-Shams prayers on the backs of yellow carnelian stones. I didn't have my carnelian ring with me in prison, but I closed my eyes and envisioned the outcome I most desired: to be free. Free as I was when I sat in my painting classes during the summertime, watching the butterflies circling the sunflowers in Feiruzeh's beautiful garden, or when I sat by her fireplace in the winter as the snow fell heavily outside. Where were those days, when did they disappear? I longed for the freedom of my youth that was gone forever, but I still hoped for a day free from threats and fear, a day I could send flowers to my mother to thank her for giving birth to me, when I could simply sit and say to God, "I am happy."

Each day that I meditated in my cell, I became more and more absorbed in my role. I had decided that I would get out of prison and that the very man who came every day to interrogate me would come to my aid. I had to store up an immense amount of energy in order to attract his attention. We never saw each other's face. My face was to the wall, and my eyes were blindfolded. Only my hands were free to move about, and I had to channel all of my energy into my hands. My role was to fall in love and make him fall in love. My freedom rested with the performance given by my hands.

Feiruzeh's soft voice was in my ear. "Camelia, be calm and think about the enormous energy you have inside you. Become strong. With this energy, you can change people." I remembered the pilgrimage we took together. Thousands of Iranians made this trip to the mosque of Jamkaran near Qom on Tuesdays, which the Shi'a believe is the day of the Imam-e Zaman. In the minibuses that carried Feiruzeh's class, all of us young women, to Jamkaran, there was more life and energy than I could now have thought possible.

According to legend, when the Imam-e Zaman first went into hiding his *babs* would take letters from his followers and bring them to his presence. Before the imam's third *bab* died, he proclaimed that he was the last *bab* and that from then on the imam would be hidden in a well. The original well used to contact him is a pilgrimate site in Iraq, but after the revolution and the eight-year war, it was impossible for Iranians to visit it. So out of their love for the imam, a new pilgrimage site was chosen within Iran's borders. One of the spiritual leaders of Qom claimed to have seen the Imam-e Zaman in a dream, and the vision told him that his dwelling was in a dry well in Jamkaran. Inspired by the blessing, he built a mosque and encircled the dry well with an iron railing, and the pilgrims throw their letters and offerings down into the well. We had been told that the caretakers of the mosque would gather all the letters in a sack and pour them into running water, believing that the imam would read them.

It was evening when we arrived at the mosque. Powerful projectors lit up the courtyard and the veranda of the mosque, and loudspeakers broadcast special prayers. Feiruzeh had told us that if first-time visitors focused, they would see the Master, the Imam-e Zaman, in some form. I had read accounts of pilgrims who had glimpsed the imam for an instant at the mosque or en route to Jamkaran, and so I made sure to keep looking. Feiruzeh and I unrolled our prayer rugs in the courtyard of the mosque to pray. I concentrated on trying to distinguish the Imam-e Zaman from amid the crowds. I saw no sign of him. We were surrounded by salt flats and there was only the raw earth and the wind throwing sand and dust into my eyes.

My mother had written a letter for me to throw in for the imam. An enormous number of women were crying and praying around the well; everyone wanted to touch the iron railing. This was the women's side, and on the eastern end of the courtyard was the men's section. I broke away from the group and pushed forward. The well was so full of letters that they were spilling out from the gaps between the rails. I thrust my mother's letter deep inside. That peculiar scent they call the "fragrance of Mecca" rippled through the air, the intense smell of cheap rose water perfume. By the time I could pull my hand back out of the railing, my chador had slipped off and fallen to the ground. When I had made my way to the side of the crush of the crowds, I fixed my chador. As I clutched the seam under my chin, I could smell red roses on my hand. My eyes were burning.

I held my hand up to Feiruzeh's nose. "Bah, bah, bah, bah," she said. "So he picked you out of all of us? The Master has taken the letter from your hand."

A few months later, we had a gathering at our house, and my

mother told our guests the story. She said that the Master had read her letter and given her an answer.

I was astounded. "Maman, what did your letter say?"

My proud mother said that she wasn't allowed to say but added, "There is a Chinese proverb that says, 'The scent of a rose never fades from the hand of the one who gives it to you.'"

Alone in my cell, I looked at my hands, and a poem by Forugh Farrokhzad came into my mind:

> *Dasthayam-ra dust daram.*
> *Dasthayat-ra dar baghcheh mikaram,*
> *Sabz khahad shud. Man midanam.*

"I love
your hands"

I will plant my hands in the garden
I will grow green, I know, I know

chapter nine Daisies in Autumn

1990

At Dabirestan-e Hoda it was fashionable to be in love. My cousin Elham told me she'd stumbled upon two girls kissing in the bathroom, and I had caught two girls kissing each other's breasts behind the wall of the courtyard. The vice principal, Khanum Haj Seyyed Javadi, had a loyal group of wildly infatuated admirers. She was unmarried and had singled out a few girls from the school for friendship, walking with them during free periods. One of the objects of her affection was Elham. The vice principal's admirers would hunch together behind her and walk along somberly through the courtyard.

I had a few admirers of my own in the freshman class, who would write me love letters and stick them on the pull-out tray of my desk. They would write poems about how they were proud to be my friend, writing about my hair and my eyes, asking for my photo. Hoda was at the center of the class and culture clashes in Tehran in the 1990s. The institution of public schools and the abolishment of private schools after the revolution had thrown together wealthy students coming from old money and new money and those from the poorest neighborhoods. Girls from upper-class families in my neighborhood, Shahrak-e Gharb, who could afford to go skiing in the winter, wore fancy sneakers, and took private piano lessons, now sat in class alongside girls so poor they came to school in the winter with cotton shoes full of holes and nothing to wear over their uniforms. These girls came from Farahzad, where their parents were seasonal workers who picked the white berries that region is renowned for or collected cow and sheep dung to dry for winter fuel. They lived in one-room shacks on their boss's property and guarded the orchards. They walked a long way or took a bus to get to Hoda, and yet, instead of seeming angry or jealous, they looked up to and adored us Shahrak-e Gharbi girls as if we were celebrities. My sweet and polite cousin Elham, whose parents were both doctors, was their deity. Sometimes Farahzadi girls would smile at me through our classroom window when they were on break, and sometimes I'd wave back at them—but they never dared to speak to me. Niknaz, who was in my year and was something of a tomboy, was the girl with the most devotees. In the grade above us was Nava Rouhani, a fourth-year student—she came in second.

The notion of girls being in love was taken very seriously. With all of the clandestine romance at Dabirestan-e Hoda, there was no place for my presumptiveness in writing poetry, even poetry celebrating the freedom of Iranian soldiers released from Iraqi prisons. And so I stood, shuffling my feet in the principal's office. "Khanum Haj Seyyed Javadi, bring Entekhabifard's file. Camelia."

My heart stopped beating. In a weak voice, I asked the principal, "Please, excuse me, Khanum Hassani, I still don't understand what I've done wrong."

"When you've been expelled you'll understand that this filthy business has no place at school. When your family gets wind of this, they'll know how to deal with you." Then she ignored me as she went about her daily business. Even my studious cousin Elham's protests had had no effect. My mother had forced me to move to Hoda, away from all my old friends at Fayazbaksh, in the hopes that Elham's influence and example would make me an obedient student. Elham kept looking over at me with a worried face, and I knew in her heart she was cursing her bad luck at having such a pain for a cousin. I motioned her to go back to class.

Principal Hassani was a nasty old girl without a drop of mercy or kindness in her blood. Dark-skinned with a blotchy face, a mouth that always reeked, and a black mustache, she wasn't the respected principal, but a demon charged with guarding the gates of the hell they called high school. And we, the damned, lived in fear of her, both inside and outside of school. In the still of the morning in Shahrak-e Gharb, she'd patrol the deserted side streets, silently and mysteriously, in her white Mercedes. Or she'd lurk around the neighborhood, waiting to jump out and grasp the wrist of any of her students she caught with a boy or with their hair showing from under their veil or laughing or even standing in a public phone booth.

"Guys, it's Khanum Hassani!" The second any of us saw a white car, we'd call out the alert, and everyone would run into the alleys to hide behind the flower bushes or a tree. At the wheel, wrapped all in black, she'd lurch out like the angel of death. If she saw us, we were done for. She was almost fifty and had never been married, and we prayed that some generous man would come along and soften her stony heart by the kindness of love. But no one showed up to ask for her hand.

The "infernal inspectors," the hall monitors, who were Khanum Hassani's envoys, found the poem after searching my schoolbag. One of the little bitches unfolded the sheet of paper and gave me a probing stare. I opened my eyes wide and stared back. "It's not a poster of Madonna! It's poetry." She studied the page in wonder. Impatiently I said, "Haven't you ever read poetry before? It's a love poem." At the words "love poem," the situation burst into flames. I was defenseless, she had me backed into a corner.

I kept my head down as Khanum Hassani asked me to explain exactly *for whom* I had composed this ode of love. I raised my chin and said, "For those who have been freed." I had written the poem that summer for the Iranian prisoners of war. Two years after the end of the war with Iraq, the first group had been released and returned via the border at Qasr-e Shirin. It was a cause for national celebration.

Brimming with pride, I asked my father if we could go to welcome them. "The town isn't open to travelers yet," he said, "and I'm sure only officials and the prisoners' families can attend." So, again, I experienced an historical moment with rapt attention to the TV screen. I wept with joy as the prisoners came home to Iran. I felt I was there with them, with the overcome mothers welcoming their sons and the prisoners leaning out of their buses to kiss the well-wisher's upturned hands and faces, with the crowds carrying flowers. I, too, was a part of their triumph, right beside them in front of the television, unable to control my emotions. When my mother came home to my tears, she thought there had been some kind of accident. I told her, "The prisoners have returned to Iran." My poem read:

Sh'eri baraye Azadegan

Daghtarin tekrar khorshid ast.
Be a'inah-ye dastanat nazar daram,
Ke hargez tekrar nakhahad shud.
Ah bar khak che ma'sumaneh ru'ideh
Shaqayeqra miguyam.
Shaqayeq man inak,
Asheqtar az anam ke yek lahze bit u sar kunam.
Be man negah kun ke dar tu man
Fikr natamam-e parandehra bekhanam.
Be payan-e asman mirasi o man dast bar pishani
Oburat ra dar a'ineh negah mikunam.
A'ineh tu ra khahad guft.

For the Free

Of all the things that cycle
Again and again, the hottest is the sun
I am looking at the mirror of your hands
Never to return.
And on the earth, so innocently sprouted,
I tell it to the bright red poppy.
Oh poppy, I'm so in love
That I cannot bear an instant without you.
Look at me,
that I might read in you
the unfinished thought of a bird in flight.
You are approaching the end of the sky
and I brush my hand across my forehead
as I gaze at your fleeting image in the mirror.
The mirror that speaks of you.

Iran is a nation of poets—you can't find a family in Iran that doesn't claim a poet. And Iranian poets love to write about love. My poem to the soldiers was in the popular contemporary style called *sher-e azad* or *sher-enou*. Yet I was also inspired by the history of Iranian poetry. Hafez, one of the most celebrated Iranian poets, writes beautifully about love and sex, and it's clear to Iranians that the women he writes about are God. People read Hafez's poems like divine fortunes, consulting them like an oracle. Through his writing they find God in their daily lives. My poem's romantic imagery was common for all Persian poets. I wondered . . . If Hafez had been a student at Hoda, would even *he* have been expelled for writing controversial poems?

My mother was called into the school, and she came out of principal Hassani's office seething. She said that I had been dismissed for the day. She quarreled with me all the way home. "Aren't you ashamed? They told me that my daughter has fallen in love with Nava Rouhani and has been writing poetry to her. I wanted to die from shame. Why aren't you ashamed?"

It was true that I cared for Nava. She liked my writing and flattered me by borrowing my notebook full of poems. She was different from the others. She had a distinct poise and was a pianist, the daughter of the famous Iranian pianist Anoushirvan Rouhani. It was because of her prominent antirevolutionary father that Khanum Hassani wanted to punish us. My "love" poem was a convenient excuse. And it was true that I had brought a rose to school for her on her birthday. But our friendship was nothing like the lurid image swimming around our principal's head.

My mother blazed ahead. "Khanum Hassani said that she's been watching you and Nava for some time now, and she's noticed that this ill-intentioned girl has been using you and"—she stopped herself midsentence and then thundered, "If we tell your father, he'll kill us all. Dirt on your head when you let them spread these rumors about you. Has anyone even once said such things about Elham? Why can't you learn proper manners from your cousin?"

I wanted to kill Khanum Hassani. I screamed back at my mother, "You! How could you let her say such shit to you? Why didn't you smack her in the mouth? Why didn't you say that this school is a madhouse and that she is a raving lunatic?" and I broke down, crying bitterly.

"What should I have said? Should I have told that Madar-e Fuladzere-ye Div that she's a liar and sick in the head? And she would have said that this Nava is a Baha'i and unclean and that she molests girls! You must never speak to her again or Khanum Hassani will kick you out of school."

For a long time after these accusations, my poetry just floated away. It was as if Khanum Hassani had banished my muse to a dark island in the middle of a vast ocean. Mandana wrote me, "Where is your new work? Don't let the typhoon carry your bird's nest away with it. It is needed in the wind." And my teacher from the club wrote me, "Be patient. Let the poetry trickle out by itself like water droplets. It will come shortly of its own accord."

I begged to be sent back to my old school, to my friends Faranak, Bita, Masumeh, and Newsha. I kept ducking out of class to go visit them. I wrote Mandana, "My house is black, and today only crows are singing in the street outside. My street is filled with a frenzy of crows." I was plagued by nightmares, and I didn't have the strength to study. I failed my exams and had to repeat my junior year. Finally, because it was so embarrassing to repeat a year at the same school, my mother allowed me to return to Fayazbaksh.

When I failed my exams, I didn't come out of my room for a week and a half. I sat and stared at the walls in misery. Shocked and confused, I thought about running away from home or killing myself. I had always been a good student, and this shameful failure hurt me and my family. Then one day my father came in, sat on my bed, and said, "Camelia, I want to talk to you." I was afraid at first that he was going to punish me, even more harshly than a few years ago when my grade in my English class fell. He'd banned me from my best friend Leila's wedding (she was married at fifteen). He never discovered that I had snuck out to attend the ceremony briefly, in a nervously planned escape that kept my blood pressure up for weeks.

On this sad day, though, I was punishing myself so much that it wouldn't have mattered if he grounded me for the whole summer. I wanted to die. Incredibly, in contrast to the wrath I expected, my father had come to counsel me about self-reliance and hope, about struggling to achieve one's goals, about success and believing in better and happier days.

He calmly asked me to follow him to the kitchen to talk, then closed the door and lit a cigarette. We sat at the table. "I don't want you and your sister to marry young. I want both of you to study hard. You have unique talents, you're different—there's so much you can achieve. In our society, where it's a sin to be a woman, I want you and your sister to be powerful and respected. Even when you do get married, if you fight with your husband, if he yells at you or treats you badly, I want you to be able to make your own decisions. If you're educated and have a job, you can take care of yourself, and you won't be forced to stay with some horrible husband for financial reasons. Learn from this failure . . ."

As I listened to him, I watched the thin line of blue smoke rising from his cigarette sitting in the ashtray, an unbroken line that rose up to the kitchen ceiling. He picked it up to take a deep puff, and the line dissolved in all directions. "The situation in our country is so uncertain and unbalanced that any day we might be forced to leave. And if we must leave Iran, your education may be your only currency. An education is cash you can spend anywhere—no one can take it away from you, it's an asset that can't be seized. Trust me, when I can't be with you anymore, it will be your education that keeps you girls safe." I was crying quietly, the tears running down my cheeks. I wanted to kiss his hands, to hold him and cry in his arms. But my father didn't like his daughters to be emotional, I knew. He wanted us to be strong. "Okay, go now and wash your face, then concentrate on the new semester. There's a solution for everything—except death. And you are alive, and I'm still with you, and you can stand up again."

When I left the kitchen, I felt I had grown years in that conversation. It was one of the few times in my life that I had seen this side of my father. My defeat had broken his usual strict composure, and he was speaking to me from the heart. My empty days of sitting in solitude and mourning my failure gradually disappeared in the confidence he'd inspired. I went back to my old school, and after a while my little butterflies of poetry also returned to land gently on my shoulder.

The cultural revolution took place a year after the revolution, and the universities were closed for two years. When they reopened, the Ministry of Higher Education and Learning was formed to investigate students and judge whether they could be admitted to college. Students who were accepted to a university still had to prove that they met Islamic moral standards before they were allowed to enroll. Every year, our neighbors whose sons and daughters had taken the entrance exams would come around begging everyone to speak generously of their children. When they were evaluating Maryam, our fourth floor neighbor in our old apartment in Shahr-Ara, the investigator knocked on our door. He had a beard and thick glasses and cotton shoes. He wouldn't look at my mother as he questioned her but turned his gaze to the wall, nodding his head and recording his findings in his file. Men who were very Islamic believed that in order to abstain from sin while talking to women, they had to abstain from looking at them directly. It was the same at all the ministries and official institutions. If you were among a few women standing together, it was difficult to guess who was being spoken to, and you had to ask, "Who are you addressing?" Or, "To whom is the brother speaking?" My mother said that Maryam was the most virtuous girl on the block and that her parents were pious and that "this girl doesn't go running around with anyone but stays at home and studies."

The investigators also visited parents' workplaces and local businesses to enquire after a family's reputation, how well they observed the *hejab*, whether they participated in Friday prayers, and so forth. And so the fates of university-bound students were in the hands of their neighbors, many of whom harbored some hostility, spite, or envy. But no matter how well we did on our exams and even in the investigative screening, it was still hard for families like ours, in the same way that it was easy for the families of martyrs, of soldiers at the front, or of prisoners of war. The only variable that mattered in the equation was the number of afflictions suffered in the war. There were special provisions for the war-torn southern provinces, but we Tehranis, who'd done nothing for the revolution, who could claim no martyrs or combatants, we had to resort to flattering those in power. I remember how, as she filled out her forms, Kati would break down. We were classified as region "one," but Kati would cry that "this 'one' stands for last, not first!" Some of her friends even transferred to dangerous war-stricken regions in their senior year just to get into college.

Luckily, by the time I graduated, the investigations had ceased. There was a new window of hope. Katayun was one of the first students accepted into the newly established Azad Islamic University. So I also submitted my exams for a program in political science at Azad while I was still in high school, during my last year. My grades weren't high enough for the Tehran campus, but I was passed to the next round where I could be evaluated for up to three alternate cities. I chose only one—the city of Shahreza. I considered this a test, an experiment. My true goal was to apply to an even more prestigious state university the next year. In the meantime, my greatest gift to my father would be for him to see my name in the newspaper among those accepted to Azad. I wanted to give him this sweet satisfaction after my bitter academic failure two years earlier. When I gave him the news that I'd passed the first round, even though I wasn't accepted in Tehran, he came home from work that evening with a big box of sweets in his hand. Grinning from ear to ear, he kissed me and said, "You've made me very proud."

We waited impatiently for the daily paper. One week passed since the promised date of the Azad University announcement, and every day the newspapers published a vague postponement. My father asked me about it every night. His restless excitement was contagious. He'd ask, "No news? When are they going to announce the names? Weren't they supposed to be announced last week?" And I'd reply, "Yes, they were. I don't know why they don't announce them. But soon, maybe tomorrow . . ."

◙ ◙ ◙

AUTUMN 1991

One of my fondest memories of my father is of visiting Maman Pari's house with him, with its red roses, grand old persimmon, and the cobalt tiling above the door that read "Nakha'i." The Nakha'i are one of the most well-known families in Tehran. My great-grandfather had the honorable title Entekhab-e Lashghar and held a high-ranking post at the end of the Qajar Era, at the time of Muzaferuddin Shah Qajar. One century ago, an Armenian youth fell in love with Entekhab-e Lashghar's beautiful daughter Zarin Taj and asked her father for her hand. But the match violated religious laws, social conventions, and moral principals, and his answer was no. The Armenian youth hired thugs and sent them under the cover of night to surround Entekhab-e Lashgar's house. They say that Zarin Taj was so in love that she opened the outer door for her father's killers. On that night, my five-year-old grandfather was asleep in his father's bed. Again and again, this is how he would tell the story of his father's death: "When I opened my eyes, there were dozens of masked men holding daggers and spears standing over us. They gestured for me to put my head under the covers. When I stuck my head out a few minutes later, I saw that the walls were splattered with blood. My father's body lay beside me just as before, but it had been punctured dozens of times over by spears."

My grandfather's childhood was plagued with nightmares of his father's tragic death and with harsh treatment at the hands of his uncles and half-brothers, with whom he waged legal battles for years over his inheritance. Disgusted with his family, he decided that he was no longer a Nakha'i, and he fashioned a family name as close as possible to his father's title of honor, Entekhab-e Lashghar. My grandmother says they sent Zarin Taj to the village of Nurabad, where she was so grief stricken by her father's death that she suffered a nervous breakdown and died there.

Every fall, the family hired someone to climb the tree and pick the persimmons. Each of my grandmother's children would get about a hundred persimmons, sometimes more, for their families, evenly divided on a large copper tray, and my grandmother would ask the gardener to leave a few persimmons up in the tree for the crows and other birds. In the beautiful Tehran autumn, the red persimmons would shine like lanterns from the ashy leafless tree. Then one year the house and the persimmon tree and the apple tree and my swimming pool and the cellar—all of it—was sold. All that is left of the cellar now are my memories of it, the cellar that, in the heat of the summer, was cool and comfortable, and where my father loved to take his midday naps. I'd follow him down there. He would take two freshly picked apples in one hand and a bottle of rose water, a grater, and some sugar in the other. He'd grate the apples and put the rose water and sugar on them, and after we'd drank the mixture, my father would go to sleep.

It was autumn at my father's funeral, and I was holding yellow and white daisies in my hand. The winds came and swirled through my black clothing. Everyone had gone forward to the grave, and I was left back a few steps on the soft earth clutching the daisies in my hand. He had been brought to me so I could look at him, so I could see him up close one last time. His eyes were shut, and where his chest had always given off a reddish hue, he was turning marble white. There was a red line underneath his left eye, evidence of his fall, and his soft black hair, which in his forty-eight years had only manifested a few white hairs around the temples, was wrapped out of sight by a white handkerchief. I had pulled him to my bosom and cried, "Baba, get up, let's go home!"

They wrested me from my father and took him away, and lying on the ground, I called out to him in a wail. Then I ran. I clenched the dirt and the daisies in my fist. They lowered him into the ground wrapped in a shroud, with only the triangle of his face exposed.

I had taken his shroud down from the top shelf of my wardrobe that morning. Some time before, one of my father's friends was traveling to Mecca and offered to bring back a souvenir. My father asked for a shroud. I had banished this horrifying souvenir to the highest and least visible spot on my shelf, until I had to bring it down so much sooner than I'd ever expected. We had wrapped the shroud in newspaper, and the print shone yellow through the plastic bag as we carried it to Behesht-e Zahra.

My uncle Ali was arranging stones on top of my father's grave. As he placed the last stone on his face, I called out and he turned. His face was covered in tears. Behesht-e Zahra was filled with the sound of our friends and relatives wailing and moaning. My uncle stood up. I opened my fists. I put the dirt on my head and the white and yellow flowers on my father's face, keeping one to remember the day. They had to drag Kati and me off by force. He had to stay, and we had to leave.

When we returned home for the memorial, my friend Negin approached me. She gave me a newspaper and squeezed my hand. "Camelia, you've been accepted. Political science at Shahreza." I didn't want to look. It was too late. I stared at the newspaper with empty eyes and then crushed it up in my hands. Very early the next morning we dressed up and went back to the cemetery for the second day of the weeklong funeral ceremonies. The grave was covered with bouquets. I held the daisy in one hand and the crumpled-up newspaper in the other. I cried, "Baba, can you hear me? I've got good news for you!" My mother's tears, and mine and Kati's started flowing again. A friend of my father's, Agha-ye Mir Eskandari, murmured to us, "Let's go. Leave him in peace. He's tired after all these years. Leave him to sleep in peace." My father slept in his fresh grave, and the smell of earth and rose water blended with the muted sounds of lamentation coming from all across Behesht-e Zahra. He had to stay, and we had to leave.

◙   ◙   ◙

SPRING 1992

On one of the last days of spring, I walked into the editorial offices of *Zan-e Ruz*. A weekly magazine, *Zan-e Ruz* had a six-page section entitled "Thirteen to Eighteen Year Olds." It seemed a good place to start, and most importantly, one of my mentors at the club told me I could mention her name. Still in mourning for my father, I was dressed in black from head to toe. I stood before the editor in chief's secretary, clutching a heavy clippings folder full of my published poems and literary pieces.

"What is your business with Khanum Gheramizadeghan?"

Making excuses for myself, I said that I was a writer and that I needed only a few minutes of her time. My voice trembled with excitement as I spoke. The office was all glass windows, and I could see women in black chadors writing busily behind their desks or chatting with each other.

When the secretary granted me entry, I realized that Khanum Gheramizadeghan herself had been watching me from behind the glass. She had a dark complexion and thick prescription glasses so wide that at their highest point they overlapped with the black veil that covered most of her forehead. Like the others, she wore a chador over her veil.

"*Salaam.* You have five minutes to tell me your business."

Khanum Gheramizadeghan leaned back behind her desk, waiting for my answer.

"I am a poet. I am a poet and a writer, and I want to be a reporter. Please believe me, I will make a good reporter . . ." I nervously placed my folder in front of her.

She started to leaf through my work. "We are not hiring. We use freelancers who write regularly. However, work for one week on a trial basis, and we'll see how you do," she said and picked up the telephone. "Tell Khanum Parsa'i to come here for a minute."

Khanum Parsa'i was a white-faced, pregnant woman with tiny green eyes that seemed even smaller through her glasses. Khanum Gheramizadeghan told her, "This girl says that she has the genes of a reporter. Put her genes to the test." I didn't even have a chance to thank her. "OK, OK. Out. Get out, I have a lot of work to do. Parsa'i knows the rest."

I went with Parsa'i to the "Thirteen to Eighteen" department. Parsa'i wasn't wearing a chador, but her long veil covered all of her hair and shoulders.

"This is not high school. We won't have any crying or whining. We take our work seriously, and we need a serious and punctual reporter. Take this tape recorder and go to the Exhibition of Exceptional Children's Art at the Behzisti Center on Khiaban-e Vali-ye Asr and get me a story. On some days we'll have a driver who can take you, and on some days, like today, you'll have to go by taxi. Go and come back by noon. And mind your *hejab*, too. I don't want to get any calls from the security office. The days when *Zan-e Ruz* chose Ms. Iran are over. As of tomorrow wear more modest clothing. And no more perfume."

My first article was published in the next issue, and less than six months later, I had my own desk and my own title. I started writing weekly articles and special reports, and I'd participate in editorial meetings. But during the first few weeks, Parsa'i would rip my reports in half and then in half again before my eyes and then hand them back to me.

"This was crap. Go and write it again. Your reporting needs to contain useful, well-supported, eye-catching intelligence, not rumors and chitchat."

Zahra Omara'i, special reporter for the magazine, would call me over. "Come on, write a new report, and I'll check on you over your shoulder. And don't cry. No one was born a reporter. Everyone starts with their work getting thrown in the garbage." My writing improved, and I got all sorts of letters from teenage readers. They would write in with feedback or send poems or opinion pieces, which we'd then publish. I was allowed to call or write them with editorial notes if necessary. Others had questions and requested help with personal situations; we sorted these letters and sent them to specialists to offer counsel. When Parsa'i went on maternity leave, three of us, all teenage girls, were put in charge of "Thirteen to Eighteen." I learned everything from writing and editing to layout and proofreading. Every morning at six thirty, I'd wait outside my house for the car service to travel to Khiaban-e Tupkhaneh, happy as can be.

When I started working at *Zan-e Ruz*, there was little variety on the newsstands; only a few papers were on display—*Kayhan*, *Etela'at*, *Abrar*, *Resalat*, *Jumhuri-ye Islami*, and *Salaam*. The Chamber of Censorship Authority administered the press in an official, or at least semiofficial, manner. In any case, the atmosphere was extremely conservative. The Kayhan Corporation, the biggest publishing corporation in Iran, owned *Zan-e Ruz*. The corporation had been requisitioned by the State after the revolution and its chief administrator appointed by the Imam. Their flagship paper, *Kay-*

han, had the widest circulation in Iran before the revolution and emerged as the right-leaning State paper afterward. People bought *Kayhan* for its classified section and, especially, its unrivaled obituary pages. How often we had found out about the deaths of friends by reading this newspaper . . . Most importantly, *Kayhan* was cheap, and its pages were big and suitable for cleaning windows and wrapping herbs at vegetable stands.

Censoring the news was part of the Kayhan Corporation's policy, and the jurisdiction of the censor extended even to our little "Thirteen to Eighteen" department at *Zan-e Ruz*. I wrote an article titled "When Will the Date Palms of Khorramshahr Be Green?" after spending the Nouruz holidays in the south, visiting Mandana in Abadan and a friend of my mother's, Maria, in Ahvaz. My mother, Kati, Kai Khosrou, and I toured the war-torn border cities, gazing at the drowned ships from the bank of the Karon River, crying when we saw the flat landscape of Khorramshahr, famous for its palm trees, without a hint of green. Just as the paper was about to go to press, the piece was pulled. I was admonished for overstepping my bounds by writing a political article. As punishment, my writing was published without my name for the next two weeks.

During the second term of Hashemi Rafsanjani's presidency a newspaper called *Hamshahri* took the drab gray blur of the other newspapers and arrested it under a beam of light. It was the first full-color newspaper in Iran and was more open and intellectual, since it was run by the cultured, immensely popular mayor of Tehran, Gholamhussein Karabashi. From then on everyone in Tehran read *Hamshahri*. Even the advertising pages in *Kayhan* dulled in comparison to *Hamshahri*'s market-savvy design. When I heard that *Hamshahri* was launching the first daily newspaper for children in the Middle East, *Aftabgardan*, I applied immediately. It was with great satisfaction that I approached Khanum Gheramizadeghan at *Zan-e Ruz* and said softly, "As of tomorrow, I will be at *Aftabgardan*." And I set my new identification card down on her desk.

I'd go to *Aftabgardan* in its chic new uptown building in the morning and attend classes at Azad Islamic University's College of Political Science in the afternoon. My classes were full of students who'd been accepted to the university without taking entrance exams as part of the television station Seda va Sima's allotment. Some were known TV personalities, news announcers, or sports commentators. A woman named Faezeh Bahremani, a visiting student from our school's Karaj campus, caught my attention. She'd show up in a white Renault, then fold up her chador and drape it over the back of her chair before the class started. I liked her attitude—none of the other girls dared remove their chadors in class, even though it wasn't mandatory to wear one.

There wasn't enough space for the university to place men and women in separate classes, so the rooms were segregated down the middle, the ladies seated on the right and the gentlemen on the left. Even when the women's side was overflowing and the men's side had empty chairs, we would squeeze in uncomfortably to avoid any unnecessary interaction with the opposite sex. Even the stairways were segregated and patrolled by Disciplinary Committee spies. If for some reason you needed to talk to someone across the divide in class, you always spoke loudly and obviously so everyone witnessed your innocent request to borrow a book or swap notes. We could be dismissed from our studies at any moment if the Disciplinary Committee reported misbehavior. In this atmosphere, Faezeh's actions struck me as brave.

Faezeh often borrowed my notes when she couldn't come to class. However, I still didn't realize who she was until another girl in class told me. I promptly spread the rumor. "Did you know that she's the daughter of President Hashemi Rafsanjani?" I whispered to my friends from Seda va Sima. "That's the president's daughter." They looked at her in disbelief. That she would be in our school wasn't all that significant, but her behavior certainly was. Her father had been Khomeini's close associate, and here she threw off her chador. We expected the president's daughter to cover herself up to her eyes like the other revolutionaries. I was amazed when I'd see her drive to school wearing only a scarf, putting on her full chador in her parked car to walk up to the school. "Go tell her to show you her identity card," someone said to me.

"Excuse me, Faezeh?" She lifted her head from her notes.

"Yes?"

"Could I see your identity card for a second?" I asked in a bold voice. "They don't believe that you're Faezeh." I knew I was being rude, but I wanted to prove how relaxed I could be with the president's daughter. By using Bahremani as her last name, the part of her full family name her father didn't use publicly, she had a little protection from scrutiny. Now I was being nosy and exposing my friend to gain popularity points.

Without saying anything, she reached into her bag and handed me her card, where it was plainly written, "Faezeh Hashemi Bahremani."

After a few months I began to feel that *Aftabgardan* was also too small for me. Just downstairs from us were the offices of *Hamshahri*, and I dreamed about a move from the fifth floor to the fourth. My editor complained that my articles were too heavy for young readers, like the one I wrote about the basement of Rudaki's hall, and how the fancy decorations from the famous celebration of twenty-five hundred years of the monarchy were gathering dust, forgotten, the elaborate parade costumes buried many layers deep under the stage. She felt the piece was too complicated and had nothing to do with children. But I didn't want to write for children any more. I wanted to go to press conferences at important ministries and write on political and social issues. For me, reporting for teens was supposed to be a stepping-stone, one I could leap over. But at *Aftabgardan* I was still being asked to know my place and keep it. So I got up the courage and submitted a story to the editor of the society desk at *Hamshahri*, Fariborz Bayat. The piece was about a couple with fertility problems, and I discussed what different hospitals offered and what Islam says about pregnancy. He accepted me as a member of his staff—all it took was a change to my identification card, and I was finally a grown-up reporter working for the most prestigious paper in Iran. I could go to work in my emerald-colored *manto* and sit with mature intellectuals like Asef Nakhai and Yousef Bani Tourof and Iranzad and talk about democracy and reform. How lovely it was!

◎   ◎   ◎

"Maman, *yallah*! Honk the horn! *Yallah*—honk the horn!"

The giddy sound filled Khiaban-e Mir Damad. My mother played along with the reassuring reply, "Honk! Honnnk! Honk!" Kai Khosrou leaned out the front window and I out the back, and we screamed, "Khatami! Khatami!" We had plastered the whole car, even the back windshield, with pictures of the presidential candidate.

Tehran was turned upside down with excitement. Khatami was the favorite candidate, and the State-supported Nateq Nuri was despised. "Don't tear yourselves to pieces! It'll be fixed, and all of a sudden Nateq will be president," a passerby shouted at us. High school–aged boys zealously tossed flyers. "For the sake of democracy, for the sake of freedom, vote for Khatami!" We were surrounded by fashionably dressed teens—the generation that was supposed to carry on the revolution but didn't. They were us. They were me. We who listened to pop music at home and danced at parties. We who had been brought before the Komité on meaningless charges, had been kicked or detained in cowardly raids on their homes, had been flogged and made to pay fines without justification. Deep inside, we hated the government and the system, and today we were baring that truth and our hope for peaceful, civilized reforms. With our votes, we were demanding human rights and social justice.

"Iran for all Iranians!" Khatami had made this his rallying cry. I knew what this statement meant for me. I, who was considered a second-class citizen, who was scorned and despised in the Ayatollah's society. Oh, I had such hope in my heart! In this unprecedented campaign the people were joyfully unified for the first time since the revolution. The fear was that if Nateq Nuri won, thugs and extremists would wreck havoc and destruction on the people, and Iran's global standing would be in serious jeopardy. Khatami's spoke eloquently of the suffering and disillusionment that we, the millions of young people of Iran, had born. If victorious, he could be our angel of deliverance.

"Maman, there's a Khatami campaign booth. Hold on a second, and we'll get more posters. Otherwise, we'll run out by this evening." When we tucked the piles of posters under our arms and hurried back, my mother wasn't there! Had it not been a legal parking spot? We searched high and low. Had she gotten tired of waiting and left?

A boy who was passing out flyers asked me, "Are you looking for the blue Renault with a lady driving?" I nodded my head. He said, "The Komité picked her up and took her toward the station."

My jaw dropped. My mother wasn't wearing makeup, and she wasn't improperly covered. But all the armed forces and Basijis, or perhaps it would be better to say all the Hezbollahis, had been mobilized to prohibit propaganda. This hard-line reaction only helped people to view the election as a referendum where Khatami's victory would represent a big "no" to the Islamic Republic. Kai Khosrou and I were worriedly conferring when we saw the familiar blue car turn the corner. It had been cleaned of any trace of campaign posters. My mother sat behind the wheel steaming with rage. "Maman, where did you go?" "Just shut up! Both of you. You and your Agha-ye Khatami! Snake venom on your propaganda! The Komité pulled me over and said, 'What is this? Is this a car or a campaign booth on wheels?' And they said putting up photos is illegal." The Komité had threatened to hold my mother and send her down to the central station, but she pleaded with them, explaining that her election-crazed children had decorated her car. And with no kids around to grab by the ear, what were they going to do with this dignified middle-aged woman?

A couple of days later, my sister and mother pulled up at the intersection of Suhravardi and Motahari. It was after eleven, and I was standing holding a billboard of Khatami that was taller than I was. My gang of boys was tossing flyers into cars as they stopped at the intersection. I had gathered a team between the ages of ten and thirteen. With only forty-eight hours left until the elections, my family was having a party for my sister's wedding anniversary, and her house was ideally situated near Khatami's campaign headquarters. So I had taken advantage of this opportunity to bring Kai Khosrou and a bunch of my other relatives out into the streets. We had until midnight to campaign. No one in my family, including me, would vote two days later. To vote would be to support the system and the constitution of the Islamic Republic, and I agonized over whether to vote until it was too late. But my brother and I campaigned until we were breathless. And on election day twenty million Iranians— many of them first-time voters, many of them women—flocked to the polling booths, and Khatami won in a landslide.

I wore my *hejab* perfectly, but even so I'd posted two scouts at the next intersection to warn us the second they saw a Basiji patrol. When the boys hailed us, we'd collide into each other as we rushed to hide in the corner store where we'd stashed our posters and flyers. This running and hiding would recur every twenty minutes, but it was worth it. Drivers would be shocked to see a woman out this late with a giant picture of Khatami, and they'd flash their brights to be sure they were actually seeing a girl.

"Camelia, give up! Get in! Tell the boys we're going home." Kati was covered in makeup for her wedding anniversary and wore a blue overcoat over her evening gown. My mother had brought her in desperation to get me. It was about the fiftieth time she'd driven down, and every time I had told her, "Fifteen more minutes!" I looked at Kati. I had certainly ruffled her feathers. "We're taking the boys!"

But my boys wouldn't budge—they weren't going anywhere without me. I cried, "This is an historic moment. Go ahead. I'll come in an hour."

This time my mother really went off. "The city is out of control! They're going to come and arrest you for being a *mujahed*, and there'll be consequences. Just like Guli. You'll end up next to her in Behesht-e Zahra. And to hell with Khatami! How worried do I have to be?"

Guli's story plagued me throughout my childhood and would later haunt me when I sat in prison. I would remember the wedding dress her mother hung on the wall, the dress that Guli had brought back from England but never had the chance to wear. My father told us the guards had delivered a bag with her clothes to her mother along with a Qur'an and a stick of candy. "Your daughter's dowry," they explained. I remembered my father's aching, futile search to discover if Guli had been "wedded" to one of the guards before she went before the firing squad, his quest to find the morticians who washed the bodies, in case they'd agree to disclose this secret. In Islam, it is an abomination to execute a virgin.

chapter ten **A Clever Bird Caught in a Snare**

FALL 1999

When we saw each other, my focused energy threaded out magically from my fingertips, drawing him into bondage. He didn't see the fine, invisible spider web coiled around his hands and feet. But he saw my hands. After a month and a half, I could feel him turning. His interrogations were no longer motivated by whether or not I was a spy. They had become about his desire to hear my voice and see my hands.

When I heard the door of the cell block open, my heart would start to throb. The story that I had written for us started with my falling in love, falling so truly in love that it would be real to the man who was my interrogator. By the vitality of my love I'd become free. This was the story inside these cell walls, I knew, but my mind was stuck when it came to sketching out what would happen outside the prison. The first condition was that I had to be free.

They were very interested in what went on in Faezeh Hashemi's house. They'd heard rumors about her affairs with a certain man and wanted to know all the details—how many boyfriends she had, how serious they were. They wanted to know if she prayed or not, did she screw her husband, Agha-ye Lahuti, at night or not? Were they against the *velayat-e faqih* or opposed to Ayatollah Khamene'i? I refused to answer for days, but then, along with everything else, I started telling them whatever they wanted to hear, from secrets I thought I'd never confess to outrageous lies to match their outrageous questions. Exhausted from the interrogations, I became confused in my own mind about what was true and what wasn't. With my face to the wall, I told as many secrets as I could fabricate about Faezeh's lovers. I also confessed the smallest details of my personal life, and giving these "shameful" memories over to my interrogator filled me with a strange sense of religious purity. I felt that my confessions were drawing him closer to me. I told him how bad my parents were, how irreligious, how they didn't believe in the government. How I drank alcohol. Then, when he still wanted more, I started telling lies.

There were only two things I promised myself that I wouldn't let escape from my lips, and I held fast to my decision. "No, I didn't see Farah Pahlavi. It's not true. I saw Reza Pahlavi and I interviewed him, but I did not see Farah!"

"You black devil! You're lying!" he shouted. "Your mother admitted to us that you'd seen her. Tell me the truth!"

I told myself that they could put me through hell, bring me to the threshold of death, but no matter what, I had to resist talking about two things: Jean, an American FBI agent who was a good, loyal friend, and my meeting with the Queen. I could never convince my interrogator that these were simple, human relationships. If they knew about these meetings, the Ministry of Intelligence would hang me from a meat hook to get me to recite whatever they wanted to hear. To keep to my role, I kept telling myself that my mother and my family must have been imagining things. I went so far as to convince myself that I really had never met the Queen.

My mother and Kati later told me about their own interrogations. My mother said, "On the second day after you were taken away, the Revolutionary Court said that Katayun and I could come to see you. We were crying and feared for your safety. But you were not there. Instead they brought me into a room with two bearded men. I asked, 'Where is Camelia? Where did you take my daughter?'

"'Hajj Khanum, keep calm. If you don't keep calm, your daughter is going to hell. Good, now tell us, what did Camelia tell you about her meeting with Farah Diba? She herself told us that you were overjoyed!'

"The wiry runt with his crooked mouth laughed and stood over me waiting for an answer. I said, 'Why are you interrogating me? It's enough that you took her away and that we don't know what you've inflicted upon her. Now you come after us and lie to us and tell us that you've arranged for us to see her—in order to put us over the rack? My daughter is innocent. She hasn't seen Farah. Take your questions and go ask Faezeh Hashemi, Faezeh, who says she's responsible for Camelia's reporting.'"

Kati told me that she heard my mother's shouting and tried to break in, but the intelligence officers blocked the door to the room and threatened her with arrest. When my mother fainted, the men carried her out and brought a glass of sugar water from the judge's office to revive her. Then they forced Kati with her two-and-a-half-year-old baby, Yasbanu, into the interrogation room. After seeing my mother fighting and arguing as she was dragged out, little Yasbanu started crying uncontrollably.

"Camelia confessed yesterday that she went to see Farah Pahlavi," they told her. And in anger Kati answered, "She never said any such thing, nor have I heard any such thing. You must have beaten my poor sister for her to be confessing to lies."

My mother told me, "That week Khamene'i led the Friday prayers, and he launched right into talking about spying and Radio Free Europe and treasonous Iranians. We went to Faezeh's house. We told her to do something to help you, or they would kill you. And even Faezeh said that this speech was hinting at the news of your arrest."

I'd heard about the Friday sermons from my interrogator. He told me, "We have reported to his eminence Ayatollah Khamene'i the big news about the spy we snagged, and he referred to this very thing yesterday at Friday prayers. Oh, you'll be in trouble if you're not cleansed in time. Everyone is disgusted with you. They want you to die. The charges against you were published in today's *Kayhan*. You don't have any friends left."

He wanted to crush my faith that I'd be released, but a sprig of hope was living inside of me. My father was very attached to one of Hafez's sayings and would repeat it often. It was a line of poetry that he'd use to give you courage whenever things looked hopeless: "*Morgh-e zirak chun be dam oftad, tahammol bayadash*" (When a clever bird is caught in a snare, it has to be strong and wait).

If I want to do something, I find a way to do it. I wanted to get of prison, and I gave myself courage, knowing that I was going to get out.

They tried to bring me to my breaking point, to the point where nothing mattered. I was moved from the damp room to a dry cell, but the same powerful light was on twenty-four hours a day. The same coarse carpet covered the floor. I had a plastic cup for drinking water and a copper plate and bowl for food. The bath schedule was once a week on Sundays, and once a week we had cleaning duty. One week we'd clean the baths and the toilets and the following week we'd sweep and mop the corridor and the space in front of the cells. On one of the Fridays when it was my turn for cleaning duty, I was listening to the sound of the guards' radio as I swept the corridor. The guest on the show was someone I knew, Afshin Aala, an author and poet who wrote for children and young adults. He started reciting a poem.

I was choking on my tears, thinking about my friends who were free to walk around in the streets and the bazaar. Who was thinking of me? Were they waiting for me?

After I was released, I happened to see Afshin in Faezeh's office, and I said to him, "Afshin, the guards' radio was playing while you were reading poetry, and I listened to your voice and cried and cried out of loneliness. If only everyone whose voices are heard in far-away places could know that someone homesick, imprisoned, and heartbroken is listening and they might offer a message of warmth."

Afshin replied, "Camelia, if I had known that day that you were listening to me, I would have told you this: at the end of the night the darkness becomes light again."

In the prison ward, I felt the whole world had forgotten about me and that all my friends had turned their backs on me. The only person left who listened to me, who seemed to care about me—though he showed me nothing but abuse—was my interrogator. I told him anything he wanted to hear. I embellished my stories with fabulous details. I even told him my best story of defiance and rebellion.

I told him how the summer before Khatami was elected, my high school friend Ghazal and I were shopping in the bazaar on Meidan Tajrish when a woman in a chador grabbed my shoulders from behind. "You're coming with us!" I wasn't wearing makeup and my hair wasn't showing and my overcoat came down to my ankles. But the woman pointed to my summer shoes and said that I wasn't wearing socks.

I told her with a sneer that she must be joking. People milling about Meidan Tajrish had gradually formed a circle around us. The woman yanked my coat and dress up above my knees to prove that I wasn't wearing stockings—she said that if a strong wind came, my underwear would show. All those onlookers saw my body exposed above my knees. It was impossible that a summer wind could blow as hard as she'd whipped up my clothing. Ghazal jumped in and said, "Pardon me, she didn't realize, she just forgot. I'll go into the bazaar right now to buy socks and will come right back."

The sisters of the Guidance stood me next to the goldsmith's shop, and one guarded me while two more were busy checking other girls and women. A heavy-set girl and her mother were walking toward us; the teen was wearing bright lipstick, and her dyed hair was hanging out of her veil. She was just too perfect for the Guidance. Two sisters marched right up and grabbed them, trying to force them into their minibuses. It ended up in a scuffle, and I looked at the woman next to me, her attention absorbed in watching her colleagues struggle. My blood was boiling in my veins. I knotted my right fist and punched her in the face as hard as I could. She lost her balance, and her face smacked into the window of the goldsmith's shop. Did I understand the gravity of what I had done? It didn't matter. The anger in that punch had been building up for twenty years.

The bitch spun toward me as I tried to act naturally, as if I hadn't hit her. But her friend who was wrestling with the mother and daughter came charging at me like a tiger. They started beating me, and the mother and the young woman came over to help me. People around us started joining in, trying to separate us, and then unbelievably, men started coming out of the alleys and the bazaar, and began to rip the sisters' black veils and chadors apart. The proprietor of the goldsmith's shop whispered in my ear, "Quick, go into the bazaar and run away through the little square in the middle. If they arrest you, you're done for." At the last minute, I stood facing the woman who'd lifted my dress. I raised my hand and brought it down on her face with all my might. "Whatever you said to me, you were talking about yourself!" And then I lost myself among the crowds in the twists and turns of the bazaar. I found Ghazal near the Khiaban-e Vali-ye Asr exit. There was a pair of cheap nylon stocking in her hand. We walked quickly south, and I opened the door of the first taxi we saw. Frightened, Ghazal asked, "What did you do? The Pasdaran have surrounded the whole bazaar."

My interrogator reveled in this story. He told me, "*Masha-Allah!*" The Ministry of Intelligence considered it its duty to help me "unburden" myself. I unburdened myself of many true secrets, and I came to believe my own lies and mythical creations. And with great dramatic elegance, I measured my voice, showing my interrogator my sensitivity, my passion, and my remorse at not having brought my moral corruption, Godlessness, and spiteful contrariness under control sooner.

I prayed at the correct times five times a day, knowing the guards were watching me. What I recited under my breath with the chador over my head was this: "Oh Lord, give me strength and endurance to bear these days. Oh Lord, don't let me be beaten and broken by these mean, chicken-hearted people."

One day, while I was performing ablutions, one of the guards, Zohreh, stopped next to me and said, "Oh my goodness, have you always done it like this? That's not how hands should be washed."

"In the treatise of Agha-ye Khui, it says only 'hands.' There's nothing about how you wash them."

She went and got a different treatise, Agha-ye Khomeini's, and as we discussed again the proper manner of performing ablutions, I slyly asked her to entrust me with the book for a few hours. I thought about the guards watching through the hidden holes drilled in the door as I prayed. I memorized the preferred manner of praying and the correct number of prostrations at each stage. I could not afford to make another mistake.

When was the sun in the sky? Summer ended, and I was still in my solitary cell. I was given religious books from the prison library to read. One of the books was about the candle stuffing of Baha'is by Amir Kabir. The book told how he persecuted them and would stuff all the orifices of their bodies with lit candles and parade them around the city in a ghastly spectacle. My stomach churned, and I shut the book in disgust. It was horrifying.

My interrogator told me that once upon a time under the rule of the Shah, Hashemi Rafsanjani and Ayatollah Montazeri had been prisoners and were tortured in the same detention center we sat in now. I thought of how, in the first week of my imprisonment, there had been many other women in the ward, and we would be brought out to bathe all together. The guards took us out of our cells without a word and lined us up blindfolded. Each of us had a bundle under our arm holding our prison uniform, underwear, shampoo, and soap. We were told to stay silent and take hold of the back of each other's chadors. There were perhaps fifteen of us, and we moved forward like a train. Down and down we went. Then they sent us to wash in a line of shower stalls separated by green vinyl curtains. We had our own showerheads but the combined dirty water would run across the slimy marble and over all our feet. It was fascinating to think that Montazeri and Hashemi had also washed in that underground shower, and even more fascinating to consider that after the revolution the new Islamic government allowed the same hidden detention center to be used. What about in the future? Would I come back as a free citizen one day to look at my cell and to read the poems written on the walls?

My romance with my interrogator was half serious in my mind and half designed just to pass the time. I knew, but he didn't know, that he wanted to be at my side. I knew, and love floated like a fresh spring breeze into Towhid Prison. To send my love letters and to nourish this relationship, I had only my hands, and it was with these hands that I spoke to him.

One Friday, Zohreh opened the door of my cell to tell me that my interrogator had come for me. She looked at me carefully and asked, "Why is he coming to interrogate you on a Friday? Don't tell me you've made this believer fall in love with you."

With my face to the wall, I crossed my legs and sat up very straight in the chair and arranged my chador.

"Don't think that I don't have a wife and children or that I couldn't stand to be away from your highness's baboon physique. I realized you would be lonely, all alone on a Friday, so I came to see you. Hold out your hand."

I was afraid. Was he going to give me lashes on my palm?

"Don't be afraid. Hold out your hand."

He put something in my hand.

"Raise your blindfold just a little. Only a tiny bit. It's a date. I've brought you a date! Tell me, what do you do in your room when you don't have anything to do? The sisters tell me you sit still for hours like a statue or an Indian yogi."

"I meditate."

"Yes. You're very bright. That's why you haven't been crying and screaming. *Masha-Allah*. You're clever."

After two months, this was my first sweet, the first outside food I'd had in prison. The food servings were always small, but I'd never asked for more. I hadn't seen the sun or the color of the sky for two months, but I hadn't complained about that either. I had never banged on the door begging to use the bathroom like the others, while the guards laughed at them. I had never complained about the condition of my room. My beloved long hair was falling out, like leaves in autumn, and I had made a big ball of it in the corner of my room. I had to stand firm to play my role.

I had always been told that I had beautiful hands. And years of dance lessons had made me graceful. Before I was swamped with work at *Zan*, I used to receive private pupils. "We lift ourselves slowly on our tiptoes. We move our hands apart, then lift and lower them softly and lightly with the music. Smile and let your hands dance. The audience looks at the dancers' hands and faces. Float on the air with your hands." My little pupils would wave their hands up and down as they watched mine.

I knew now that the man in the corner at Towhid Prison was watching my hands, and all of my artistry flowed into them.

chapter eleven **Zan**

SUMMER 1998

In Tehran, a brand new newspaper, *Zan*, was about to be launched. A friend arranged a meeting for me with the newspaper's distinguished owner and editor, Faezeh Hashemi. Yet again I found myself waiting to talk to a new editor in chief, with my clippings in hand, this time at the guard post in front of *Zan*'s building on Kucheh-ye Simin off of Khiaban-e Vali-ye Asr. On the second floor, I knocked on the door to Faezeh's office. Her hoarse voice sounded from inside, "*Befarma'id.*"

We sat facing one another at her conference table. She studied my face. "Haven't I seen you somewhere before?"

I smiled. "We were classmates at the university." Once I mentioned it, she remembered me well, and I asked about another girl from our class, her close friend Maryam. She told me Maryam was now working for her at the Women's Solidarity Association, which Faezeh headed. Faezeh divided her time between *Zan* and the Majlis. She had been elected a member of the fifth Majlis with more than a million votes in Tehran. Many of the women I'd gone to college with were now gaining prominent positions in various fields. The job at *Zan* was competitive, and Faezeh quizzed me in the interview with detailed questions about my work and background.

The mood of the country was fresh and progressive during the promising early period of Khatami's reform government. Working under Faezeh's bold, intrepid direction was perfect for me. The first issue of *Zan* included my exclusive report from Bosnia and the war in Kosovo. I was given the title "special correspondent," a largely unknown term in the Iranian press, and my picture appeared in the paper above my article.

I was emboldened and sought to be the first journalist on the scene at major political events. In June 1998 I was watching the news in Sarajevo when suddenly a headline flashed on the screen. Mazar-e Sharif had fallen to the Taliban, and the Iranian embassy had been taken in a surprise attack. The embassy staff and a journalist from an Iranian news agency were being held hostage in an undisclosed location. All it took was a call to Faezeh, and I was en route to Afghanistan.

Two days later I left for Karachi, Pakistan, and from there on to Peshawar. But I still needed a visa. For several days, I found myself at loose ends, sitting on the curb in front of the Taliban consulate in Peshawar. The Taliban were now Iran's premier enemy, and after the seizure of fourteen Iranian citizens, the possibility of a direct attack on Afghanistan by Iran loomed ominously. At Friday prayers in Tehran, there were murmurings about the threat posed by the Taliban, and the military held maneuvers along the border. As I waited, a journalist from a Taliban news agency helped me file my daily reports with *Zan*. Finally, a man emerged from the consulate and said, "Mulawi Ahmad will see you now." Two Pashtun men with long beards and big black turbans waited inside, the shadows of their eyes to the ground except for once or twice when they gave me a sideways glance.

"You don't have a *mahram*," they announced. A male relative was required as a chaperone. "It is not possible for you to travel alone in the Islamic country of Afghanistan. Become *mahram* with one of the brothers, and we'll even give you a car and a driver, and you can go all over, wherever you want." This was their awkward marriage proposal. I smiled at them and said, as I walked out the door, "I swear by the Qur'an that I'll get over that border. I'm going to Afghanistan."

I was determined to uncover the truth about the seized Iranian journalist and diplomats. Two days later, an Iranian friend in Peshawar found me a pair of reliable Afghans to accompany me over the dirt road into Afghanistan. My escorts were closely connected to the Iranian consul general in Peshawar, and they themselves were going over to collect the latest intelligence for the Iranian embassy. But instead of waiting for them in Peshawar for any news, I decided to go with them to make my reports firsthand. I bought a burqa and cheap used shoes and clothes at the bazaar, and we headed off to Jalalabad. I posed as the wife of one of my traveling companions, and we crossed the border in an elaborately painted Pakistani bus, full of Afghans on their way home. They all had long beards, and some wore large turbans.

We spent half a day in Jalalabad, and in the evening we went directly back to Peshawar. My presence increased the risk for the two Afghans that their mission could be exposed, so we had to return to Pakistan quickly. Agents in Jalalabad had entrusted my guides with video footage of the murder of the hostages in Mazar-e Sharif. In Peshawar I found the first available opportunity to call Faezeh and relay the news.

"Are you sure?" Faezeh asked me. "This is going on the front page!"

I was sure. My report went off like a bomb in the unsettled atmosphere of Iran. A large group of the captives' relatives gathered on the street outside of the newspaper, desperate for more information. That evening the Iranian Ministry of Foreign Affairs issued a statement denying *Zan*'s report, proclaiming that they were in contact with the Taliban and guaranteeing the safety of the captives.

In Peshawar, I arrived safe and sound at my friend's house, covered in mud and dust and drenched in sweat. The following day I talked to Faezeh.

"Camelia, you're in for it if you screwed up. I'll have your hide. The phones have been swamped all day with calls from the Ministry of Intelligence and the Ministry of Foreign Affairs. They want you to get back here fast."

"I know what I'm saying. I saw the footage of their bodies."

In Islamabad, the Iranian undersecretary of foreign affairs, Agha-ye Amini, who had come to Pakistan to try to work things out between Tehran and Islamabad in the face of this crisis, exploded the second he saw me. "You! What made you think you could mess around with our national security? Don't you understand what will happen if you are captured or killed in Afghanistan? People are upset enough at the seizure of the diplomats. The murder of an Iranian girl—for them it would be a declaration of war. I'm really surprised at Khanum Hashemi. Did you want to cause a war?" A Pakistani journalist brought me the same message from the other side, from the conservative side of their government who supported the Taliban: if I wanted to save my skin, I'd better leave Pakistan immediately.

In Tehran, I walked into the newspaper's offices like a hero in a blue burqa. Several weeks after my article was published, the Foreign Ministry officially announced the murders. The people of Iran were better prepared, psychologically and emotionally, to bear the horror of the news because of my reports in *Zan*.

The women who worked at *Zan* enjoyed total freedom in choosing what they wore. Faezeh believed the *hejab* was a matter of personal choice. As a member of the Majlis, she spoke out about such issues as women being allowed to ride bicycles in public. I was proud to be working for her, and I'd leave for the office in the morning humming to myself. One after another, new newspapers followed our lead and added to the ensemble of reformist voices. The tension between the free press and the Ministry of Intelligence grew and grew. I wanted to face the problem head on, to write about the tension that was building instead of keeping quiet about it. I wanted to write about all the pressing issues that had been forbidden to me since my first day as a journalist. And Faezeh never said no.

"Faezeh, you should be president. Twenty million people would vote for you. And I'll run your campaign."

"You're crazy," she'd laugh. "I'd better ask Hamid to check your head." Hamid Lahuti, Faezeh's husband, was a psychiatrist who was as different from his brazen, boisterous wife as night from day. They had two children: Muna, who was the spitting image of her mother, and Hassan, who was the spitting image of his father. Our personal friendship grew closer and deeper. On Fridays, Faezeh and I would go to Karaj or up north with her kids. I'd stay over at their house some nights, and some days Faezeh would stop by our house to eat lunch and chat with my mother. This friendship was kept strictly personal and totally distinct from our professional relationship at *Zan*. When people would ask me about the salacious rumors that dogged Faezeh, I'd simply knit my eyebrows and reply, "I'm not interested in hearing that gossip." I'd had to answer their stupid questions a million times. "I swear to God. I swear on the Qur'an that Faezeh lives with her husband. Yes, he's the only husband she has, and no, she hasn't been divorced two or three times." But they would squint at me and say, "OK, you're right to stick up for her. She's your friend, and she takes care of you." Faezeh and Hamid married when she was eighteen, and she'd never had another husband, but for some reason this particular rumor of divorce was relentless, even passing through the thick walls of Towhid Prison, where it was one of the first things my guards asked me about. Because she was a successful woman and because she was Hashemi Rafsanjani's daughter, people wanted to trash her. There was a certain man she was close to in our office, and in typical Iranian fashion, the rumors had followed their friendship. She didn't care to defend herself against these accusations. She stood above this kind of talk, and I followed her lead.

When the invitation arrived from the *Boston Globe* for Faezeh to travel to America, she selected me to go in her place. It was the first exchange program for journalists between Iran and America since the Islamic Revolution. Khatami's victory with twenty million votes and the subsequent lessening of the restrictions on freedom of the press had taken the world by surprise. In 1998, journalism in Iran was itself a hot news topic in the global media. Just about every week, the BBC's Persian service or Voice of America or Radio France interviewed me. A German television station filmed a segment on me, and I was interviewed by the Japanese newspaper *Asahi*. "How lucky I am," I said to my mother. "Today I have everything I've always wanted."

Five of us were chosen to participate in the American exchange: the editor in chief of *Hamshahri*, Mohammed Atrianfar; the editor in chief of the monthly magazine *Zanan*, Shahla Sherkat; the editor of the foreign edition of *Iran News*, Mojghan Jalali; a member of the editorial board of the newspaper *Salaam*, Karim Arghandeh Pour; and myself. I had worked for Agha-ye Atrianfar at *Hamshahri* and hated him. He had been an oppressive figure, always carrying a *tasbih* in his hand. He'd given me such a hard time that I had resigned from the paper in part just to get away from him. But in America, where I could finally give him a piece of my mind, he said, "Forgive me—those days have passed, and today has come, and you are successful."

We became friends on the trip, and I began to confide in him. Our program in New York consisted of speaking at Columbia University's School of International Affairs and at the Asia Society. At Columbia when a few Iranian girls, students at the journalism school, volunteered to give us a tour around the campus, I looked sadly at the buildings and said to Atrianfar, "You know, what I want more than anything is to continue my education here. Do you think that's too much to ask? But with all that's going on in Tehran, how could I leave now?"

We had serious journalistic work to do to reclaim our civil liberties and turn forward the wheels of reform. I couldn't leave Iran just as our freedoms were expanding. But I still dreamed and made hopeful plans, never realizing then that I would become an exile before I could return and become a student.

After we gave our presentation at the Asia Society, our American hosts were showing us around, when one of our escorts, Cynthia Dikstine, excitedly told us that we had been invited to George Soros's house for tea that evening. None of us were overwhelmed with joy. She got impatient and said that he was the most important man in America and had paid for our trip. We still had no idea who he was. I racked my brain and only vaguely recalled an article I had read someplace. As we hailed two taxis to Soros's house on Fifth Avenue, I whispered into Atrianfar's ear, "Now I know who he is! He's Jewish and the wealthiest man in America, and he has an empire in central Asia." He absently nodded his head, but my wild description didn't seem to impress him.

In Soros's magnificent home, a servant brought us tea in fantastic china teacups. I sat with the other women and looked at Khanum Shahla Sherkat and smiled. Mojghan looked at us, too, and giggled. And then for some reason that to this day is unclear to me, the three of us started laughing in a most ridiculous and idiotic fashion. The whole time we sat in Soros's apartment, we couldn't stop laughing. I went to the washroom and took a deep breath and went back to my seat. It was useless. We were laughing so hard we couldn't even bring the teacups to our lips, and all three of us were pouring tears. Giving us a disapproving look, Atrianfar asked us in Persian to mind our manners. Even Soros interrupted himself midspeech to say, "The ladies must have spotted something quite interesting . . . It would be nice if you'd let us in on it so that we might benefit from the joke, too." We were still overcome with laughter, making it impossible for us to answer. As we were saying good-bye and Soros was signing a copy of his book for each of us, we apologized in nervous flurries.

A few days later, Agha-ye Atrianfar had amassed enough information about George Soros to panic. In the distinctive Esfahani accent that he was always trying to conceal, he warned us, "Soros is one of the most prominent Zionists in the world, and there may have been some kind of conspiracy behind this meeting." He worried that by going to his house without knowing who he was, all of us would be in danger when Tehran got wind of the visit. He implored us to get rid of Soros's book so we wouldn't be caught when our luggage was searched in Mehrabad airport. Mojghan and Shahla Sherkat bit their lips nervously at Atrianfar's predictions, but I only cursed my silliness and stupid laughter, and wondered why I couldn't have shown better character. Who knew that only two years later I would end up as a freelance correspondent for Soros's news Web site, EurasiaNet.

Before I flew back to Iran, I stopped over in London. My first piece of unfinished business was to set up an interview with Salman Rushdie. I lay stretched out on my friend Susan's bed in London, wondering how I could possibly track him down. In what I thought was a flash of brilliance, it came to me that I should contact the press office of the Iranian embassy. When I called, they wouldn't give me any information over the phone and told me I needed to come in person, so I tied on a head scarf and calmly went to the embassy. But the official in charge of the cultural center challenged me immediately, wanting to know what business I had with Rushdie. The foreign ministers of Iran and England had shaken hands at the United Nations and the *fatwa* against him had been lifted, I explained, so it was quite natural that I, as an Iranian journalist, would be interested in interviewing a man who had lived in the shadows for years, fearing for his life. I assured him that Khanum Hashemi had given me permission.

At two in the morning the phone rang, waking me to Faezeh's sharp voice on the other end. "Camelia, whatever steps you've taken to meet with Salman Rushdie up to now, keep them to yourself. As of tomorrow, you will deny them. I just got a call from the highest level of the Ministry of Intelligence about this. Wherever you are, whatever you're doing, put a stop to it. Got it?"

Despite these midnight calls, relative to what I'd grown up with, the Iranian press was in full bloom, burgeoning with unprecedented freedom and gusto. It was a time when it seemed we could expose all the old taboos, when it appeared that the red tape had been rolled up and stored away. I felt like I was exposing what had always been captured in my mind, like I could step into the darkroom of the revolution and put whatever forbidden subjects caught my gaze under the light of an enlarger. Whatever I proposed to Faezeh, she had always supported me. I had built up so much courage that I had even contacted the head of Farah Pahlavi's office in New York to ask for a future interview with the Queen. And from London, I reminded Faezeh that we'd planned for me to take a train to Paris to try and meet Abulhassan Bani Sadr, the first president of the Islamic Republic of Iran, who'd fled Tehran for Paris in 1981.

◉　◉　◉

It was snowing in Paris as my French friend Sonia and I stood at the door of a large house, waiting for the police to finish going over our identity papers. We were ushered into a cold waiting room where the fireplaces had been lit only minutes before. A young boy apologized and said that "the President of the Republic" didn't have enough fuel to heat the whole building and that he rarely used this room. He brought us tea and *gaz* from Esfahan on silver trays.

When Bani Sadr entered the room he evoked in me an immediate sense of nostalgia for the time of the revolution, the days when my father would read to us about him from the newspaper and my uncle would brag about his coming to his practice to get his teeth fixed. Now, there was no longer an invisible red line that bound my expression, and it was strangely intoxicating. This was true freedom—to be able to use the power of the press to bring the message of our hope after Khatami's election to the world.

Bani Sadr recognized my last name and asked after my uncle, expressing homesickness for my uncle's excellent medical treatment. He also knew my father, and so I told him that he had passed away just a few years earlier. We continued in polite conversation, and he asked about *Zan*. I explained that I had come to interview him for an article, and to the complete surprise of his staff, with whom I'd prearranged the interview, he placed two bags full of books at my feet and said, "These are books and articles that I've published. Please read them all the way through first and become acquainted with my thinking and writing and then come back for the interview another time." We bid our farewells, and I lugged the two heavy bags back to Sonia's in a taxi. When I was leaving Paris for London, Sonia cried, "You forgot your books!" I laughed. "Like I'm that crazy that I'd bring two hundred pounds of books with me. Give them to the library!" I also asked her to keep George Soros's book and the applications I'd picked up to Columbia's and Harvard's school of journalism, so they wouldn't be found when I entered Tehran.

Listening to Persian-language radio weeks later, I was completely astonished when Bani Sadr said in an interview that former president Hashemi Rafsanjani had sent a woman in the guise of a journalist to Paris carrying a special message for him. God knows what he meant—that I was there to invite him to join the government?

At Mehrabad airport, when I presented my passport, the policeman wouldn't return it. He brought a man in civilian clothing to take me into a room marked, mysteriously, The Presidential Section. The man wrote a telephone number on a scrap of paper and told me I'd need to call the Presidential Passport Office the next morning. I think they couldn't call it "The Ministry of Intelligence Secret Passport Office" or everyone would panic at the airport. I was outraged and afraid. "But *why* have you taken my passport?"

"You'll be informed."

That night I went with my mother to Faezeh's house, and she promised that tomorrow she would look into it herself. I went to work as usual the next day, and at noon Faezeh called me into her office. "It was the Ministry of Intelligence that took your passport. I spoke with Agha-ye Moghadam, a friend of mine who is their representative at the Majlis and told him that any questions they have about your reporting, they can ask me. I told them I'm directly responsible for your work. But he said they'll only deliver the passport to you in person. A man will wait for you in front of the Presidential building, the stone building on Khiaban-e Jordan. Watch out—once they have you in their grasp, nothing will save you."

At noon in front of the stone building, I met the man, and he looked like an ordinary person. That this guy was an intelligence agent would never have crossed my mind. He had a mustache and was wearing a casual short-sleeve shirt. He put on a cool act, slyly asking me, "Are you really so afraid of what's inside?"

"I'm smart enough to know I don't want to see it," I responded.

"I want to tell you, you should appreciate Khanum Hashemi.

You're lucky she's looking out for you," he said. I took my passport and left.

◙ ◙ ◙

FALL 1998

Suddenly, writers for reformist papers and intellectuals opposed to the government were enveloped by fear like never before. It seemed that every day the earth-shattering news of the killing or seizure of a writer would reach us or the tragic fate of a colleague who had disappeared years before would be revealed. From Sa'idi Sirjani, a writer who they claimed had died of heart failure in prison, to Piruz Davani, who suddenly called his mother and said he was going to Mashhad, then disappeared like a drop of water in the ocean. His body never turned up. Dariush and Parvaneh Foruhar were stabbed to death in their home. Dariush had been in line to be minister of labor in the cabinet of Doctor Bazargan's provisional government directly following the revolution. Khomeini had charged Bazargan with nominating the first Islamic government in Iran, but Bazargan resigned after the American embassy hostage situation. In the years that followed Dariush Foruhar had earned a reputation as a critic of the Islamic Republic and became the leader of the Mellat Iran party. The heartbreaking killing of the Foruhars heralded the dangers in store for political and social activists. Mohammed Mukhtari was seized, and it surfaced in the media that his body had been dumped in the desert of Karaj. His throat had been cut, and gradually we heard murmurs that a segment of the government had had a hand in his death. Many more writers had received death threats over the phone. We asked ourselves who was responsible for this string of killings.

Khanum Simin Behbahani, a renowned poet, and I sat together at the shrine of Taher at Karaj. The two of us had come, along with the rest of the writers and journalists of Tehran and thousands of others, to escort the body of the greatly respected writer Mohammed Ja'far Puyandeh to the *imamzadeh*.

As they interred his remains, I shielded my body and pushed my way forward through the folds of the crowded mass, which was encircled by plainclothes agents from the Ministry of Intelligence. I wanted to see his face when they uncovered it once he was in the grave. His white shroud had turned red with fresh blood leaking from his slit throat. We had all heard that he and Mukhtari had been killed in the same fashion. They had both been snatched off the crowded streets of Tehran and silenced with a metal wire.

I couldn't bear to see anymore, and I went back and sat next to Khanum Behbahani at the edge of an open grave in the newly expanded section of the cemetery. We were talking about our shock and apprehension at the complicity of the Ministry of Intelligence in this wave of killings when she unexpectedly fell backward into the grave. I controlled my impulse to laugh as a young man helped me pull her out. She was shaken and dazed, but luckily, she hadn't been hurt. Her clothes were covered with dirt. "This fall is a sign that I will be next," she kept saying. "I, too, am in danger, and today I've been given a sign."

In the midst of all these killings, I continued to take risks. I knew that by insisting on freedom of the press, I was also helping to ensure freedom for ordinary Iranians. One especially dangerous interview involved several visits to the home of the former secretary-general of the Tudeh party, Nureddin Kiyanuri, and his wife, Maryam Feiruz, on Khiaban-e Karimkhan Zand. Kiyanuri and his wife had been freed after years of imprisonment in Evin, but Kiyanuri was still under house arrest. This elderly couple cheerfully welcomed me into their home, and I would sit for hours talking with them, recording all their stories and memories. Kiyanuri was about eighty-five, and though he used a walker around the apartment and couldn't always hear me clearly, his memory and intelligence were still sharp. He listened to all the foreign radio broadcasts and read the paper daily, keenly analyzing recent social and political news. "Aren't you afraid these killers will come after you?" I asked him.

His answer was clearheaded. "We're being monitored from the building across the street, so if any stranger comes to our door, the Ministry of Intelligence would be watching. And that would mean *they* wanted us killed, and who could escape their wishes?" He felt the government condoned, or likely participated in, the recent spate of deaths of writers and intellectuals. As he told me about the guards holed up across the street, I felt again how much danger I was in, as their home was very likely bugged with secret microphones. But I hoped only to fashion a worthy-enough investigative piece from the interviews. I would go at night and bring my photographer friend, Vahid, and when we left under the cover of darkness we hid my tapes and his film in our clothes. If I saw anyone coming or if a car turned its lights on, I'd shout, "Vahid, run!" We were ready to literally run for our lives.

The editorial departments of all the independent and reformist newspapers came together in a single harmonious, cohesive movement bent on exposing the perpetrators of these crimes. At *Zan*, I began my column with headlines such as "Who Knows Whose Turn It Will Be Tomorrow?" There I wrote about my own investigations into the series of murders. When finally, under pressure from Agha-ye Khatami's commission of inquiry, the Ministry of Intelligence confessed that there were soiled hands within their ranks, the press never rested. We now set our sights on the resignation of the minister of intelligence.

A source leaked to *Zan* a list of people marked for punishment and death, names that had been gathered from the interrogation of prisoners. The list had been faxed to the paper addressed to me. Our newspaper broke the story, announcing, "Ministry of Intelligence Has Compiled a 'Black List' of 179 Intellectuals, Writers, and Political Activists to Be Punished and Killed." Some of the people listed had already disappeared, and some had been killed. Among the well-known figures listed, such as Nushabeh Amiri, Ebrahim Nabavi, and Mehrangiz Kar, was my own name, number 164. I shuddered.

The story shook Iran. It was a courageous, incendiary story. The constantly ringing telephone drove me crazy. Thousands of people called to be reassured that their names were not on the list. Still others insisted that their names must have been mistakenly omitted. One well-respected man came to the office, and swearing that he had been targeted time and time again, kept begging, "Please put my name on this list and, *in sha' Allah*, I shall repay your kindness."

"Sir, please leave," I said angrily. "We are reporters doing our job—this is not a private printing outlet." And then there were the terrifying calls from the Ministry of Intelligence asking me how I'd gotten the list.

I remember one evening in particular when I left for home, exhausted from the excitement. Before getting into the car service provided by the newspaper, I had called my mother. "Maman, I'll be home in fifteen minutes." As we drove up, I could see her waiting for me in the kitchen, outlined in the lit second-floor window. All I had to do was walk from the car to my front door, and I'd asked the driver to wait to make sure I got into the house. But my hands still trembled as I took my keys out of my purse. The sharp, menacing shadows of the trees seemed to leap out at me, and I kept turning to look for the cold flash of a dagger, a vision that kept rising from the darkness. Try as I might, I was shaking so hard that I couldn't find the keyhole. Helpless and numb, I finally got inside and collapsed in a chair while my mother fretted over me, repeating her conviction that the Ministry of Intelligence would show up any day.

On the flimsiest pretenses, the "second of Khordad" newspapers (referring to the date of Khatami's election), were being shut down one by one and their contributors dragged to court. *Zan* had been banned from publishing for two weeks based on charges made by the head of police security, Mohammad Naghdi, in response to an article that accused him of having been involved in an attack on two prominent governmental figures. Several of my more provocative articles were put on hold indefinitely after the ban was lifted. It seemed that every day we were about to run a piece I'd written on the re-virginization of girls in Tehran, we'd hear the newest reports of Hezbollah sympathizers demonstrating and attacking newspaper offices. Faezeh would loom over my editor, Agha-ye Balafkan, and say, "Tomorrow they're coming down on *Zan*, so pull this piece from the issue. Schedule it for next week."

One of the most inflammatory pieces I was working on at *Zan* would never be published in its pages. Everyone knew about my series of trips to the holy city of Qom. Before I finished the article, *Zan* was shut down permanently and I was in detention, where my interrogator asked me again and again, "What were you doing in Qom?"

A co-worker tipped me off to this sensational story as a way of repaying my help in obtaining an identity card for his daughter. He was a specialist in religious issues and would write religious polemics refuting cases where Islamic jurisprudence was abused. He was a *hojjat ul-Islam* who would wear short-sleeved shirts and jeans—the only indication of his religious status was his full beard. When he showed us a picture of himself in a robe and turban, I couldn't help gaping in surprise. He had named his baby daughter Saghar, literally, "a cup for serving wine," and no registry would issue an identity card. He had gone to court, bringing with him books of poetry by Hafez and Khomeini as evidence in his favor but all to no avail.

"Get ready," I'd said to my mullah colleague, who sat with his arms wrapped around his knees in despair. "We're going together to the registry on Khiaban-e Niyavaran. I'll get you the card."

"It's no use. I've been there, too."

"But now we're going there together."

At the registry, I told him to go sit in the corner and stay put. I put on a big, coquettish smile as I went up to the window. Half an hour of flirting later, I handed Saghar's identity card to her father. In return, he gave me a gift fit for a journalist: a terrible story to tell about the lives of women prostituting themselves in the religious city of Qom. He'd been a student in Qom and knew the right places to go, so he volunteered to help me make the trip.

FEBRUARY 1999

Before I visited Qom, I started by investigating prostitution in Iran's bigger cities. In Tehran I was introduced to a nurse who performed illegal abortions in her middle-class home. She worked in a hospital during the day. The new Renault sedan she had bought with the money she made in her off-hours sat outside. One afternoon, she allowed me to pose as her assistant and watch one of the operations.

The patient entered the nurse's home, where dirty dishes were piled up in the sink and the smell of old cooking oil filled the air. The nurse asked her, "Did you shave?" The young woman said no, she had only trimmed her pubic hair. The nurse sent her to the bathroom with only an old razor and common soap. She came out again and the nurse told her to come into the bedroom, where the woman stripped and lay down on the examination table, her face white with fear. She spread her legs apart and dug her nails into the hands of the friend she had brought along for support.

The nurse injected her patient with an anesthetic, placed a plastic bucket on the floor below her, and began her work. The girl's face and body twisted and turned in pain. She screamed for her mother. Suddenly the nurse stopped. She called the girl a slut and told her to shut up. "If you scream," she said, "I will leave you just as you are." Her friend stuffed a piece of cloth into the girl's mouth. Instantly, the white cloth turned red as she bit her lips from the pain. Blood seeped out from between her legs, running down into the plastic bucket as the nurse yanked and twisted with her metal forceps. When it was over, the girl's friend had to help her to her feet. Dazed, she staggered out of the room.

JULY 1999

"Welcome to the City of Blood and Uprising." Only about an hour from Tehran, Qom is like the Vatican for the world's one hundred million Shi'a Muslims and home to the seminary where mullahs are groomed for their chosen vocation. My guide motioned for the driver to stop at the tollbooth so we could pay the entrance fee. I walked out and adjusted my black chador.

Wrapped in their own black chadors, I could see the women— "the hidden attraction of Qom"—milling among the crowd. There was nothing to set them apart from the flow of students, teachers, and bureaucrats. It was their purpose that made them different— that they had come to agree to a *sigheh* to lie beside a Muslim man for a few miserable minutes and earn the pittance that sustained their wretched lives. It is for this that Qom is known as a place of both pilgrimage and pleasure.

When I went to visit Qom for the last time, *Zan* had been shut down only a few months before. I was planning to leave Iran within ten days to return to America and I knew that coming back to the holy city put me in great danger. The situation for reformist papers wasn't getting any better, and every day more and more journalists were losing their jobs. But this article had become so important to me that I couldn't just set it aside. I knew that if I could take down these women's stories, with the help of Faezeh or the foreign journalists I had befriended around the globe, I would find a newspaper or magazine to publish them.

My investigations soon led me to the Sheikhan cemetery located in the courtyard of an ancient mosque in the city center. The burial ground is not far from the resting place of a *masumeh*, whose shrines draw seas of pilgrims every year. The women sat silent and motionless on the dirt graves, so entirely covered in their chadors that only their faces and hands revealed that these pitiful masses of fabric were in fact women. From the four corners of the courtyard, clusters of young seminary students clad in the traditional turbans, robes, and mantles worn by mullahs teemed into the courtyard, some smiling as though they were setting off on vacation, others looking at the women to see who was new. Some surveyed the pictures of the martyrs from the war with Iraq that were displayed everywhere, but most of them surveyed the human wares. A thin young boy, with a watering can in his hand, washed the floor of the courtyard, looking for a customer in need of an introduction.

I didn't need his help. I approached them myself. A woman named Mehri pulled her chador aside for me, and I could see she was a young woman in her midthirties, her hair streaked with cheap blond dye, her brightly colored blouse cinched tight to reveal her cleavage. Her face was a mess of garish makeup that betrayed her poor, rural background. Another woman I spoke to could hardly have been more than twenty. When the women uncovered their faces, the murmurs of the young men hovering around us intensified. With their lips they recited blessings, but their eyes were glued to the bare faces and necks of the women. In Shi'a Islam, a man who intends to marry—even if only for a day—is allowed a single glimpse of the woman's face to make his choice. These brief unveilings would be their only chance.

My presence among the women was disturbing to the students' otherwise casual approach. I wanted Mehri to step outside the cemetery to speak with me, but I told her I was worried that the men would get suspicious. She fixed the seminary students circling around her with a look of anger and contempt. "I don't care," she said, almost spitting. "I hate these kids." Safely outside the courtyard, she told me how she had ended up selling herself. She had been married to a truck driver who died in an accident a few years before, leaving her to take care of seven small children and a teenage daughter who had a baby girl of her own. She also weaved carpets, but the money was never enough, so three times a week she would take the bus to Qom. While she talked to me, she looked my driver and guide up and down to see if they might be in the market.

Need, sadness, and regret filled her eyes. She smelled pungently of sweat; she was soaking after hours of waiting under the hot sun. She told me that in the tourist months of summer she might take a temporary husband three times a day. "Locals don't pay much," she said. "Outsiders are better customers." I asked her where these "marriages" are consummated. "If they have a home, they take me there," she said. "If they don't, we go to the New Cemetery."

A cloud of dust and wind churns through the ancient, forgotten New Cemetery, which is located outside the city limits. No one goes there anymore to visit the dead, only the women with temporary husbands in tow. For a few minutes, until the man is finished and they have their money, they lay their bodies next to their client on an old wooden bed covered with a thin mattress. Inside the dusty, cob-webbed tombs, they receive between 20,000 and 40,000 rials ($2 to $4). The participants no longer even follow the rules of the *sigheh*, which call for a mullah to read a particular blessing. The man just calls, and the woman comes to him. The temporary brides are supposed to remain celibate for three and a half months after each divorce to ensure they aren't pregnant, but many disregard this convention. They have no choice. They need money to survive.

They make what passes for a living, enough for their own needs and those of their children and other loved ones, away from the prying eyes of neighbors. None of them believes in selling her body, and unlike prostitutes in other parts of the world who try to attract customers by baring more of themselves, these women clutch their chadors more and more tightly from shame and humiliation. At least in the cemetery, they feel secure. "The home of the dead is a safe place to be," Mehri says.

MARCH 1999

As part of an internship program funded by the European Union, I joined nearly thirty other young reporters from all over the world in the main hall of Radio Free Europe in Prague to participate in a month of intensive training in radio journalism. The Persian-language division, Radio Azadi, had been launched recently and had become known in Tehran as "Radio Overthrow the Government." After the welcoming ceremonies, a Mr. Calhoun, the director of Azadi, introduced me to the other Iranian staff members. They had all left the country years before, and it was eye opening for them to see a woman from the Islamic Republic with such a modern European appearance. Especially a reporter from *Zan*, closely connected to Faezeh Hashemi.

I'd promised myself that I wouldn't ask anyone what their name was or where they lived, that I'd focus only on my work. The Iranian reporters used false names on air, and it was clear that many were terrified they might expose their families in Iran to risk. I'd take the train straight from my hotel to the radio station to attend daily workshops. The only money I made was about twenty dollars a day for food and transportation. But slowly the staff warmed up to me and asked me to go to lunch with them on their break, if only because with my little book full of telephone numbers, I could breath new life into their programming. At first they only showed me around. Then they wanted to take advantage of my connections and have me produce a program for them.

"You can use a false name like everyone else."

I knew it would help keep me safe, but I didn't want to use a false name. Why should I stay undercover? I was already well known in Tehran, and I wanted to use my own name. The temptations of being a commentator, of the microphone, of having a faraway audience listening to my voice, it all got the better of me. I compromised. "*Salaam* dear listeners, this is Camelia Nakha'i and you are listening to Radio Free Europe, Radio Azadi from Prague."

I turned into an unofficial but vital member of the radio station. With Gholnaz I'd sit in street-side cafés and drink coffee and eat carrot cake, chatting about Iran and girlish things like fashion and makeup. With Ardalan I joined the nightlife, drinking tequila in the bars downtown and dancing. I remember how happy I was, feeling I was joining the group, thinking everyone was being friendly and open. On only twenty dollars a day, I still bought a small fresh bouquet of wild violets every morning from a lady who sat outside the train station, and I'd fix them to my wrist or the collar of my jacket, or sometimes put them in my hair. I was blind to how unhappy most of the Iranian broadcasters really were. I couldn't yet understand how terrible it had been for them to flee Iran under death threats or how hard it was for them to see me acting careless and free with my opinions with a bunch of flowers tied around my wrist. I often talked on the phone with Faezeh and defended her against their criticisms of her father. A week before the end of the internship, Calhoun said that if I was interested, he would hire me and I could stay in Prague.

It was an attractive offer—the most a newspaper reporter in Tehran could hope to make was a hundred thousand tomans a month (about $120 at the time). A stable future earning three thousand dollars monthly and living in Prague hovered before my eyes—while *Zan* and my struggle for civil rights beckoned from Iran.

I explained to Mr. Calhoun that I first had to travel to America to cover a trip planned for Faezeh to speak at the Asia Society in New York and that I then had to go to Iraq to interview Saddam Hussein. I had sweated for months trying to get a visa to Iraq and it had finally come through at the Iraqi embassy in Tehran. A German television reporter, Faramarz Qazi, offered to send a crew with me to Iraq and to buy the license to broadcast my interview. I felt I had to do this historic interview even if Radio Free Europe offered me the best job in the world. But I decided that from Iraq, I would return to Prague, and I was elated as I left Calhoun's office. A girl working in the Persian division asked me when I was going back home. I smiled and said, "I'm hired. I'm staying here."

Then a couple of days before I was scheduled to leave for America, Calhoun asked to speak with me in private. He was playing with something on his desk to avoid eye contact with me. "I'm very sorry to tell you that there is strong opposition to your working here. The women who work here say that if we hire you, they will resign. You have such close ties to Iran that they're afraid you'll disclose their identities. Unfortunately, I have to tell you that I can't offer you the job." It is always hard to hear such a thing said to you—to lose a job, to fail an exam—but as my father once told me, those losses don't make your life. I shrugged my shoulders, strangely more relaxed at first than angry, strangely glad to be released from the decision. I realized then that I wanted, more than anything else in the world, to be in Iran working at my newspaper. But I was also afraid, as I realized that the reason I hadn't turned down the offer originally was that I was nervous about returning to Tehran. My voice had been broadcast over a foreign radio station. Certainly Faezeh would help me, I assured myself; when we met in America I could explain everything to her. Yet I pictured the faces of the women I'd worked with at the station. Had they lied about their fear out of jealousy? Or was I really the only one ready to take such a risk? I was suddenly furious.

"They'll have my scalp in Tehran. Why did you let me produce a radio program for you? Why did you let my voice be broadcast? These people who wear black overcoats and hats to come to work so they won't be recognized, these people who are afraid to even sit by the window in case they are targeted for revenge by agents of the government . . . How did they not think that it's possible I might get into serious trouble in Tehran just like they would?" I looked boldly at Calhoun. He was playing uncomfortably with his fingers.

"You produced the show under the name Nakha'i. They won't know who you are."

"How many Camelias do you think there are there in Iran? And Nakha'i is my family name." The story of our name was told daily in our household when I grew up, the tale of the famous feud surrounding my grandfather, and we all struggled between the two last names, introducing ourselves as "Entekhabifard," then immediately explaining, "We were Nakha'i, but our grandfather changed it over a family fight." The Nakha'i name was well known and respected, and many of us were angry to lose it. I'd long wished I could become a Nakha'i again, and the broadcast was a way to become, in that moment, the person I'd always wanted to be. I didn't believe Calhoun was ignorant of the significance of my last name and certainly must have known the threats I'd face returning to Iran. I went back to my room, and of all the friends I thought I'd made at the radio station, only Ardalan called to help calm me.

APRIL 1999

I'd met Dr. Hushang Amir Ahmadi on my first trip to America, when I'd interviewed him for *Zan*. He was a close supporter of Hashemi Rafsanjani and had taken a stance against Khatami, proclaiming he was a powerless figurehead and that the real money was behind Rafsanjani. It was Rafsanjani, according to Dr. Ahmadi, who had the power to warm relations between the United States and Iran. He had devised an elaborate program to bring Faezeh to New York, to speak at Asia Society and to meet a number of congressional representatives in Washington as well as the first lady, Hillary Clinton. I'd flown directly from Prague, and as I walked into JFK international airport, I saw FBI agents waiting for Faezeh, who they expected would be coming with me.

But Faezeh wasn't due to arrive until the following evening. I was awakened in my hotel that morning by a panicked call from Dr. Ahmadi. "Camelia?" he frantically asked. I'd developed a nasty cold overnight and had a high fever. In a weak, muffled voice, I replied, "*Salaam* Agha-ye Doctor. I'm very sick." He wasn't listening to me.

"I'm done for! Faezeh's not coming. *Zan* was shut down. Tomorrow evening I have a thousand guests coming. I'm screwed! My reputation will be ruined . . ." It sounded like he was screaming underwater.

"Hang up and I'll talk to Tehran." I dialed Faezeh's cell phone number.

"No, I'm not coming. My father is against it. The newspaper's been closed, and I have a thousand people being held down at the Revolutionary Courts. We're all out of a job."

"Amir Ahmadi is going to give me hell," I said.

"Fuck Amir Ahmadi and his guests!" Faezeh snapped. "You worry about yourself. Sit tight for a few days while this whole thing blows over. They're saying that you obtained the Nouruz greeting from Farah Diba and that you faxed it to the paper and that running it was your idea. I have to take the fax down there and show it to the Revolutionary Court and say that it wasn't you . . . You take care of yourself and stay in touch with me." I was devastated. *Zan* was my last hope, and I had been waiting for Faezeh to arrive so I could tell her about all my disappointments in Prague. I wanted to cry like a frustrated little girl and hide behind her chador so she could take me home to Tehran. Now nothing was turning out as I'd expected, and I cursed Calhoun, the women at the radio station, Amir Ahmadi, the Revolutionary Court, and my terrible luck all at once.

I asked Amir Ahmadi to call off the event, but he convinced me to speak in Faezeh's place. "I can't tell all these guests that the evening's been canceled. All the dinner arrangements have been made." Quite a crowd turned out, and I stood on the stage and apologized to everyone for Faezeh's absence and answered questions about *Zan* and the reformists. Sick and overwhelmed, I thought of *Zan* being closed down, and I wondered if I'd ever be able to return home. I couldn't stand any longer, and they had to bring me a chair to sit in to finish the talk.

◙   ◙   ◙

SPRING–SUMMER 1999

During the troubled days that followed, as I debated whether to return home, I studied English at Columbia University and furthered friendships within the Iranian community in New York. I met Golriz for the first time in person, though we'd corresponded before. She worked for a human rights organization, and when I was working on the series at *Zan* about the mysterious killings of intellectuals, I wrote a piece about her group's plans to investigate the murders. The article caused quite a stir. Now with the typical hospitality Iranians show each other outside the country, she and I often met for lunch.

I was still interested in following the trail of those murders. My research led me to an FBI agent, Jean, and she became my most loyal friend during this difficult period. I was looking into Sa'id Emami, the former deputy advisor to the minister of intelligence and the primary suspect accused of the murders. After his arrest in Tehran, Emami had—or so it was claimed—committed suicide by drinking cleaning fluid, thus evading justice. In New York I'd found an article on the Internet that described how he'd been a student in America during the time of the Shah, attending a school in Washington, DC, where he was a member of the Muslim Student Union. The secret behind the killings had died with him, but I decided to research his tenure as a student and hopefully come up with some stories that could keep the issue alive. One of the surviving reformist papers had expressed interest in the piece. Hesam Zarafshar, a relative of a friend of my father's who I'd met in New York, helped me track down various leads. I even called the former Iranian ambassador to the U.S., Ardashir Zahedi, in Switzerland. It was important to me to keep working, though *Zan* might be lost.

Eventually, a source led me to Jean and Tom, FBI agents who asked to meet me in the lobby of a hotel in Washington to discuss my article. They couldn't find any information on Emami, though, and by our third meeting Tom stopped coming. I eventually abandoned the article on Emami after a series of dead ends, but Jean and I began to meet as friends whenever I traveled to Washington. My English wasn't very good, and she suggested that I read books expressly for the purpose of learning the language. She told me about her family, her dogs, and her beautiful children and their singing lessons, joking that they sounded more like they were chirping than singing. We both knew our friendship had to remain a secret, that it could be incredibly dangerous for me if I returned to Tehran.

Jean urged me to stay in America. And when I called Faezeh weekly, she warned me that the Revolutionary Guard considered me a prime culprit in the charges facing the paper. I was unofficially charged for interviewing Farah Diba and sending her Nouruz greeting to the paper and encouraging Faezeh to publish it. I was completely innocent—I hadn't even met the Queen yet, though ironically, I would meet her soon after the charge was leveled. But through all this I was burning to return, as students rioted in protests against the government's fresh assaults on freedom of speech. My mother told me that martial law had been imposed in the neighborhoods around the University of Tehran. Students had gathered in front of their dormitories to demonstrate against the shutting down of the paper *Salaam*, and they were taunted and beaten by the Basij. The strikes continued in the hopes of a second revolution. People were waiting for Khatami to stand up and fight—but he remained silent, losing many supporters. I yearned to be in the city so I could report in person at this historic moment. I didn't see myself as an exile; I felt like I was standing by, waiting for the right moment—any moment—to return.

◉   ◉   ◉

It was a rainy day in May 1999 when I got a call from Kambiz Atabay, the head of Farah Pahlavi's office in New York. I had met him several times in the past months as he arranged my interview with Reza Pahlavi. For monarchists outside of Iran, it seemed unbelievable that Rafsanjani's daughter would approve of my interviewing the "young Shah," but I'd done it all with Faezeh's full support in the hope that when *Zan* reopened we'd have a unique story in our hands. I'd secreted away my recordings of Reza with a friend in America, and I left them there when I returned to Iran, but *Zan* was never able to publish the piece. The paper stayed closed forever.

I had told Atabay of my ambition to someday also meet Farah, who lived in Paris. But it was still an incredible surprise when he called the family friend I was staying with in New Jersey and informed me that the Queen would receive me in his New York apartment the next morning. I rummaged through my wardrobe for something suitable to wear to meet a queen and settled on a gray coat and skirt and woke up early to fix my hair and makeup.

The weather was terrible. In between getting off the bus at Port Authority and getting into a taxi, my shoes were soaked, and my hair was a mess. I bought a bunch of red roses at the bus terminal. As soon as I opened the door to get out of the taxi at the appointed block, Kambiz Atabay pushed me back in and got in the cab. He told the driver to keep going; the true location of the meeting was being kept secret from me. I was soaking wet when we arrived. I put the roses on the table in the reception room and went into the bathroom to hurriedly wipe the raindrops off my black leather shoes with a tissue.

Busts of the Shah and exquisite paintings and photos were displayed in every corner of the sitting room. Mina, Atabay's wife, came in with a tray of tea. Lovely fragrant steam rose from the silver teacups decorated with Takht-e Jamshid engravings. She placed another tray of pastries at the edge of the table. I picked up a teacup and a crunchy roll covered in powdered sugar and walked over to the window. I'd taken a big bite of the pastry and was about to sip my tea when Atabay called me from behind. "Camelia."

Farah was waiting, framed by the doorway. She was stunningly elegant. Fumbling, I put the teacup down. My mouth was so full I couldn't even say *salaam*. I gulped it all down and stood on tiptoe to kiss her. She was tall and beautiful, a thousand times more beautiful up close than in any of her pictures. There's never been a good picture, I thought to myself. I didn't know what to call her. Khanum? Shahbanu? Your Highness?

"You are very thin and beautiful," is what I finally came out with. "How are you?"

She asked that I convey her greetings to Faezeh, who she'd heard was modern and progressive. She seemed very interested in my views as a journalist about how Tehran had progressed under Khatami's reform programs. She was keeping in touch, via e-mail, she told me, with many young people in Iran and that sometimes she was so homesick she'd dial a number at random just to hear a voice speaking her language from inside her country.

"The roses are for you," I said and held them out to her.

"Thank you." She ran her hand over the petals and patted my shoulder. "They're beautiful, just like you. I'm pleased to see that Iran has such brave girls. I wish you success." Then she took her leave and disappeared behind the wall, and Atabay escorted me out. I wondered, was I brave enough to return to Iran? Later, in prison, I'd think of how, in those few polite exchanges, I was risking my life.

JULY 1999

My mother had made a *nazr* that if I emerged from Mehrabad airport safe and sound, we'd all make a pilgrimage to the shrine of Imam Reza in Mashhad. She had implored me not to come. "You're making a mistake. I'm not opening the door for you. You don't understand how crazy Tehran is. It's not enough the nonsense *Kayhan* printed about you? Didn't you read that you're a monarchist and an American spy?"

I expected to return to New York within ten days. Despite my mother's, Jean's, and other friends' urgent warnings, I had been persuaded to return to Iran by the assurances of Golriz. She'd asked me to accompany and assist her in her work for the human rights organization on this short trip. I trusted her. Then she abandoned me three days after we'd arrived in Iran, when the Ministry of Intelligence agents showed up at my mother's door to take me to prison. Much later, people told me that while I was sitting alone in my cell, Golriz did nothing to help me and claimed that I had come to

America not as a reporter, but as a spy for the Ministry. It's not really very funny, but it is ironic: at the same time the Ministry was accusing me of spying for the Americans, in America I was being accused of spying for Iran. I have never forgiven Golriz or understood her motives. But I know that while she let me believe I would be safe with her, it was also my own choice to return. I wanted to be free to visit my country any time I wished. I trusted more than anything that I could return to the home that I had always known. I trusted that I would be safe among friends.

Among the pieces I was working on, I was especially determined to finish my article about Qom, to tell the story I'd begun before I left for Prague. I could find a newspaper in New York to publish my articles. I knew now that I couldn't continue to hope for their publication in *Zan*. The open atmosphere in the Iranian press had disappeared. Every day the judicial authority shut down another paper, and an increasing number of journalists were being dismissed or threatened. Newspapers no longer had the courage of those heady first few months after Khatami's election.

I spent half of the second day after my arrival in Qom. Then my mother, my sister and my niece, and I went to Mashhad to make the offering my mother had promised. My mother bought millet and poured it onto the ground for the doves. We put on chadors and went to pray for health and for the strength to stick together. How I had missed my family! I longed to have a satisfying, heart-to-heart talk with my mother and my sister but still hadn't found an opportunity by the time we got home the next day. We returned to Tehran at dawn, and Kati went home to her husband after she had dropped my mother and me off, exhausted from our excursion.

It was six o'clock in the morning when there was a knock at the door of our apartment. When my mother came in softly a few seconds later and stood over me, I knew what she was going to say.

"There are two men at the door. They say they have a letter for you."

"I know. They've come for me. Keep calm." I followed my mother, grabbing an overcoat from the rack and putting it on over my nightclothes. I coolly opened the front door, and the men said they had a search and arrest warrant from the Revolutionary Courts. They showed me the warrant, and I read it. I stepped aside and told my mother again to stay calm. They woke Kai Khosrou and got him out of bed and herded us into the hall, telling us to be quiet and sit still. They unplugged the phone and went into my bedroom. I could hear them keeping in touch with their headquarters by radio as they poured all my things, including books and family photo albums, into big bags. They took things from all over the house— from the kitchen, the dining room, from inside the silverware cabinets. They took my passport.

"Put on some pants," they told me. I looked around my room. I looked at my suitcase lying open in the corner—I still hadn't even fully unpacked. I looked at the doll that my dear mother had bought me. In the hallway, my mother sobbed and said, "Where are you going to take her? Take me, too!"

"Hajj Khanum, you stay at home. You will be contacted."

I leaned my face close to my mother's. "*Khoda hafez*, don't worry . . . *Khoda hafez*."

I looked at the picture of my father on the wall as I walked out the door. There were a few more guards standing along the footpath. I sat in the back of the Peykan as they emptied the bags of evidence into the trunk. I could see even more men standing in the shadows of the trees lining our street. When they were given a sign, they too got into their cars. I turned and looked behind me, at my mother's flower boxes, at the lace curtains tied back in the windows. I knew she and my brother were watching us.

"Am I ever going to see my street, my house, or my mother again?" I asked myself.

One of the men sitting up front turned around and held out a gray canvas blindfold.

"Please put this over your eyes and lay down in the back." I lay down, and they threw a blanket over me. Softly I said, "For God's sake, take me wherever you're going to take me. Just don't kill me."

chapter twelve

Save Yourself by Telling
the Truth

One day, right after I'd returned to my cell from the interrogation
room, the guards were sent again to get me. "Your interrogator is
here. Get ready quick." I put on my chador and my stockings again
and followed him up the stairs. What did he want with me now?
Had something happened?

When we were back in the room, he asked, "Good, so you say
you're ready to do whatever the organization needs. Do you want
to become one of the nameless soldiers?" I nodded my head.

"Take these confessions by Manuchehr Mohammadi and his
friend Qolamreza Mohajeri-Nezhad and read them. They are
about their meetings with Reza Pahlavi. Mohammadi has not
admitted to taking money from Pahlavi to start the student riots, and
you must help us. He has been told that we have abducted one of
Pahlavi's employees in Turkey and brought her to Tehran. You are
Shiva Batmanqelich. When you're in front of Mohammadi, tell
him that you were Reza's accountant and that you wrote a check out
to him for twenty-five thousand dollars."

He forced me up, still blindfolded, and to walk ahead of him and
into another room as he spoke to me. Then I could hear another man
talking to him, and someone behind me said, "Lift up your blindfold
and look at the person in front of you, but don't look behind you."

I lifted my blindfold. A blindfolded young man stood before me.
He, like me, was wearing prison clothes. He was upset and was
squeezing his fingers. I knew that this was Manuchehr Mohammadi.

A voice said, "Put your blindfold back on." I obeyed, and that same voice, coming now from another direction, said, "Boy, now you lift up your blindfold." Evidently, Mohammadi was looking at me now. "Put your blindfold back on."

"Very well, Khanum, did you recognize this gentleman?"

I launched into my role as instructed by my interrogator. I said that he was Manuchehr Mohammadi and that I had seen him in Washington and that I had signed a check for him from Reza Pahlavi. They asked Mohammadi if he recognized me. He cried and wailed that by God this was a lie—that this woman was a liar and that he had never seen me before, that he did not recognize me. He cried very hard.

His interrogator shouted at him and started punching him, and Mohammadi howled and swore at me. "Why are you lying?" I didn't know how to answer. They pulled me out of the room. My interrogator growled at me, angry that I hadn't acted well enough. He said Mohammadi hadn't confessed because he saw through me and understood that it was all a trick.

"Why did you beat him?" I couldn't stop myself from asking.

Surprised, he answered, "Beat? Who did we beat? He's crazy. He's always hitting himself. You have enough sense to know you'd better mind your own business."

My senses were all there, and I *was* minding my own business. I was getting more positive signals from my interrogator as he listened to my confessions. I knew by rote now how to list my crimes, and I'd confessed to every one. Among my primary offenses were having relations with Reza Pahlavi and publishing Farah Diba's Nouruz greeting in *Zan*; having relations with an Israeli; working for the CIA at Radio Azadi in Prague; spying for a human rights agent in Tehran (meaning Golriz); seeking action against national security through attempts at interviewing Salman Rushdie; and seeking to harm the government of the Islamic Republic by inspiring fear and dissent among the people by disseminating the black list. Among my secondary offenses were prostitution, wanton behavior, and alcohol consumption; Godlessness and spreading atheism to the blameless; making a mockery of Islam; and opposition to the *velayat-e faqih*.

"Any one of these crimes could mean execution. You should receive forty lashes for the crime of the consumption of alcohol alone. Now, what do you think should be done with you?"

Bravely I answered, "I'm going home—I know that these days are ending soon, and I will be set free."

He laughed. "*Masha-Allah*, I like you, you're very cheeky. But I'm sorry to say I think the only way you'll be getting out of here is dead. How are you so sure you'll be freed?"

"I dreamed of a letter written to my mother that read 'this is a letter from the Imam-e Zaman' and of my mother crying from joy."

"Ha! Haven't you heard the saying '*khab-e zan chap ast*' (a woman's dreams deceive her)?" Then he pounded his briefcase against my head and said angrily, "When the imam comes to your dream, dirt on your head, he's coming to tell you to correct your path!" He quickly became calm again and said, "Probably the letter your mother received was news of your death. Don't be so optimistic."

Love, like a wisp of fresh air from paradise, had been blown deep into the heart of this hardened man. I knew, even when he punched me, that he felt he was touching a delicate flower. His mood swings were harsh because this love confused him. He had given his whole life to the Imam and the war and the Islamic Revolution. The fires of love consumed this "man of God." And they consumed me as well. I was really in love with him. With my whole being, I could feel my freedom though the halls of the prison, the halls that seemed to lead nowhere. The dream I meditated so long on sprang forth with boundless energy.

"The brothers who see you on the walkway say they have worked in this prison for twenty years, and they have never seen a prisoner like you. They say you walk up the stairs behind me with your head held high."

This was true. I hadn't broken. I looked at prison, at the difficult days of interrogation, at the contempt and the hunger, at the solitude and the suffering as a performance. A great performance—the performance of my life. But after three months, I was tired. I had sung all the songs I knew.

My interrogator was able to obtain the order for my conditional release through convoluted negotiations with high-ranking colleagues. I first had to be tried in a formal proceeding. The Ministry of Intelligence told the judge assigned to my case to enact certain formalities and to release me on bond. He was told that I was willing and able to work for the Ministry of Intelligence, and they wanted to start me on a trial basis. I would monitor other journalists inside the offices of various newspapers and report back to them. I signed all my confessions and filled out my *tak nevesi*, each page reading on top "Save Yourself by Telling the Truth."

I was told that if I turned on the Ministry and revealed our secret agreements, I would be subjected to the worst punishments imaginable and killed.

The next step in my conditional release was for me to appear in a videotaped court proceeding. They wanted to shoot two different films. We rehearsed dozens of times as I read my statements off a script.

"It's not natural. You have to speak naturally."

They explained that I could perform *taqiah* on the day of the shooting. I didn't understand and asked what *taqiah* meant.

"It means you must lie for the good of your religion. In your heart you intend to lie, purposefully, so your lies will not be seen as wrong by God, because it is for the sake of your religion."

On the day that my rehearsals were deemed satisfactory, they gave me my old clothes back to put on, along with a chador I wore on top of my scarf and overcoat. My interrogator brought me into a room and told me to take off my blindfold. The room was divided by a thick curtain. The camera lens stuck out through the seam of the curtain, and a table and a chair were positioned in front of its gaze.

"Sit in the chair and start the interview."

He was on the other side of the curtain, filming. On my side, I played the role of the errant girl, distraught and repentant. The first tape was about me—my role in lashing out at the government; my corruption and inability to control myself; descriptions of my sexual relations with an Israeli spy and of how I took advantage of my voice as a newspaper reporter to create opposition to the State and to undermine the revolution and the *velayat-e faqih*; and an acknowledgment that I knew that the crimes I had committed carried a death sentence. They wanted the second tape to be about Faezeh and the rest of my colleagues. In this segment, I admitted that Faezeh was irreligious and uncommitted to the Islamic Revolution and that she had numerous boyfriends, and I mentioned one of them by name and said that I had seen them alone together in Faezeh's office. I talked about whomever else they asked me to.

"What are you going to do with these videotapes?"

"I'm going to put them in a special drawer in my office. No one has access to it."

"What are they for?"

"For someday, just in case. This is standard procedure with the Ministry of Intelligence. We have to tape all the accused."

OCTOBER 1999

At the court I told the judge, as planned, that I didn't need a defense attorney and that I would defend myself. He and the clerk sat up there and read my charges, and I answered each of them. They admitted my mother and sister after the hearing. I hadn't seen them in seventy days. My mother looked like Afsar Khanum, Guli's mother. Her hair had gone white in spots, and one of her eyes was drooping. I found out later that she had suffered a mild heart attack in her sleep and that the nerves in her left eye were paralyzed. And my sister, thinner and paler than ever, pressed me to her bosom like a baby chick and sobbed. We weren't allowed to talk; I could only whisper, "I'm coming home soon."

When they left, my mother was limping, and my niece, Yasbanu, cried out that auntie had to come with them, too. My heart was bursting out of my chest. Why had they been torturing my family like this? Why was I here?

But when she first held me, in the middle of our weeping, my mother noticed one of the guards and abruptly changed her tone. "Hey, aren't you Agha-ye Amir? Your house was in Manzeriah, next door to my aunt Nargess." Everyone stared at her.

"Yes, yes, Zahra Khanum. *Salaam aleik.* What a good aunt you had, God rest her soul. I remember you. And your brother, Ali Agha. God rest his soul, too."

I started laughing. My mother, even in the most dangerous of places, in the middle of the Revolutionary Court, couldn't stop being a busybody.

"You better watch out. My daughter is in your hands. For God's sake, tell them not to hurt her."

I jabbed my mother in the side.

That afternoon, in the prison, my interrogator laughed. "Today your mother found her relations from Jamaran."

◙　◙　◙

Then one day the guards came for me, not to take me for more questioning, but to send me home. They gave me back my old clothes and wallet, then covered my face for the ride from the prison. "Don't touch your blindfold yet," one said. "You will take it off only when I tell you to go. After that you must get out of the car. Above all, don't look back." They let me out in the middle of the street somewhere in downtown Tehran. It was a rainy fall day, and I was wearing a threadbare chador, clutching a plastic bag with my few belongings. Strangely, nobody seemed to notice me. I hailed a cab for home.

My mother rarely locked the front door to our apartment—I simply turned the knob and stepped in. Yasbanu looked up from where she was playing on the floor, her face frozen in amazement. Every day the courts had promised my mother I would return, but at last I had really come home. She came from the kitchen, crying and pulling me close. I was shocked when I looked in the mirror; those long weeks under the artificial light had turned my skin a pale and pasty color. My eyes were locked in a squint. For the first few days I could barely sleep. Every day, I stood at the window and watched for the officers to return, waiting for him to call . . .

◉ ◉ ◉

At our fourth or fifth meeting after our disastrous first encounter in the offices of *Zan*, when he threw me out for wearing perfume, "my commander" asked me to sign a slip of paper. There-after he carried it, hidden in his planner, whenever we met, in case anyone arrested him and charged him with having an improper relationship with me. It was a temporary marriage certificate, a *sigheh*, though he'd just written it out himself. We never saw a mullah.

"We'll be spending many hours together alone, and it's not right. I'm a religious man. I must answer to God." This moment changed the meaning of our relationship irrevocably.

"Okay. What am I suppose to do now? Shall we stop seeing each other?" I pretended I didn't understand what he wanted. I thought about those women in Qom. I waited, wanting him to be the one to say it.

"I mean, it'll be good for both of us. I'll feel more comfortable, and we can talk freely when we work together." And he slid the paper toward me to sign.

I wasn't sure what this meant to me. I still didn't know his name, he always told me to call him Farmandeh whenever I asked him. I thought about how people joked in Iran about *zan-e sighehi*, how they show clients they're waiting by wearing their chador turned inside out. Should I be ashamed at this point in my life, after all I'd been through? I had dragged this man to this spot, and now what was I supposed to do? Though he might have believed it protected him from God, his little piece of paper didn't mean anything to me. I thought it might perhaps strengthen our relationship, help keep me safe, keep him committed as my protector. But what would my family think? I calmed myself by thinking that the *sigheh* was shameful for him, too, for his wife and family and that we would never let anyone know about it unless he was arrested.

Later, I think the *sigheh* also helped me escape him when I left for America. It gave him the confidence to trust me when I promised that I'd come back to him. It let me become closer to my commander and to gain some command over him. He changed after he had that paper signed. He was gentler with me and let me flirt with him more directly. But signing that paper also made it clear to me that though I was out of prison, the game hadn't ended. This was a new beginning. I wondered how long could I go on leading two lives.

In contrast to our first painful meeting when he made me scrub my face, he now started asking me to wear makeup for him and attractive clothes when we met. "A Muslim woman should save all her beauty and talent for her husband." That was his word and the word of the Prophet Mohammed.

My job was to return to work at a reformist newspaper and secretly gather information for the Ministry of Intelligence about relations between Seyyed Mohammed Abtahi and Alireza Nourizadeh in London.

"Will they hire me?"

He wrinkled his eyebrows. "What do you mean?"

"I mean they're afraid of me. They say that Intelligence is after me, and my working at a newspaper is as good as that newspaper getting shut down." I was lying. I didn't want to go back to any of my former jobs. I didn't want to spy on my friends. I knew I'd have to stay in the shadows for a while, so in the daytime I arranged with Faezeh to help her run a small women's NGO newsletter, *Saba*. I was the only writer, and Faezeh was the editor in chief. It was only about four pages long and quite a step down from my previous work, but it kept me away from the spotlight and away from the people that Intelligence was most interested in, except Faezeh.

Laughing nervously, I'd told her, "Faezeh, I'm meant to spy on you." She answered with grace, "Tell them the worst things you can imagine. I know they have problems with me, not with you. They brought you in because of your friendship with me."

Soon, the carefully planned agenda for my work for the Ministry turned into mostly taking long romantic drives with my interrogator. Sometimes we drove far out of Tehran to find places where we could sit together in public. We'd travel up north or northeast to small shops where only tourists on their way to the Caspian Sea would stop and where there was almost no chance we'd be recognized. At first, it was enough to spend this time together talking, to drink *doogh* on Jade-ye Ab'ali or to go to a teahouse in Lavizan.

Then we also started to meet more often in different hidden "security offices" around Tehran. I wouldn't leave until nightfall. As the shops of Tehran began to pull down their rolling shutters, I would put on my chador to wear home. My chador was a deeper shade of black than the shadows on the walls, and I'd dart from dark corner to dark corner through the streets of Haft-e Tir to be sure no one was following me. He'd told me, "It's possible that you are being followed by Intelligence task forces!" His eyes filled with hunger and desire as he instructed me on how to go to and from our rendezvous, telling me to change cars a few times, to take different routes, and to put on or take off my chador in hiding so no one would be able to recognize me. I felt like a prowling stray cat as I slipped through the night.

We'd gone to a film studio on Khiaban-e Karimkhan. To a gyne-cologist's office on Haft-e Tir, where a friend of his was the practicing doctor. We had to be careful so no one suspected we ever did anything but talk. We'd sit, chatting softly, listening for anyone in the hall. One time by accident I came face-to-face with his son when he came to find his father. It was in a medical office we were using. By mistake his son opened the door, and our eyes locked.

As he and I became closer, sometimes we did more than just talk. He'd press up against me and then break away suddenly if we heard anyone coming. We stole some private moments in those public offices, terrified of being caught if we stayed quiet too long. But those short hushed moments were never enough. Just as my heart had begun to leap in Towhid Prison when I heard his steps coming down the hall, now I waited anxiously for his calls to set up another meeting. But he always wanted more, and I was never sure how far I was willing to go. He kept making more demands, wanting to find a more private place for us. . . .

◙　◙　◙

NOVEMBER 1999

"Who are these children? They must be your son and daughter." I stood facing a framed picture of a boy and a girl on the wall. I was being nosy, looking around his parents' home. The little girl was wearing a puffy pink dress and sitting in a chair. The little boy was standing up. He was wearing a coat and pants and had very short hair. "My commander" had been tempted to take me to his mother's house a thousand times, as he had the key. Then this particular Friday, his parents had gone to Behesht-e Zahra to pray for his brother, who he told me had been martyred at the front. He'd never been able to fulfill his desire to sit and look at me undisturbed, as long as he wanted, as if we were in his own home. He wanted me as if I was his wife.

"Keep your head down so you don't know where you are," he had said as we approached the building. I knew exactly where I was. I had come to this neighborhood time after time with my father. We'd park here to go see my uncle at his dental practice. I'd put my little hand in my father's as we'd cross the street. My father took big steps and I took small ones, lagging behind him as we crossed the broad Khiaban-e Sepah.

Now my father wasn't with me, and I had to cross the street by myself. When we stood in front of the house, he'd said, "Keep your face covered. The neighbors have been here for ages, and everyone knows us. I'll leave the door open. You come in a minute later."

It was a large, old house. There were dozens of pairs of shoes in the entryway. "You have to take your shoes off in a house where people pray." he reminded me. I took my shoes off by the doormat and carried them with me. In the entryway hung a picture of a young man dressed as a Pasdar. "This is your martyred brother." He didn't answer. In their large dining room, like in most Iranian homes, there were objects adorning every surface—bowls with birds engraved on them, religious wall-hangings, and a piece of black fabric in an elaborate inlaid frame. He pointed to the latter and said, "This is a piece of the covering of the Ka'aba."

We were going upstairs when I stopped on the way up to look at the picture of his children. I dared to ask him again, "What's your name?"

"Same as always. Nothing . . . Farmandeh!" His eyes sparkled from behind the bushy line of his eyebrows.

"Really, I don't know what to call you."

"Take off your chador and let me see how beautiful you are. Amir. I'm not going to say more than that." Then he came closer. Too close. I shut my eyes. Even now, I can close my eyes and see every detail of his face. I hated myself for being weak. I wondered why I didn't kill myself. Why would I want to live like that—like a rat? Even now I can't answer that question. I shut my eyes and repeated the mantra I used when I meditated every morning: "Camelia, you are dreaming . . . What's happening to you is only a dream . . ."

Afterward, I noticed he was praying under his breath as he tucked in his shirt. He was looking down at me, where I sat on the thick rug. I couldn't hear what he was saying, but I saw his lips moving, and I knew it was a prayer. Then he asked, "Do you want some water?" I nodded, and he went back down the stairs toward the kitchen. I started looking around the upper floor of the house and found another fancy room, obviously used for parties and special occasions. Every corner was decorated with bowls and plates. I shuddered. What else did he want to do with me in this empty house? How many hours would he keep me here? I tried to guess how long his family usually stayed at the cemetery—perhaps half a day? I hoped I'd be allowed to leave sooner than that. But I couldn't tell him, "Please take me home." I couldn't let him see I was disgusted. I kept myself deep in my role as the perfect lover, pretending that I couldn't get enough of him either. And I waited, silently making my own prayer, asking God that he'd come back with the water and say, "OK, get dressed and go."

I heard a commotion below, and he came scrambling back up the stairs. "Where are your shoes?" They were in my hand. He moaned, "My parents came back. On the way, my mother couldn't decide whether she'd turned off the gas or not. When they were halfway there they turned around and came home." He was trembling. "Oh God, my reputation is ruined. Lord, have mercy, I repent. Go hide under the sofa. Don't make a sound. Don't even breathe till I call you."

My heart was beating so hard that I could hear its sound filling the room. Would I have to stay under the sofa all day? Two days? As I lay there I thought of my French classes and of all of my mother and father's other efforts to raise a proper, worthy, sophisticated daughter. And now where had I ended up? Under a dull brown couch in a house at the end of one of Tehran's historic back alleys.

After what seemed an eternity, but was about five minutes, I heard his voice. "Come out. Be quick. Put on your chador. They're sitting in the courtyard. Go downstairs and get outside, hurry like the wind! Go down the hill. I'll come in fifteen minutes. Get as far away as you can."

He stood watch on the stairs. I was sweating as I ran, but I thanked God to be out of there. Fifteen minutes later, his gray Peykan pulled up in front of me.

"That was too close . . . After a respectable, pious life, how close I came to total devastation. Thank God." He took a deep breath and looked at me. "Why did I fall in love with you?" I knew, but I replied only with a charming smile.

◎   ◎   ◎

After much coaxing, Amir agreed that I had greater potential to spy for the Ministry outside the country's borders. He agreed to let me go to London and from there to America. In return, I promised him that I'd get the tapes from my interview with Reza Pahlavi, collect information on Manuchehr Mohammadi, and look into the ties between Nourizadeh and Abtahi.

"How are you going to get a visa to America?"

"My friends at the university in America will take care of that, don't worry," I assured him. In truth, I planned to call Jean from England, and she'd help me secure a visa.

Before he'd allow me to travel to America, Amir ordered my mother and I to go back to the Presidential building on Khiaban-e Jordan to hand over her passport and the title to her car. Only then did I receive my own passport back, which had been confiscated when I was arrested. I had been released from prison on a thirteen-million-toman bond (about $13,000). The deed to my mother's apartment had already been put in the custody of the Revolutionary Court to make bail (it was worth about ten-million and she'd paid cash to make up the rest). Compared to other released prisoners, the cost wasn't that much—Amir had handled everything to let me out relatively easily and quickly.

As he waited with me at Mehrabad airport, he gave me one last warning: "Remember that your family is here. Keep in mind that if you betray my confidence, I will do something that you won't forget for the rest of your life. You will be gone for only ten days."

▣   ▣   ▣

DECEMBER 1999

In New York, people were passing freely by me, so why didn't I feel free? I traveled to Washington, DC, to tell Reza Pahlavi the truth, that I had seen Manuchehr Mohammadi in Towhid Prison and that even now I had come to spy on him. I spoke so frankly that I don't know if he was able to believe what I told him. Many of the Iranian friends I'd made on my first trip to New York wouldn't speak to me anymore because of rumors Golriz had spread while I was in prison. I heard that she claimed I'd never even been in Towhid—that it was all a set-up, that she hadn't abandoned me but had instead escaped some trap herself. She thought I was lounging by the Caspian Sea for three months. Her betrayal of our friendship overwhelmed me with anger. But it was as if her gossip had predicted my fate. On this trip, I actually *had* agreed to come to New York to spy for the Ministry of Intelligence. But I didn't intend to give Amir any useful information—I didn't think of myself as a spy at all. I'd only agreed in order to get out of prison and out of Iran. Now I didn't know how I could begin to defend myself and set the record straight. I didn't have the courage to open up and admit to the affair. I felt completely alone with a truth that no one would accept, and I fell into a deep depression. How could I tell anyone about the debasement, the humiliation, and the suffering that I'd endured to restore my freedom?

Jean, one of my few remaining friends, was a great comfort. "Don't go back—you should stay here in America. They'll kill you in Tehran," she said, tenderly putting her arm around me. "I've been so worried about you."

"I'm not ready to stay here," I told her. "I have to be sure that my family is safe." I remembered Amir's warning and feared for my mother and sister. And I began to think that if I went back home, maybe by some miracle it would turn out that nothing with Amir was really as dangerous as I imagined. I was furious with everyone in New York who'd turned against me. I felt angry at the whole world. A hundred thoughts ran through my mind—and I had only ten days to decide.

On the eve of the new millennium, I stood in Times Square cheering with millions of people around me, witnessing the end of a thousand years. I said to my friend next to me, "I always wanted to be here in New York for the millennium . . . Always. And here I am." But in the middle of this dream come true, I was pulled backward by the painful love I felt, the role I'd convinced myself to play, and by all the dreams I'd had to leave behind.

I returned to Iran. I returned to my savior. I don't know what kind of shape my mind was in—I was both in love and not in love. My ambivalence was consuming me from within. I would tell my friends and family that I was fine, that I felt normal, but I wasn't fine or in any ordinary state. I was consumed with dread. I'd wake in the night with cramps, my leg muscles tight, and I would be beside myself with pain. I would limp the next day, and when anyone asked, I'd just say I was fine.

JANUARY 2000

In Tehran we faced each other again for the first time in the office in the Club for Creative Literature, as I made my report. He glowed at my return. "You seem to have genuinely repented." We talked for what seemed like hours. But I didn't have much to tell. I told him that Golriz had completely ruined my reputation. I told him I'd gone to Washington, DC, to speak to Reza Pahlavi and that he really hadn't given any money to Manuchehr Mohammadi. I set the tapes of my interview with Reza down on his desk.

Now he started to grow surly. "Nothing? You're giving me nothing? This is what you meant when you promised you could be a great spy in America? You could have done this in Iran."

In fact, I couldn't do this anymore at all. I knew I didn't want to work for him—why had I even come back? I wanted to live, and I wanted to get back to my real work, to my life as a journalist.

While I was away, he'd also been traveling. He'd gone with his family to Karbala in Iraq to visit shrines, along with one of the first groups of Shi'a pilgrims after the war. He'd brought me souvenirs, a silver ring and a piece of green fabric, which he told me came from a holy shroud. The green swatch wasn't bigger than his palm. "This ring is identical to the one that I bought for my wife. I think I should go knock on your mother's door soon and ask for your hand. There have been many cases where repented *mujaheds* have married the single brothers who interrogated them. But what are we going to do when this time the brother who has fallen in love with his charge already has a wife and children?"

I wasn't in love anymore. Whatever I'd done—self-deception or self-defense, meditation or role playing—whatever I had told myself to make me *feel* I was truly in love, it was over. It was over as soon as the captain of the plane announced we had reached Iranian soil. At that moment I'd woken up. I changed my mind, and I was amazed at how naïve I'd been to come back and take this risk. Come back for what? To be the mistress of some unknowable, mysterious, nobody of a man? To hide under a black chador, sneaking through the back alleys of Tehran? My eyes were finally opened, but it was too late. By then, the plane was already circling Mehrabad airport. In that moment of clarity, I promised myself I'd plan carefully how I could leave. The love I'd felt disappeared like fog before the sun. Where was I going with this man?

He was still in love, and though I was not, I was still his lover. He called me his Persian miniature rose. . . . He kept asking me, "Are you tired of this job?" and promising that if I was tired of the job or of him, I could simply tell him and he'd release me, that no one would harm me. I wasn't stupid. I wasn't going to say, "Yes, I'm sick of this. Please let me go back to my life, *khoda hafez!*" But I was deeply depressed, and he could see it. I hated being without my real work as a reporter and instead writing daily reports for him that were full of nothing, of boring details that were less than lies: "I went to a café by the Caspian Sea with Faezeh and her daughter and son, and we talked about sports and my assignments for *Saba*." He'd shake his head and say, "What kind of a spy are you?"

APRIL 2000

He found a vacant apartment building in Sa'adat-abad and convinced the realtor to give him the key. He told me he was planning to show the apartment to his wife. Maybe he was, but he also took me there a few times. He'd lay cardboard down over the bare floor. I remember we spent the morning of Ashura in that apartment, the holy day when the Shi'a mourn the martyrdom of the third imam, Hussein, the hero of Karbala. My mother had asked me to go with her to Jamaran for Ashura, but I told her, "I have something very important to do, I'll join you later. I'll be there by noon."

Amir picked me up early, not far from my home. The Tehran streets were silent. Everyone was in the mosques or *tekiyeh*s, beating their chests in lamention for Hussein. It was traditional for the pious to prepare meals to share with the masses as a *nazr* to the imam. People would stand outside their doors and invite passersby inside, and mourners would stand in line with pots held out to take the food home to their families. As we drove, I saw that he had a couple of cooking pots on the backseat. He must have told his wife he was going out to collect food for the family, but instead he was driving to Sa'adat-abad to spend the national holiday with me. He giggled like a child getting away with something and then said with a serious voice, "What am I doing with you? This is the first time in my life I haven't been in the Bazar Mosque on Ashura. God forgive me. You are a devil."

I smiled sweetly, but in my heart I felt awful. The game had gotten away from me. How could I tell him that after our meetings I'd stand under the shower, crying and washing myself a hundred times, asking God why he'd given me this destiny? As we drove toward the apartment I felt like vomiting. I couldn't say a word. Quietly, I followed him up the stairs to the third floor. . . .

It was around noon when he dropped me off at Meidan Tajrish, where I took a cab to Jamaran. Mader-jan had passed away in the spring of 1997, but my mother's family still gathered in her beautiful old home in front of Jamaran's *husseinya* during the Ashura and Tasoa holidays, watching the chest-beaters from the courtyard. It was the first time I'd seen some of my more distant relatives since I'd left prison. Though it had been almost six months, they examined me as though I'd been freed yesterday. Their stares and questions were even harder to bear as I'd come directly from seeing Amir. "God, you've really changed! Your face seems a little swollen—did they beat you?" they asked. Someone looked at my expression and whispered in my ear, "Did they do anything . . . *wrong* to you?" Uncle Ali's widow, Iran-Dokht, told everyone to leave me alone. She walked with me to the mosque and said, "Ask the imam to give you peace. Pray to be happy and free."

I didn't want to act like a good Muslim any longer for Amir. He even asked me to refuse the invitation to my cousin Elham's wedding because it was mixed, with both men and women as guests. I couldn't imagine missing my first cousin's wedding—what would my mother say! I lied to him, telling him that my aunt Avid, the mother of the bride, had decided to separate men and women at the wedding. I danced to the live band all night, dancing so hard that at two in the morning, when my mother, Kai Khosrou, and I drove home, I had to take off my high-heeled shoes to walk barefoot from the car to the front door. I met with Amir the next day, and my stomach twisted when he asked me about the party. But I coolly replied, "It was nothing special—a quiet, traditional wedding." I felt sick— I had to stop lying, even if it meant ending my life. I wasn't a journalist anymore. I was no one.

I never told my family about the affair. Even now, I still haven't told my mother and sister all the details. But despite the risk, I decided to seek the advice of someone outside the family who I could trust. Korosh was an influential man I'd known for many years. I visited his office, and he told me, "Go, Camelia, don't stay here a minute longer. You are playing with fire. When he gets enough of you, when he wakes up from your spell—or if you ever reject him in any way—you'll simply vanish. They'll kill you to protect this secret. It will be a car accident, or it might look like a suicide. Think about it. You tell me that he told you himself that he had signed death warrants for young girls in prison not all that long before you were arrested. He might have been 'in retirement' for ten years, but people like him don't change that much in a decade. These days, he doesn't need to send you to the firing squad. It's easy to kill someone. Find a way to leave as soon as you can—you don't want to play this game out to the end."

◙ ◙ ◙

"You teach at the university. I know," I told him once. Amir looked at me curiously.

"How do you know? Maybe you follow me around instead of me following you! How did you guess?"

"I knew. I knew long before this. From the clothes you wore in prison and the educated philosophical discussions you'd have with me. I can even guess what your field is!"

"That's enough. That's enough. The prying stops here. Believe me, you're the strangest case I've ever worked."

There were a lot of things I had figured out. I'd figured out that he enjoyed high status in the Ministry as a special consultant, that he was the chief investigator on my case. I'd figured out that only his wife knew that he worked for the Ministry. For the rest of his family and friends, he was an academic. I'd also figured out that the Ministry wanted to do away permanently with reformist journalists and intellectuals—that I had no future in Iran. And with Korosh's help, I'd figured out that I had to end my relationship with Amir before I wound up dead, wrapped in a plastic bag on the side of the road or hanging with a forged note in my hand.

My mother found smugglers who would take me across the border for four million tomans (about $4,000). But crossing the border was risky—I knew what would happen if they took me alive. I told my mother to be patient. And I told Amir, "I've been invited to a conference in New York. They want me to participate in a program in America." It was true. I had sent my request when I was still at *Zan* to attend a special session of the UN's general assembly in New York, "Beijing +5," and the invitation had arrived in response, though *Zan* no longer existed. Faezeh's office called the conference and asked them to change the invitation to *Saba*, her newsletter, so I could still join the group representing Iran.

"Ha!" He looked at me in disbelief. "The one time I let you go was a mistake. We're not having anymore coming and going. You need to get to work right here." But I arranged through a connection of Korosh's to buy plane tickets and planned to again call on Jean during the London stopover to arrange my visa. When I left New York the last time, she'd promised to help me whenever I needed her. I kept putting the bug in Amir's ear. "It's a prestigious program and could be very useful for us. You know that Ayatollah Khomeini's granddaughter Zahra Eshraqi-Khatami is going as well?" That set off a bell. She was suspicious alone for being Ayatollah Khomeini's granddaughter, and in addition she was now President Khatami's sister-in-law. It most certainly was of interest to the Ministry of Intelligence to track her.

It was hard to tell my family I was leaving. We had survived in Iran from the day the Shah left through all the infernal trials of the revolution and its aftermath. Now, I was fleeing under threat of death. All they could do was sit and pray. If Amir didn't give in, I might never get another chance to leave the country legally. My mother of course knew something was wrong. How could she not? I'd leave home almost every day with a black chador in my bag, telling her, "I still have more interviews with the Ministry and the courts."

She'd say, "My stomach is boiling with nerves. You call me if you need to stay out late. Please call me, wherever you are."

Amir would eye me suspiciously when I'd leave the room to phone my mother at eleven. He'd ask, "What did you tell her? Where did you say you are?"

"With Faezeh." My mother knew that the line might be tapped. She'd say, in a strained voice, "Thanks for checking in, say hello to your friend." I'm sure she knew that I wasn't with Faezeh. No matter how late I'd come home, she'd be standing in the dark kitchen, watching out the window for me. She would tell me, "Whatever you're doing, think of your father. Do what he would agree with, were he still alive."

MAY 2000

Then it happened. Amir told me, "Your trip has been approved." I convinced him I had to leave immediately. I knew I wasn't coming back. At home in my room, I took a last look around at all the things that I loved. I looked at my bed, thinking how I'd never sleep there again; out the window to the neighbor's courtyard and their beautiful rose garden, which I'd watched so many summers sitting in my room; at my father's clothes still hanging in my closet. I had kept one of his coats and one of his shirts in his memory. I looked at the framed photos on my wall and at my unfinished watercolor paintings. I packed a very small bag. A large suitcase would have aroused Amir's suspicion.

He was waiting for me at the airport. I took the plastic bag he handed to me with presents he'd brought, and when I looked inside I saw he'd given me pistachios packed in a little heart-shaped bamboo box. I knew he was still in love. There was also an envelope with two hundred dollars inside—about a month's salary in Iran. "It's very little, but buy something for yourself with that," he said. He took my passport over to the immigration officer to be validated, and when he returned, he asked, "What would you say if I told you you couldn't go?"

"Nothing. I'd walk out of here with you." My whole body was drenched with sweat.

"Go. Go. You're my homing pigeon. Wherever you go, you'll come right back to me."

There were two Pasdars standing next to the plane. My legs could barely support me. Who could they be after? Did they know what I was doing? Were they going to take me away? My mother was there to say good-bye—she was as white as a sheet. She was turning a *tasbih* over in her hand with her thumb and praying under her breath. She whispered into my ear, "Go, and don't look back. Go, and get out of this hell. Go, and be free. Fly away, my daughter. Fly."

On the British Airways flight, I covered my eyes until the pilot announced that we'd flown over the border. Then I took off my head scarf.

epilogue "I Brought This Star for You"

I haven't returned to Iran. Spring came to an end, and it was summer. Amir had somehow gotten hold of my number and was leaving messages that made my hair stand on end. In Persian and in English, sometimes threatening, other times in a soft, kind tone. The only answer he got was silence. Then the e-mails started.

He wrote that my life and the lives of members of my family were in danger. He promised he would come after me, even in America. Then he said I was free to stay in the United States only if I stayed in touch with him regularly. Once he asked me if I was healthy, if I needed anything he could give me. Another time he wanted to know if I would be returning to Tehran to visit my family for the Nouruz holidays, as he could arrange this visit without any problem—I only needed to get in touch with him. They started summoning my mother to court and threatening her. Should I go back to Tehran? Where did the performance end? Where would my story end?

In September 2000, during a session of the General Assembly at the United Nations, I waited in the lobby of the hotel where the Iranian delegation was staying. There was one person I had to tell my story to. I had to talk to Agha-ye Khatami. I looked around, trying to spot the person most likely to help me arrange a presidential meeting. A portly, jolly man appeared in the lobby, and I recognized him from his picture in the newspaper. He was Seyyed

Mohammed Abtahi, the president's chief of staff (and later the Vice President of Iran). He had a big smile on his face, and his eyes glimmered like polished marbles. We sat next to one another on a sofa in the lobby. I trusted him, and I cried as I told him my whole story, detailing the long days and months of crisis and worry.

"I'll help you meet President Khatami. I'm terribly sorry for everything that's happened to you."

On the day Khatami was to fly back to Tehran, right before they took him to see the Statue of Liberty, it was arranged for him to receive me in his private suite. Khatami kept his eyes down as I spoke, only occasionally looking up and meeting my gaze. It wasn't easy for him to listen to what I had to tell him. I started crying so hard that I couldn't keep talking.

"My daughter, don't cry. God is a friend to those who are wronged. I'll put Agha-ye Abtahi in charge of your case. Stay in touch with us."

Pouring my heart out in this private meeting was a great release. I found renewed strength in my journalistic work and was encouraged to cover Khatami's travels and Iranian foreign relations, mostly for the Associated Press and the *Village Voice* in New York. The next time I met Abtahi in person was at an OPEC summit in Caracas, where he told me he'd held several meetings with the Minister of Intelligence, Agha-ye Ali Yunusi, and that Khatami had requested all my files from the judiciary.

Working for the AP, I embarked on travels throughout the Middle East. Khatami continued to treat me with special kindness, and I had the distinction of interviewing him at a summit of leaders from the Muslim world in Qatar. How satisfying it was for me to have Agha-ye Khatami address me personally by name and ask me how I was doing in front of hundreds of people. I was happier than I had ever been in my life. I traveled freely from Qatar to Saudi Arabia and from Saudi Arabia to Egypt and from Egypt to the

United Arab Emirates. But I never returned to Iran. I posted translations of my articles on an Iranian Web site to share my liberation with those still working under censorship and fear.

"Your files have been lost by the judicial authorities," Agha-ye Abtahi told me finally. Apparently, the Ministry of Intelligence had been displeased that Khatami was investigating my case. He had helped me as much as he could, but it was shocking to realize again the limits of Khatami's power.

In Qatar, I approached Khatami as he was leaving his hotel, and said, "*Khoda hafez*, Agha-ye Khatami." He smiled and said, "Come along, let's go to Tehran together."

"If you give me a letter guaranteeing my protection . . ."

He answered, "I don't know whether anyone can protect any of us when we get to Tehran."

I stood at the hotel entrance and watched Khatami walk away, as the delegation that had come with him passed me by. Another cleric, Agha-ye Du'ai, stopped and told me, "Pray for us *and* for Agha-ye Khatami."

◙　◙　◙

And thus immigration and self-imposed exile led me unexpectedly to the life I'd always wanted, full of freedom, security, and journalistic opportunities. In prison, I'd begun a metamorphosis, and now my cocoon was breaking open. It wasn't easy, but I slowly spread my wings. Jean helped me with my visa and encouraged me to apply for political asylum. Other new friends helped me find a place to live and freelance writing jobs.

For a year I had the same nightmare that I was back in the airplane on the tarmac at Mehrabad airport, returning to Tehran. I would suddenly realize that I wasn't going home to my family but returning to Amir. I imagined he would torture me to death, and I would beg the British Airways crew to let me stay on the plane. Then the nightmares receded as I turned my full attention to continuing my studies.

No one in my family could attend my graduation ceremony, only a few friends. But I knew that my father could see me walking up to receive my diploma, just as he'd watched me hiding under a sofa in a stranger's home and all the rest of that dangerous game, and that he could now finally find peace in his grave.

The last e-mail from Amir came in the spring of 2004. I have no idea whether he still has his job and his rank or if he has been dismissed. Perhaps his heart is full of hate. Maybe my silence over the past six years led him to believe that I would never tell this story. But I do know that, until the last moment of his life, he will remember my hands. The hands that spoke to him of love. The hand that he lifted up in his own on one of those days when we drove aimlessly through Tehran. The hand that he placed on the gearshift and covered with his own hot grasp when he said, "You don't know what extraordinary hands you have. I've fallen in love with your hands."

◙   ◙   ◙

SPRING 2001

My niece, Yasbanu, now four years old, was firmly clenching a gift for me in her hands. We were in Dubai, and it was the first time I'd seen my family after a whole year, the first of my exile. She had grown so much.

I asked Yasbanu, "What is this, little auntie? Open your hands so I can see it."

"A star," my sister said. "She's brought you a blue star."

It was a funnily shaped piece of blue paper. Katayun said, "It's *like* a star. She painted it and cut it out for you herself."

Yasbanu was waiting anxiously for my reaction, her upturned face yearning for approval. I kissed her. "You are a star. My little star."

Glossary

Abrar: The Righteous, the name of a newspaper.

Afarineshha-ye Adabi: Literary Creations, the name of a creative writing center.

Aftab-e Yazd: The Yazd Sun. Yazd is a city in central Iran.

Aftabgardan: Sunflower.

agha: Equivalent to "mister" or if used to address a stranger, "sir."

alif: The letter "a."

alif to yeh: Equivalent to "a to z."

Allahu Akbar: God is greatest.

aluche-ye kisa'i: Mashed prunes sold in plastic wrappers.

Ashura: The tenth day of the lunar month of Moharrem when Shi'a muslims commemorate the martyrdom of Imam Hussein.

ayatollah: High-ranking Shi'a cleric.

Azadi: Liberty, the name of a radio station and various squares and other landmarks in Tehran.

bab: Literally "gateway." Used here to refer to the people claiming to deliver messages to the twelfth imam.

bah, bah, bah: Exclamation of admiration or extreme approval.

Bahman: February.

Basij: Volunteer militia.

befarma'id: A polite entreaty to "help yourself" or "go ahead."

Behesht-e Zahra: Literally "the paradise of Zahra, daughter of the Prophet." A large, well-known cemetery outside of Tehran.

Bulvar-e: Boulevard.

chador: Clothing worn by women in Iran to ensure that the hair, neck, and body are properly covered.

Chahararshanbeh-ye Suri: Literally "the Wednesday of the red rose." The last Wednesday before the Iranian New Year.

chelow kebab: Grilled meat (usually lamb) with rice and grilled tomatoes on the side.

dabirestan: High school.

dawyus: Cuckold.

djinn: A spirit, often evil or mischievous.

dokht: Daughter.

doogh: A sour yogurt drink.

Etela'at: Intelligence, the name of a newspaper.

fal: A kind of fortune telling, where hidden knowledge is divined, for instance, from coffee grounds or poetry.

Faravahar: A winged disc that represents the Zorastrian deity Ahura Mazda.

Farmandeh: Commander.

fatwa: An Islamic ruling by a religious authority that may forbid certain practices or condemn the actions of an individual.

fesanjun: A stew made of chicken, walnut, and pomegranate.

Forqan: One of the militant groups that opposed the Islamic Republic. Literally "The Distinction between Truth and Lies."

Forugh-e Javidan: The Eternal Radiance.

gaz: A kind of nougat.

ghazal: A poetic form with a specific meter and a recurring rhyme.

hajj or hajji: A title bestowed upon one who has made the pilgrimage to Mecca during the hajj. Also a title of respect for elderly individuals or persons of stature who are politely presumed to have made the pilgrimage.

Halabiyabad: Slum neighborhoods in south Tehran.

Hamshahri: One who inhabits a city, a fellow citizen. The name of a newspaper founded by the popular mayor of Tehran, Gholamhussein Karabashi, who was linked to the reformist movement.

hejab: Both the practice of covering oneself appropriately in accordance with Islamic doctrine and the clothing used to do so.

hojjat ul-Islam: Literally "proof of Islam." A middle-ranking Shi'a cleric, lower than an ayatollah.

husseinya: A religious gathering space where sermons are delivered or the martyrdom of Imam Hussein is described.

imam: A descendant of, and successor to, the Prophet.

Imam-e Zaman: The twelfth imam. He is expected to return "when the world is full of sin" to kill all the infidels.

imamzadeh: The tomb of someone related by blood to one of the Shi'a imams.

in sha' Allah: God willing.

jadeh: A medium-sized street.

Jumhuri-ye Islami: Islamic Republic, the name of a newspaper.

Ka'aba: The structure housing the black rocks around which the pilgrims perambulate at Mecca.

Kakh-e Javanan: The Youth Palace.

Kayhan: The World, the name of a a large circulation, syndicated newspaper in Tehran with conservative politics.

Kermanshah: A province in western Iran.

khanum: Lady or miss.

Khavaran: An unofficial cemetery in Tehran, much further from the city than Behesht-e Zahra, where the munafiqin are buried.

kheirat: A small gift or refreshment given in honor of the dead.

Khiaban-e: A major street or avenue.

khoda hafez: Good-bye. Literally "God protect you."

Khordad: May.

khoresht-e badamjan: Eggplant stew.

khoresht-e qorma sabzi: Green-herb stew.

Komité: The military body in charge of enforcing Islamic decorum among the citizenry.

kucheh: Narrow street or lane.

kuku: A type of casserole.

kuku-ye sabzi: An herb casserole.

lavash: Iranian flatbread.

Madar-e Fuladzere-ye Div: A mythical armor-plated monster invoked to describe difficult people.

Mader-jan: An affectionate form of address for an old woman, literally "mother dear."

madresseh: School.

mahram: A close male relative such as a brother, father, husband, son, or uncle who in Islamic law is authorized to accompany a woman and see her without her chador.

Majlis: Parliament.

Maman Bozorg: A variation of *madar-e bozorg*, which means grandmother.

manto: Long Islamic overcoat.

masha-Allah: Well done.

masum(eh): One of the blameless, (eh implies female) such as members of the extended family of the Prophet and imams.

meidan: Square.

Mellat Iran: People of Iran, a political party.

Mersad: Ambush.

mofsed: Corrupt, seditious, subversive.

Mordad: August.

muhandes: engineer.

mujahed(in): An individual (or individuals) engaged in a struggle, often armed, for the sake of Islam.

Mujahedin-e Khalgh: A group that continues to oppose the current Iranian regime.

mullah: A Shi'a cleric.

Mumtaz: Excellent.

munafiqin: Muslims who stir up trouble with other Muslims.

musala: Public prayer ground.

nazr: Votive offering.

noql: Sugar-coated almonds, a wedding candy thrown like rice.

Nouruz: The Iranian New Year, March 21st on the western calendar.

Omid: Hope.

Omur-e Tarbiyati: A body charged with maintaining Islamic values in the school system.

Pasdaran: Revolutionary guard.

Peykan: An Iranian car model.

qama: Double-edged sword.

qand: Sugar cubes.

qibleh: The marking of the direction of Mecca, which muslims face in order to pray. In mosques, it is a special niche in the wall or corner, while in hotel rooms (or prison cells) it is usually an arrow painted on the ceiling.

Qur'an: The holy text of Islam believed to have been a direct revelation to Mohammed from God delivered by the angel Gabriel.

Resalat: Prophetic Mission, the name of a newspaper.

rezai: Similar to a foster sibling, the relationship carries the privilege of a *mahram.*

rial: Iranian monetary unit.

rowzekhan: The singer of a *rowze,* laments that recount the martyrdom of various religious figures, including of Hussein at Karbala.

Ruba'yat: Quatrains.

saba: Zephyr or morning breeze. The name of a newsletter edited by Faezeh Hashemi.

salaam: Hello. Literally "peace."

salaamu aleik(um): Peace be upon you, the typical Islamic greeting.

salvat: Praise uttered to the line of Mohammed.

SAVAK: Sazeman-e Etela'at va Amniyat-e Keshvar (National Security and Intelligence Organization).

SAVAKi: Intelligence agent of the Shah.

Seda va Sima: Sound and Vision. An Iranian television station.

Shah: King.

shahanshahi: Royal (of the Shah).

Shahnameh: Abu al-Qassem Ferdowsi's *The Epic of Kings*, an epic Persian poem from around the 10th century.

Shahbanu: Queen, literally "Lady of the Shah."

Shah-Dokht: Princess.

Shahpur: Prince.

Shahyad: Shah's memory.

Shaqayeq: Poppy.

Shemiran: A neighborhood north of Tehran.

sher-e azad: Free poems.

sher-e nou: New poems.

Shir-e Pak: Pure milk, the name of a factory that produces dairy products.

sigheh: A Shi'a contractual marriage, which may be specified to be valid for a limited time.

taghuti: From the Qur'anic *toghut*, used by Khomeini to refer to those who live well at the expense of others and therefore deserve to be destroyed.

tak madeh: A one-time-only allowance in school whereby a failing grade is disregarded.

tak nevesi: Short for Towbeh Kardeh Nevisi, a statement of repentance.

Takht-e Jamshid: Persepolis, the ancient ceremonial capitol of the second Persian dynasty.

taqiah: Shi'a concept of concealing one's identity for pragmatic purposes that have religious validity.

taryaki: Opium addict.

Tasoa: The ninth day of the lunar month of Moharrem when Shi'is commemorate the martyrdom of Imam Hussein. The eve of Ashura.

tasbih: Rosary.

tekiyehs: Ceremonial spaces specially built in the month of Moharam for the public mourning of Ashura and Tasoa.

timi: Literally "team," *timi* describes homes occupied by groups of insurgents operating secretly in residential areas.

toman: Iranian monetary unit equal to ten rials.

tudeh-i: Communist.

Vali-ye Ahd: The Crown Prince.

Vali-ye Asr: The Master of Time.

velayat-e faqih: Rule by Islamic jurisprudence.

velgard: A vagrant, a loitering good-for-nothing.

Ya Sar-e Allah: A religious expression meaning "Oh Movement of God."

yallah: Expression of impatience or incitement to proceed, similar to "let's go!"

yeh: The letter "z."

Zan: Woman, the name of a newspaper. *Zanan* is the plural form, also the name of a publication.

Zanbaq: Iris.

Zan-e Ruz: Woman of the Day, the name of a weekly magazine.

zan-e sigheh: The brides of temporary marriages.

Zeinab: The daughter of the first Shi'a imam and the sister of the imam Hussein. The Sisters of Zeinab were female Revolutionary Guards.

Zoroastrianism: A pre-Islamic religion in Iran still practiced by a small minority. The faith espouses a dualistic view of the world, where creation is divided into good and evil.

CAMELIA ENTEKHABIFARD was born in Tehran in 1973. In Iran she was a reporter for the leading reformist daily, *Zan*, among other papers. In 1999 she was arrested for her journalistic activities and spent three months in prison. She has been a contributor to *O, The Oprah Magazine*, and reported on Iranian and Afghan affairs for AP, Reuters, Eurasia Net, *The Village Voice*, and *Mother Jones*. She holds an MA in journalism from New York University and an MIA in international and public affairs from Columbia University. She lives in New York.

GEORGE MÜRER is a graduate from the Bard College film department and has spent time in Iran as a student of Persian literature and music. He is currently conducting documentary research on the music of the Persian- and Kurdish-speaking worlds.